The War Conspiracy

Books by Peter Dale Scott

Poems
The Politics of Escalation in Vietnam
(with Franz Schurmann and Reginald Zelnik)
Education at Berkeley
(with Charles Muscatine and others)

Translations
Zbigniew Herbert, *Selected Poems*
(translated from the Polish with Czeslaw Milosz)

The War Conspiracy

The Secret Road to the Second Indochina War

by Peter Dale Scott

The Bobbs-Merrill Company, Inc.
Indianapolis / New York

Chapter One of this work first appeared in *Ramparts* magazine (February 1970) and was subsequently reprinted in Nina S. Adams and Alfred W. McCoy (eds.), *Laos: War and Revolution* (New York: Harper, 1970). Chapters Two and Three first appeared in the *New York Review of Books;* Chapter Two was subsequently reprinted in Marvin Gettleman *et al.* (eds.), *Conflict in Indochina* (New York: Random House, 1970).

The Bobbs-Merrill Company, Inc.
Publishers: Indianapolis / New York

*To the people of Asia, and above all to the
victims of the American war conspiracy*

Table of Contents

Preface

No doubt this will be called an anti-American book, particularly since its author is a Canadian. The charge is absurd. At a time when cynicism is widespread both in Washington and among certain segments of the American left, only a residual optimism could have inspired this inquiry into some of the contradictions between the commonly affirmed values of the American people and the activities of certain American institutions. If indeed America were the enemy, then this book was a waste of time.

Once a year my family and I visit a county fair in California. Usually it is that of Alameda County, a mixed county of farms, suburbs, and large cities. That Berkeley is located in such a representative cross-section of America is an important fact often overlooked by both Berkeley's detractors and its beleaguered denizens. But I have found these annual pilgrimages to middle America strangely reassuring, in a way that would hardly please President Nixon or Vice-President Agnew. To be sure, middle Americans today, when seen among their pickled tomatoes and flowers made from old nylons and copper wire, do not seem very radical. Usually the only political table is manned by friendly salesmen from the John Birch Society, who ply me with extra literature because I am a professor and "read books." But one has the impression of an essentially humane people not so deeply vindictive or alienated, concerned with a multitude of small sustaining projects from hydroponics to tap-dance, and also deeply unsettled about the war.

I am aware that such comforting scenes from Alameda or Contra Costa or Grass Valley do not represent the whole of America, any more than does Berkeley itself, where the FBI now raids homes at night without warrants. No doubt one could have found idyllic counterparts in Bavaria on the eve of Hitler's first plebiscite. But for ten years I have known and taught and learned from the children of middle America at the University of California, the children of motel-keepers and miners and bakers. Although education is a slow process, and the education of a people is a matter of generations, I am convinced that through its system of mass higher education America is embarked on a historic and revolutionary enterprise.

In the sense both of betrothal and of combat, the war has engaged the public university. Specifically it has made more urgent a choice confronting public education in any case: the choice whether to aim at a new generation of technical and bureaucratic robots or of more conscious and sensitive human beings. The outcome of the war (and the peace) will affect the future of the university, for imperialism and free mass education cannot tolerate each other for long.

The seeming complacency of the preceding paragraphs will not be echoed on all of the pages that follow. At times my mood is more desperate, and that is one reason for returning to each year's county fair. But the book is an act of faith, as anyone will see who reads it carefully. It is written in the faith that American people, if they study and understand what they have been inflicting on Asian people for more than twenty years, will act to end the wholesale destruction of Asians and their environment.

All faith, all coherent action, is built around unverifiable propositions concerning the future. To have faith does not require a closed mind. To those who will claim that this book is too single-minded, that it looks only for what corroborates its own analysis, I can only answer that the prevailing media have also been too single-minded, the time is short, this book is already too long.

It may well be that the whole truth is more irrational than the recurring patterns developed in this book. What matters is that the patterns do recur and must be eradicated. I have however striven to be honest, to focus on actual processes in a manner that is selective but never misleading.

Whatever vast chain of social forces responds to the challenge of the war conspiracy, I hope it too will do so in the faith that truth and humanity are on the same side, so as to engage facts rather than abstractions, with fervor but without hatred.

A word about method. I began by relying on traditional sources: memoirs, newspaper articles from many countries (including the English-language Asian press), and the reportage of experienced Asian observers like Stanley Karnow and the late Bernard Fall. I came soon to appreciate the importance of congressional committee hearings (even more than reports), the annual reports of chartered corporations (such as Air America), available for a small fee from state secretaries of state, and such basic reference works as Poor's *Register of Directors and Executives,* Moody's Manuals, the *World Aviation Directory,* Martindale-Hubbell's *Legal Directory, Who's Who in American Politics* and *Asia Who's Who,* etc. (I unfortunately came too late upon the excellent *NACLA Research Methodology Guide* published by the North American Congress on Latin America.) A complex society like America's cannot be a closed one; there is material in such sources for a hundred critiques more profound than what I have written.

Living in Berkeley, I have had fewer interviews with the protagonists of this story than I would have wished. It is true that the resulting perspective is somewhat print-bound and academic, in dealing with matters where public libraries do not reach very far. But inside stories on covert matters are notoriously unreliable; more than one critic of American foreign policy has relayed planted stories, because of the pleasure in hearing them personally from important sources. The result of impersonal research in libraries, though admittedly at a disadvantage, is not all loss.

Among the countless people I must thank for their help and support, I think first of the late Robert Ockene, my first editor at Bobbs-Merrill; Sonia Robbins, his very patient successor; and Robert Silvers, editor of the *New York Review of Books.* Yet it has been a book written from a Berkeley rather than a New York perspective, thanks to the stimulation of such thinkers as Franz Schurmann, David Horowitz, Fred Crews, and a younger generation in the local Committee of Concerned Asian Scholars. I owe much to the careful criticism at various times of Carl Dawson, Roger Hamilton, David Kolodny, Howard Hugo, Norman Rabkin, Masao Miyoshi, and above all my wife. I have been immensely helped by the cooperation of the UC Library staff, particularly in the newspaper room, the map room, and above all in the documents department under the incomparable Mr. George R. Davis. I am also indebted to the ingenuity of my research assistants, Bill Snow and Chris Jenkins, and of my chief typist, Mrs. Willow Taylor.

Introduction

In the two decades since 1950, the year of the Korean war and the China Lobby, there has never been a genuine US de-escalation in Southeast Asia. Every apparent de-escalation of the fighting, such as in Vietnam in 1954 and Laos in 1961–62, has been balanced by an escalation, often unnoticed at the time, whose long-range result increased America's war effort. In 1954, for example, America's direct involvement in the first Indochina war was limited to a few dozen USAF planes and pilots "on loan" to Chennault's airline Civil Air Transport (CAT), plus two hundred USAF technicians to service them. Though Dulles, Radford, and Nixon failed to implement their proposals for US air strikes and/or troop intervention, Dulles was able to substitute for the discarded plan for immediate intervention a "proposal for creating a Southeast Asia Treaty Organization."[1]

1 Chalmers Roberts, "The Day We Didn't Go to War," *Reporter* (14 September 1954), p. 35; reprinted in Marvin E. Gettleman, *Vietnam* (New York: Fawcett, 1965), p. 101.

SEATO soon became a cover for US "limited war" games in Southeast Asia, which in turn grew into the first covert US military involvement in Laos in 1959—the start of the second Indochina war.

In early 1961 Kennedy resisted energetic pressures from his Joint Chiefs to invade Laos openly with up to sixty thousand soldiers empowered, if necessary, to use tactical nuclear weapons. (Nixon also conferred with Kennedy and again urged, at the least, "a commitment of American air power.")[2] Unwilling with his limited reserves to initiate major operations simultaneously in both Laos and Cuba, Kennedy settled for a political solution in Laos, beginning with a cease-fire which went into effect on 3 May 1961. On 4 and 5 May 1961, Rusk and Kennedy announced the first of a series of measures to strengthen the US military commitment in South Vietnam. The timing suggests that the advocates of a showdown with China in one country had been placated by the *quid pro quo* of a build-up in another. In like manner the final conclusion of the 1962 Geneva agreements on Laos came only after the United States had satisfied Asian and domestic hawks by its first commitment of US combat troops to the area, in Thailand.

In 1968, finally, we now know that the "de-escalation" announced by President Johnson in March and October, in the form of a cessation of the bombing of North Vietnam, was misleading. In fact the same planes were simply diverted from North Vietnam to Laos: the overall level of bombing, far from decreasing, continued to increase.

One has, unhappily, to conclude that up to 1970 there was simply no precedent for a genuine US de-escalation in Southeast Asia, though there have been illusory appearances of it. This conclusion does not of itself prove that "Vietnamization" of the war is impossible, or that a deception has been practiced in order to delude the American electorate. It does, however, suggest that a twenty-year search for a successful war in Southeast Asia will not be easily converted into a search for the means to withdraw. The Cambodian and Laotian adventures are only more proof, for anyone who still needs it, that our current crisis in Southeast Asia is only the outward manifestation of a continuing crisis of government at home in America.

This book will attempt to outline the hidden history of these US escalations in Southeast Asia by focusing on key crises that have helped to bring escalation about. Though each of the chapters is a

2 Richard Nixon, "Cuba, Castro, and John F. Kennedy," *Reader's Digest*, November 1964, p. 291.

separate essay, I believe that an understanding of each episode will contribute to the understanding of all the rest, particularly as they help break down the false picture of these events that has been carefully impressed upon America.

The initial false picture is of a peace-loving America reluctantly drawn into Asia through a series of "responses" to various acts of aggression by socialist countries, such as: a "massive" North Vietnamese invasion of Laos in 1959, an impending invasion of Thailand in 1962, an unprovoked attack on two US destroyers in 1964, and an imminent invasion of South Vietnam from Cambodia in 1970. Today every single one of these separate allegations is now generally recognized to be untrue, and their refutation (in Chapters Two, Three, Four, and Seven) need not delay us here. They will, however, not be understood until they have been seen in their context as part of a process or syndrome, the repeated use of intelligence agencies and their allies to prepare the conditions for escalation. This covert preparation, through provocation, connivance, and deceit, is the process which, at the risk of oversimplifying, I have called "the war conspiracy."

A second false picture of these same US escalations is found even among elements of the US peace movement. According to this version, US involvement arose accidentally through a series of "mistakes." The distorted claims of aggression to which the US "responded" arose through mistakes of perception on our part, to be attributed to American naïveté or anti-Communist paranoia, to failures of communications or of command-and-control procedures, or to the clumsiness of mammoth bureaucracies and the difficulties of handling the vast amounts of information they deal with every day. Every one of these incidents is now attributed to a breakdown of US intelligence, and by an interesting corollary the same incidents can become grounds for increasing the US intelligence establishment so that such "mistakes" will not occur in future.

But, as we shall see, it is precisely the activities of US intelligence personnel (including those with responsibilities for covert or "special" operations) that have repeatedly given rise, deliberately and conspiratorially, to these false perceptions in Washington. It would appear that the very apparatus that should have relayed intelligence has instead manufactured its opposite and supplied false pretexts for unilateral US aggression. In every one of the critical escalations mentioned (as well as in other episodes for which we have little or no space) US intelligence personnel have been chiefly responsible for escalating our involvement.

Today those who vainly expected US involvement to end with the exposure of the "mistakes" have been mostly disillusioned. Revelations about the second Tonkin Gulf "incident" have led to the repeal of the Tonkin Gulf Resolution but have done nothing to affect the conduct of the war. The military's stubborn disregard of recent congressional limitations on the war are only the latest indications of a more deeply ingrained internal crisis in America, of an apparatus bent on war regardless of the public wish for peace.

To correct this picture of accidental or mistaken involvement I have spoken of a "war conspiracy," by which I mean the sustained resort to collusion and conspiracy, unauthorized provocations, and fraud by US personnel, particularly intelligence personnel, in order to sustain or increase our military commitment in Asia. I mean no more than this. I am aware that the total picture is more complex than any single phrase or narrative could suggest, and that other factors, not so covert, have also contributed to our Asian involvement. War conspiracy itelf is as much a symptom as a cause of the war mentality it furthers, for where the management and censorship of news are commonplace, the manipulation and outright invention of it are invited. The war conspiracy is to be seen as a general syndrome, not as the work of a single private cabal; nor is it necessary to think that war was always the intention of these collusions, as well as their result.

On the contrary, both the personnel and the concerns of the war conspiracy have changed widely over the last twenty years. Until recently this change has been continuously in the direction of militarization. In the 1950s our concealed involvement was mostly restricted to a few enterprising individuals like General Chennault and his "private" airline, Civil Air Transport (now known better as Air America), or such flamboyant CIA field operatives as Colonel Lansdale or Robert Campbell James (a cousin of the Socony president, B. B. Jennings). In the 1960s the picture is militarized. CIA field operatives were supplemented or supplanted by the primitive cadres of "special forces," while the labors of military ELINT —electronics intelligence—personnel contributed to our soon being involved in a full-scale US ground and air war. Today the once aggressive CIA seems to include some of the stronger voices for peace within the administration, while the war conspirators seem to be located chiefly within the competing DIA (Defense Intelligence Agency). In other words, the conspiracy must be seen as a continuing process on the model of a long-lived vital organ in which the organizing functions survive the transient cells which make it up. A more down-to-earth analogy would be that of a floating illegal crap game in which he players (and dealers) change, but not the motive of gain.

In a like manner, even though one can talk of US imperialism in Southeast Asia, the specific objectives of this imperialism seem to have varied widely in the last two decades. In the early 1950s the desire to secure stocks of scarce war materials like tungsten seems to have figured largely in our covert backing of Chinese Nationalist guerrillas in Burma through Chennault's airline. Later the same airline seems to have been used in Laos as part of a new US preoccupation with the technology of a covert or limited war. Doubtless in 1971 US intervention in Asia is backed by the economic prospects of quick-term profits (in the range of 35 percent per annum or even more) from investments in the region, particularly by hopes of new oil discoveries off the shores of Thailand and Cambodia in the South China Sea. Since late 1968 offshore drilling activity in Southeast Asia has doubled, and there are predictions that the area may soon "emerge as the world's most active exploration and drilling area."[3] Today nearly all of the South China Sea floor north of Java and Sumatra has been allocated in concessions to the international oil companies, with the exception of a particularly promising area off the coast of Cambodia and South Vietnam, where offshore drilling has also begun.[4] These economic concerns may well dictate a de-militarizing of the Indochina War in the 1970s, and a concomitant return to covert operations.

Despite the apparent diversity of groups and interests in these successive phases of US involvement, the story of covert war conspiracy in this book reveals a latent continuity underlying them. Take, for example, the private law firm of Thomas G. Corcoran, which organized both Chennault's Flying Tigers and CAT.[5] In the early 1950s Corcoran represented CAT, the insurance interests in Asia of C. V. Starr (a former OSS agent) and United Fruit; and was said by *Fortune* to maintain "the finest intelligence service in Washington":

3 *World Oil*, 15 August 1970, p. 186; cf. *Ocean Industry*, December 1969, p. 63.

4 *Oil and Gas Journal*, 28 April 1969, p. 56; map of concessions in *Ocean Industry*, December 1969, p. 64.

5 It is indicative of Corcoran's deep involvement in covert CIA activities (such as CAT) that throughout the 1950s his Washington law firm of Corcoran and Youngman was not listed in the Martindale-Hubbell *Law Directory*. In contrast Desmond FitzGerald, the CIA agent in Indochina with whom CAT worked, *was* listed in Martindale-Hubbell under the cover of a private practice. Yet we know that in practice FitzGerald "spent many of the ensuing [postwar] years in Vietnam or elsewhere in Asia" (Stewart Alsop, *The Center*. New York: Harper & Row, 1968, p. 157).

Most of [his clients] are companies with international interests and he
has a choice clientele in this field. It includes United Fruit Co., American International Underwriters Corp. (part of the C. V. Starr interests in Asia and elsewhere) and General Claire Chennault's Civil
Air Transport, Inc. In late 1951 Corcoran, for one example, was
working his intelligence service overtime keeping up with American
policy on Iran—what the State Department did in this affair would
be a guide to what it might or might not do to keep his client, United
Fruit, from being thrown out of Guatemala.[6]

After the successful CIA coup against Mossadeq in Iran, Chennault's
partner Whiting Willauer went from CAT to be US ambassador in
Honduras, where he helped United Fruit officials and the CIA overthrow Arbenz in Guatemala. Miguel Ydigoras Fuentes, an anti-
Communist who later succeeded the CIA's Castillo Armas as president of Guatemala, tells how a retired executive of United Fruit tried
to recruit him for the coup, and how, when in office, a "Washington
law firm" told him: "they had financed the 'liberation movement' of
Castillo Armas, who had committed himself to certain payments. On
his death he still owed them $1,800,000, and as they considered me
to be his heir they held me responsible for payment."[7]

In 1960, while Willauer and United Fruit officials were partici-
pating in the CIA's preparations for the Bay of Pigs, Chennault's
airline Civil Air Transport (soon to be better known as Air America)
took part in the CIA's overthrow of Souvanna Phouma in Laos, and
it has served since as part of the infrastructure for the CIA's secret
Laotian war. Previously one of the principal US financial interests in
Indochina was the Compagnie Franco-Americaine d'Assurances of
Saigon owned by Corcoran's client C. V. Starr and Co., whose president by 1960 was Corcoran's law partner William S. Youngman. But
since 1950 Corcoran has also represented some of the oil companies
which since 1963 have been expressing more and more interest in
offshore drilling in the South China Sea. One of these is the Tenneco
Corporation, which already holds two concessions in the Gulf of
Siam between Thailand and Cambodia and has acquired further
interests in the concession of Frontier Petroleum near Singapore.

Thus, on the functional or operating level of the war conspiracy,
diverse intelligence operations such as in Guatemala and Laos, and
diverse overseas economic interests such as in bananas, insurance,
and oil, are revealed to be part of one continuous story. At least

6 "Lawyers and Lobbyists," *Fortune,* February 1952, p. 142.
7 Miguel Ydigoras Fuentes, *My War with Communism* (Englewood Cliffs, N.J.: Prentice-
Hall, 1963), pp. 49–50, 63–64.

through 1968 Corcoran's law partners Ernest Cuneo (ex-OSS), Robert Amory (ex-CIA), and James Rowe (one of Lyndon Johnson's earliest advisers along with Corcoran himself) continued to keep closely in touch with Asian developments through both the CIA and the White House. Furthermore, the apparently diverse economic interests who have chosen to be represented by Corcoran's firm (like United Fruit, CAT, and C. V. Starr) turn out, on closer examination, to be less differentiated than the usual pluralistic models of American society would have us think.

Robert Lehman, for example, was for years a director both of United Fruit and of Pan Am Airlines, which after supplying the operating cadres for CAT went on to profit directly as the back-up for its Indochina operations. And at least two Pan Am officials associated with Chennault (Gordon Tweedy and John S. Woodbridge) have also been intimately involved in C. V. Starr's worldwide insurance operations. The private influence of Corcoran's law firm on US policy appears to be one good reason why in 1957 *Fortune* could report that Robert Lehman's family investment firm of Lehman Brothers (also involved in international oil operations) had experienced by 1957 "the greatest postwar growth of any Wall Street house," and was "one of the biggest profit makers—many believe the biggest."[8]

In other words, powerful economic interests have from the outset been behind the covert instrumentalities such as CAT which contributed to our initial involvement in Southeast Asia. The simple fact of their hidden association with these efforts does not of itself prove to what extent US involvements were motivated by hope of private profit. This is a complex question, and the reader will have to decide for himself (see Chapter Eight) whether to call CAT (alias Air America) a private "cover" for the implementation of public US policy, or, alternatively, an instrument whereby public resources have been committed to the support of private interests. (One cannot talk here narrowly of "private U.S. interests": we shall see that Nationalist Chinese capital, often said to derive from the Soong family, helps to pay for the total Air America operation, just as Nationalist Chinese pilots and personnel help to man its planes.) The power of intelligence networks is not simply bureaucratic, but arises in particular from their close alliance and interaction with private wealth as well as public authority.

But the story of the intelligence conspiracies to escalate US involvement becomes much more complex in the 1960s, when it be-

8 T. A. Wise, "The Bustling House of Lehman," *Fortune,* December 1957, p. 157.

came militarized and intensified. Since 1959 private economic motives for staying in Indochina have been reinforced by bureaucratic motives, the latter sometimes at variance with the former; and US intervention has involved far more than the operations of a single agency and paramilitary airline. Air America (which lost its monopoly on covert air operations in 1960) is no longer the central US intelligence enterprise in Southeast Asia combining private wealth with public authority. In the 1960s its wealth and importance were surpassed by those of industries specializing in intelligence technology, such as Itek (the CIA-linked electronics firm) and Ling-Temco-Vought, which supply the super-secret electronic equipment for ELINT operations such as those of *Maddox* and *Pueblo*. Personnel of these intelligence industries are often intimately concerned in preparations for, and occasionally even of the operations of, ELINT missions. There are many other ways in which private companies supply covers, personnel, or infrastructure for intelligence operations.

Once again, however, this polymorphous and perverse picture of private-public relations is not so pluralistic as at first it might appear. Underlying both the military intelligence operations of the 1960s and the "civilian" intelligence operations of the 1950s, we find the same financial interests. As only one example of this continuing financial base for US involvement, I shall cite the fact that Harper Woodward, who served in the 1950s as a director of CAT, continues to this day to serve as a director of Itek. This is not just because Woodward specializes in offering services to the CIA. He is where he is as an "associate" (i.e., employee) of Laurance Rockefeller, a member of a family whose oil and financial interests (chiefly in Standard Oil of New Jersey and Socony Mobil) are worldwide.

It is assuredly no coincidence that Nelson Rockefeller helped sound the alarm about scarce raw materials in 1951,[9] nor that Laurance Rockefeller headed the Rockefeller Brothers Fund Panel Two which first offered a public blueprint for limited war spending in 1957, nor that the Rockefeller and Socony Mobil hosted Diem and Thai officials in America in the 1950s. (John D. Rockefeller III's Asian Society supplied a forum in 1963 for a Socony Mobil employee who, in the company of several spokesmen with intelligence backgrounds, called publicly for the kind of overt US intervention in Vietnam affairs that began a year later after the assassinations of Ngo

9 Nelson Rockefeller, "Widening Boundaries of National Interest," *Foreign Affairs*, July 1951, pp. 523–38.

Dinh Diem and John F. Kennedy.)[10] Robert Lehman and the Rockefellers, Wall Street financiers, were personally financially involved in
the whole range of economic interests that have been served by the
Vietnam war. (James Rockefeller, a cousin, was a fellow-director
with Lehman of Pan Am.)

In the face of such pervasive economic interest in the background
of intelligence operations, particularly those contributing to the Vietnam war, one is tempted to retreat from the "accidental" fallacy about
US involvement to the opposite conclusion: acceptance of it as
inevitable and unopposable. In the introduction to his valuable essay,
Gabriel Kolko asserts, as "a central reality," that "a ruling class
makes its policies operate" through a pervasive "business-defined consensus"; and he adds that "to understand this essential fact is also to
reject conspiratorial theories."[11] From such arguments it is all too
easy to conclude that the rest of us do not have the means or institutions to oppose this class. But the recurrence of intelligence conspiracies is a fact, not a theory; and this fact challenges the assumption
that there exists in America a single-minded national ruling class.

It is certain that Kolko underestimates the contradictions underlying US policy in Vietnam since 1944, as for example when he
states that: "Despite the almost paranoid belief of the French representative that the O.S.S. was working against France, the O.S.S. only
helped consolidate Washington's support for the French. They . . .
were unanimous in believing that Ho is . . . a Communist."[12] An
Institute of Pacific Relations article by OSS veteran George Sheldon
in 1946 spoke favorably of the Viet Minh and critically of French
atrocities in the postwar period. It observed that Ho Chi Minh was
"formally elected by a vast majority" in the elections of January
1946, and added that: "Neutral observers, including Americans,
testified that the election was conducted in an efficient and orderly
fashion and that the overwhelming popularity of President Ho was
undeniable."[13] It is true that such surprising candor from intelligence
officers has become much rarer since the persecution of the Institute

10 William Henderson, "Some Reflections on United States Policy in Southeast Asia," in
William Henderson (ed.), *Southeast Asia: Problems of United States Policy* (Cambridge,
Mass.: MIT Press, 1963), pp. 253–63.

11 Gabriel Kolko, *The Roots of American Foreign Policy* (Boston: Beacon, 1969), pp.
xii–xiii.

12 *Ibid.*, p. 92; in *The Politics of War* (New York: Random House, 1968) Kolko is more
cautious: "The [OSS] reports [that Ho was Communist] helped to consolidate Washington's
support for the French" (p. 610). His later addition of the word "only" seems to be a logical
leap without empirical justification.

13 George Sheldon, "Status of the Viet Nam," *Far Eastern Survey,* 18 December 1946, pp.
373–77.

of Pacific Relations for its heresies by the right-wing McCarran Committee in 1952. But that successful campaign by the China lobby, in which Owen Lattimore was defended by top Washington lawyers Thurman Arnold and Abe Fortas, was only one of the many signs in that era of contradictions and struggle *between* powerful American factions.

In like manner, if a single-minded class-explanation of US policy were adequate, then there would have been no need for intelligence conspiracies, no Laos invasion fraud in 1959, no second Tonkin Gulf "incident" in 1964. US forces would simply have then moved into Laos and Vietnam as nakedly and as arrogantly as the Soviet tanks moved into Czechoslovakia. It may be that we shall see such naked US aggression in the future, but the past suggests that the issue of escalation has up till now divided the US government. The same incidents that show the grave challenge to our constitutional processes also reveal, by their very resort to connivance and collusion, that these processes are not yet meaningless. The intelligence incidents between 1959 and 1970 studied in this book suggest a sequence of related conspiracies to deceive, not only the US public, but the Congress of the United States, and at times even recalcitrant elements within the administration itself. Thus we may speak of conspiracy in violation not only of morality but of domestic US law. The result has been an erosion of congressional authority which can only be checked by a thorough congressional investigation and exposure. In addition, where the statute of limitations does not apply, there are grounds for possible further actions by the courts.

Sections 956–60 of the US Criminal Code, for example, forbid conspiracies to injure the property of any foreign state, the hiring or retaining of persons within the United States for enlistment in any foreign military service, and the furnishing of money for any military enterprise against the territory of any foreign state. These laws have been violated at least six times in the course of our covert intervention in Southeast Asia: with respect to Taiwan (1950 and 1952), Vietnam (1953), and Burma (1951–53 if not later), Indonesia (1958), and Laos (1959).

In all cases a pretext of legality was supplied by the same fiction: US military officers in foreign service were not employed by the foreign country directly but by a private company with a foreign government contract. This legal cover was first devised by President Roosevelt for Chennault's Flying Tigers in 1941, but he secretly authorized it by an unlisted Executive Order (15 April 1941).

It would appear that in late April 1953, when USAF planes and pilots were "loaned" to Chennault's CAT for use by the French in Indochina, this procedure was again authorized "at the highest level."[14] Thus the United States involvement in the first Indochina war was covert but not conspiratorial: no private individuals had plotted *against* the authority of the United States government.

The legal picture was different in 1950, when Admiral Charles M. Cooke, as head of a private military advisory group for Chiang Kai-shek's government on Taiwan, was employed by a firm known as CIC or Commerce International (China). Cooke himself later revealed that he sought, but *failed to obtain,* any presidential authorization for his plans ("I never received any action one way or the other on these recommendations; no red light, no green light").[15]

The picture was again different in August 1959, when USAF "volunteer" pilots in the "American Fliers for Laos" returned to a second Indochina war in Laos, again under cover of Civil Air Transport (whose American operating company, CAT, Inc., had five months earlier changed its name to Air America). Rather than risk lacking an authorization, certain individuals relayed false evidence of a North Vietnamese "invasion" to Washington. I shall argue that this evidence seems not only to have been deliberately staged, but even deliberately timed to coincide with Eisenhower's one-day seclusion in Scotland.

In like fashion Section 1001 of the US Criminal Code, dealing with fraud and false statements, states that

> Whoever, in any matter within the jurisdiction of any department or agency of the United States knowingly and willfully falsifies, conceals or covers up by any trick, scheme or device a material fact, or makes any false, fictitious or fraudulent statements or representations, or makes or uses any false writing or document knowing the same to contain any false, fictitious or fraudulent statement or entry, shall be fined not more than $10,000 or imprisoned not more than five years, or both. (18 USC 1001)

In the case of the Tonkin and *Pueblo* incidents, we shall examine the indications in these remarkably similar scenarios that US authorities were presented by intelligence agencies with "unimpeachable" evidence of enemy aggression, in the form of alleged corroborating

14 Department of State, *Bulletin,* 18 May 1953, p. 708.
15 US Congress, Senate, Committee on the Judiciary, *Internal Security Report for 1956,* p. 197.

"intercepts" of enemy orders, which were so distorted as possibly to be fraudulent. Similar misrepresentation of intercepts contributed to the 1970 invasion of Cambodia.

And we shall look more closely at the forgotten *Turkestan* affair of 2 June 1967, when US airmen, in the midst of delicate Washington-Moscow negotiations on the eve of the Six-Day War, shot up a Soviet ship in Haiphong harbor and killed one of its seamen. For that episode three US airmen were ultimately court-martialed. One was convicted for "destroying US government property" (the flight film in the planes' gun cameras) and "processing the film in an unauthorized manner." Even this penalty, a $600 fine, was ultimately set aside. This bizarre episode of escalation becomes much more ominous when it, too, is seen as part of a recurring sequence.

To some it may seem pedantic to dwell on such isolated examples of conspiracy to break the law. The true barbarism of the war is to be found elsewhere, not only in isolable massacres such as at My Lai, but generally in the systematic air war that has become central to the so-called Vietnamization program. Can one write a whole book about the Vietnam war that focuses on technical illegalities, while remaining silent about the larger crimes of napalm raids, the wholesale generation of refugees, and possibly even genocide?

Undoubtedly such crimes are in human terms far more serious than those which are the subject of this book. But they have been amply exposed, although their exposure, hitherto, does not seem to have been efficacious. Even the My Lai revelations, chilling though they are, expose only those who are responsible for carrying out a war, not those who are responsible for starting it. The aim of the present book is exposure on a higher level, that of those who have used provocation and escalation as an instrument to sustain an imperialist policy, and have resorted to lies and illegalities to achieve those ends.

Working only with the resources of a university library, I am conscious that I have cast only the light of one candle where a floodlight is needed. Ultimately the full job of exposure can only be done by men in Congress or the courts, who have the power to subpoena witnesses and documents. On their ability to rise to the occasion may well depend the larger question of whether this country is to issue from a course of war and imperialism in Asia by constitutional or by revolutionary means.

Postscript: This introduction, like nearly all of the chapters which follow, was written before the appearance of the Pentagon Papers. I believe that my arguments are substantiated by the facts contained in these more recent revelations (some of which I have added as corroboration in the following pages). But, just as I have not found that my contentions need to be altered, so I do not find them to have been rendered superfluous or out of date.

On the contrary, I have written a brief Epilogue, contending (in the too little space available) that the selective editing and misrepresentation of certain key documents in the Pentagon Papers represent yet one more manipulation of "intelligence" in order to influence public opinion and policy.[16]

---

16 A lengthier and more adequate exposition of this argument will be published by Beacon Press in a forthcoming collection of essays to be edited by Noam Chomsky and Howard Zinn.

Civil Air Transport (Chinese Nationalist). *CAT is a commercial air line engaged in scheduled and non-scheduled air operations throughout the Far East, with headquarters and large maintenance facilities located in Taiwan. CAT, a CIA proprietary, provides air logistical support under commercial cover to most CIA and other US Government agencies' requirements. . . . During the past ten years, it has had some notable achievements, including support of the Chinese Nationalist withdrawal from the mainland, air drop support to the French at Dien Bien Phu, complete logistical and tactical air support for the [1958] Indonesian operation, airlifts of refugees from North Vietnam, more than 200 overflights of Mainland China and Tibet, and extensive air support in Laos during the current crisis. . . .*

Lansdale memorandum, July 1961, in *The Pentagon Papers* (New York: Bantam, 1971).

Chapter One
CAT/Air America: 1950–70

In the closing days of the 1968 presidential campaign, the Democrats made an eleventh-hour bid for the presidency through a White House announcement that all bombing in North Vietnam was being stopped and that serious peace negotiations were about to begin. This move was apparently torpedoed within thirty hours by President Thieu of South Vietnam who publicly rejected the coming negotiations. Three days later, the Democratic candidate lost to Richard Nixon by a narrow margin.

After the election, it was revealed that a major Nixon fund-raiser and supporter had engaged in elaborate machinations in Saigon (including false assurances that Nixon would not enter into such negotiations if elected) to sabotage the Democrats' plan. It was also revealed that, through wire taps, the White House and Humphrey knew of these maneuvers *before* the election and that a heated debate had gone on among Humphrey strategists as to whether the candidate should exploit the discovery in the last moments of the campaign. Humphrey declined to seize the opportunity, he said, because he was sure that Nixon was unaware of and did not approve of the activities of his supporter in Saigon.

The supporter in question was Madame Anna Chan Chennault, the widow of General Claire Chennault (d. 1958) and now an intimate friend of his lawyer Tommy Corcoran. Her covert intervention into the highest affairs of state was by no means an unprecedented act for her and her associates. General Chennault had fought in China with Chiang Kai-shek; after the war he formed a private airline company called Civil Air Transport. Both husband and wife have, through their involvement with the China lobby and the CIA's complex of private corporations, played a profound role throughout our involvement in Southeast Asia. General Chennault's airline was, for example, employed by the US government in 1954 to fly in support for the French at Dienbienphu. It was also a key factor in the new fighting which began in Laos in 1959; moreover, it appears that President Eisenhower was not informed and did not know when his office and authority were being committed in the Laotian conflict, just as Nixon did not know of the intrigue of Mme. Chennault. But such are precisely the ways of parapolitics and private war enterprise.

In its evasion of congressional and even executive controls over military commitments in Laos and elsewhere, the CIA has long relied on the services of General Chennault's "private" paramilitary arm, Civil Air Transport or (as it is now known) Air America, Inc.

How Air America Wages War

Air America's fleets of transport planes are easily to be seen in the airports of Laos, South Vietnam, Thailand, and Taiwan. The company is based in Taiwan, where a subsidiary firm, Air Asia, with some eight thousand employees, runs one of the world's largest aircraft maintenance and repair facilities. While not all of Air America's operations are paramilitary or even covert, in Vietnam and even more in Laos it is the chief airline serving the CIA in its clandestine war activities.

Until recently the largest of these operations was the supply of the fortified hilltop positions of the forty-five thousand Meo tribesmen fighting against the Pathet Lao behind their lines in northeast Laos.

(The Meos are hill tribesmen on both sides of the Laos–Vietnam border with little sympathy for their Lao rulers.) Most of these Meo outposts have airstrips that will accommodate special short take-off and landing aircraft, but because of the danger of enemy fire the American and Nationalist Chinese crews have usually relied on parachute drops of guns, mortars, ammunition, rice, even live chickens and pigs. Air America's planes also serve to transport the Meos' main cash crop, opium.

The Meo units, originally organized and trained by the French, have provided a good indigenous army for the Americans in Laos. Together with their CIA and US Special Forces "advisers," the Meos have long been used to harass Pathet Lao and North Vietnamese supply lines. More recently they have engaged in conventional battles in which they have been transported by Air America's planes and helicopters.[1] The Meos also defended, until its capture in 1968, the key US radar installation at Pathi near the North Vietnamese border; the station had been used in the bombing of North Vietnam.

Farther south in Laos, Air America flies out of the CIA operations headquarters at Pakse, from which it has reportedly supplied an isolated US Army camp at Attopeu in the southeast, as well as the US and South Vietnamese Special Forces operations in the same region. Originally the chief purpose of these activities was to observe and harass the Ho Chi Minh trail, but recently the fighting in the Laotian panhandle, as elsewhere in the country, has expanded into a general air and ground war. Air America planes are reported to be flying arms, supplies and reinforcements in this larger campaign as well.[2]

Ostensibly, Air America's planes are only in the business of charter airlift. Before 1968, when the US Air Force transferred its operations from North Vietnam to Laos, air combat operations were largely reserved for "Laotian" planes; but it has been suggested that at least some of these operated out of Thailand with American, Thai, or Nationalist Chinese pilots hired through Air America. In addition, many of Air America's pilots and ground crews have been trained for intelligence or "special" missions: a reporter in 1964 was amused to encounter American ground crews whose accents and culture were unmistakably Ivy League.[3] And for years Air America's pilots have flown in a combat support role. As early as April 1961, when US "advisers" are first known to have guided the Laotian Army in com-

1 *New York Times,* 26 October 1969, p. 24.
2 *New York Times,* 18 September 1969, p. 10.
3 *New York Times,* 27 August 1964, p. 6.

bat, Air America's pilots flew the troops into battle in transports and helicopters supplied by the US Marines.[4]

The 1962 Geneva agreements on Laos prohibit both "foreign paramilitary formations" and "foreign civilians connected with the supply, maintenance, storing and utilization of war materials"; Air America's presence would appear to constitute a violation under either category. In calling Air America a paramilitary auxiliary arm, however, it should be stressed that its primary function is logistical: not so much to make war, as to make war possible.

The Early History of Air America

To understand the complex operations of Air America, one must go back to 1941 and the establishment of the "Flying Tigers" or American Volunteer Group (AVG), General Claire Chennault's private air force in support of Chiang Kai-shek against the Japanese. At that time President Roosevelt wished to aid Chiang and he also wanted American reserve pilots from the three services to gain combat experience; but America was not yet at war and the US Code forbade the service of active or reserve personnel in foreign wars. The solution was a legal fiction, worked out by Chennault's "Washington squadron," which included Roosevelt's "Brain Truster" lawyer, Thomas Corcoran, and the young columnist Joseph Alsop. Chennault would visit bases to recruit pilots for the Central Aircraft Manufacturing Company, Federal, Inc. (CAMCO), a corporation wholly owned by William Pawley, a former salesman for the old aircraft producer Curtiss-Wright, Inc. and head of Pan Am's subsidiary in China. According to their contracts, the pilots were merely to engage in "the manufacture, operation, and repair of airplanes" in China; but Chennault explained to them orally that they were going off to fly and fight a war.

In theory, the whole contract was to be paid for by the Chinese government; in practice the funds were supplied by the United States government through Lend-Lease. The operation was highly profitable to both of Pawley's former employers. Curtiss-Wright was able to unload a hundred P-40 pursuit planes, which even the hard-pressed British had just rejected as "obsolescent." Pawley nearly wrecked the whole deal by insisting on a 10 percent agent's commission, or $450,000, on the Curtiss sale. Treasury Secretary Morgenthau protested, but was persuaded by the Chinese to approve a payment of

---

4 *Washington Post,* 6 April 1961, A9; *New York Times,* 25 March 1961, p. 2. Americans still pilot helicopters for the Laotian Army (*New York Times,* 24 September 1969, p. 1).

$250,000.[5] For its part, Pan Am's Chinese subsidiary was later able to use many of Chennault's pilots in the lucrative charter airlift operations over the "hump" to Chungking.

It was agreed that Pawley's new CAMCO corporation could not take American pilots into the private war business without presidential authorization, and there was some delay in getting this approval. But on 15 April 1941, Roosevelt signed an Executive Order authorizing the enlistment of US reserve officers and men in the AVG-Flying Tigers. Thus CAMCO became a precedent for the establishment of a private war corporation by government decision. It does not appear, however, that the CIA was quite so fastidious about obtaining presidential approval in the postwar period.

After the war Chennault saw that a fortune could be made by obtaining contracts for the airlift of American relief supplies in China. Through Corcoran's connections—and despite much opposition—the relief agency UNRRA supplied Chennault not only with the contracts but also with the planes at bargain prices as well as with a loan to pay for them. One of Corcoran's connections, Whiting Willauer, promptly became Chennault's Number Two man. With the generous financing of the American taxpayers, Chennault and Willauer needed only a million dollars to set up the new airline. Recurring rumors suggest that CAT was originally bankrolled by Madame Chiang and/or her brother, T. V. Soong, then Chiang's ambassador to the US, whose personal holdings in the United States—after administering Chinese Lend-Lease—were reported to have reached $47 million by 1944.[6]

World War II was over, but the Chinese Revolution was not. CAT, established for relief flights, was soon flying military airlifts to besieged Nationalist cities, often using the old Flying Tigers as pilots. Chennault himself spent a great deal of time in Washington with Corcoran, Senator William Knowland, and other members of the Soong-financed China lobby; he campaigned in vain for a $700 million aid program to Chiang, half of which would have been earmarked for military airlift.

5 Anna Chan Chennault, *Chennault and the Flying Tigers* (New York: P. S. Eriksson, 1963), pp. 76–83; Russell Whelan, *The Flying Tigers* (New York: Viking, 1942), pp. 31–32; Claire Lee Chennault, *Way of a Fighter* (New York: G. P. Putnam's, 1949), pp. 100–01, cf. pp. 131–33. Corcoran's private law firm dates from this maneuver, when Roosevelt released him from the White House to become counsel for the Flying Tigers' supply corporation, China Defense Supplies, and thus T. V. Soong's contact with the White House (Barbara Tuchman, *Stilwell and the American Experience in China, 1911–45* [New York: Macmillan, 1971], p. 220).

6 *San Francisco Chronicle,* 2 April 1970, p. 31; W. T. Wertenbaker, "The China Lobby," *Reporter,* 15 April 1952, pp. 9–10.

After the establishment of the Chinese People's Republic in October 1949, Truman and the State Department moved to abandon the Chiang clique and to dissociate themselves from the defense of Taiwan. By contrast, CAT chose to expand its parabusiness operations, appealing for more pilots "of proved loyalty."

To help secure Taiwan from invasion, Chennault and his partners put up personal notes of $4,750,000 to buy out China's civil air fleet, then grounded in Hong Kong. The avowed purpose of this "legal kidnapping" was less to acquire the planes than to deny them to the new government pending litigation. It is unclear who backed Chennault financially in this critical maneuver (Soong denied that it was he). But it is known that shortly before the Korean war CAT was refinanced as a Delaware-based corporation by "a group of American businessmen and bankers." By the winter of 1950–51 CAT was playing a key role in the airlift of supplies to Korea, and Chennault (according to his wife's memoirs) was into "a heavy intelligence assignment for the US government."[7]

Chennault's Ambition of Rolling Back Communism

Chennault's vision for his airline was summed up in 1959, the year of CAT's entry into Laos, by his close friend and biographer, Robert Lee Scott: "Wherever CAT flies it proclaims to the world that somehow the men of Mao will be defeated and driven off the mainland, and all China will return to being free."[8]

As late as March 1952, according to Stewart Alsop, the Truman administration had failed to approve the "forward" policy against China then being proposed by John Foster Dulles.[9] Yet in a CIA operation in 1951, CAT planes were ferrying arms and possibly troops from Taiwan to some twelve thousand of Chiang's soldiers who had fled into Burma. In his book[10] Roger Hilsman tells us that the troops, having been equipped by air, undertook a large-scale raid into China's Yunnan province, but the raid was a "colossal failure." Later, in the "crisis" year 1959, some three thousand of the troops moved from Burma to Laos. On another CIA operation in 1952, a CAT plane dropped CIA agents John Downey and Richard Fecteau with a supply of arms for Nationalist guerrillas on the mainland.

---

7 Anna Chan Chennault, *A Thousand Springs* (New York: P. S. Eriksson, 1962), p. 248; cf. Anna Chennault, *Chennault and the Flying Tigers*, p. 275.

8 Robert Lee Scott, Jr., *Flying Tiger: Chennault of China* (Garden City, N.Y.: Doubleday, 1959), p. 282.

9 Stewart Alsop, *Saturday Evening Post*, 13 December 1958, p. 86.

10 Hilsman, *To Move a Nation* (Garden City, N.Y.: Doubleday, 1967), p. 300.

In 1954 Chennault conducted a vigorous political campaign in support of a grandiose but detailed proposal whereby his old friends Chiang and Syngman Rhee would be unleashed together against the Chinese mainland with the support of a 470-man "International Volunteer Group" modeled after his old Flying Tigers. "Once Chiang unfurls his banner on the mainland," promised Chennault, "Mao will be blighted by spontaneous peasant uprisings and sabotage."[11]

Chennault actually had a list of pilots and had located training sites for the group in Central America, where his former partner Whiting Willauer, now US ambassador to Honduras, was playing a key role in the CIA-organized deposition of Guatemalan president Arbenz. (Willauer was also one of the two chief officials responsible for the planning of the Bay of Pigs operation under the Eisenhower administration.) Chennault's plan was sponsored by Admiral Radford, Chairman of the Joint Chiefs of Staff, and seems to have had CIA support. It was defeated, however, by opposition in the State Department, Pentagon, and Nationalist Chinese Air Force.[12]

CAT, however, had by no means been idle. It flew twenty-four of the twenty-nine C-119s dropping supplies for the French at Dienbienphu. The planes were on "loan" from the US Air Force, and some of the "civilians" flying them were in fact US military pilots. According to Bernard Fall, who flew in these planes, the pilots were "quietly attached to CAT to familiarize themselves with the area in case [as Dulles and Nixon hoped] of American air intervention on behalf of the French."[13]

CAT's C-119s were serviced in Vietnam by two hundred mechanics of the USAF 81st Air Service Unit. Five of these men were declared missing on 18 June 1954. Thus the CAT operation brought about the first official US casualties in the Vietnam war. Senator John Stennis, fearful of a greater US involvement, claimed the Defense Department had violated a "solemn promise" to have the unit removed by June 12.[14]

From the passing of the 1954 Geneva agreements until Chennault's death four years later, CAT seems to have played more of a waiting than an active paramilitary role in Indochina: its planes and

11 Claire Lee Chennault, "Voice of the Tiger" (as reported by Tom McClary), *Flying,* October 1954, pp. 64–68. See also *Look,* 7 September 1954, pp. 80–83; *Flying,* May 1955, p. 69; *Newsweek,* 26 April 1954, p. 41.
12 Neil Sheehan *et al.* (eds.), *The Pentagon Papers* (New York: Bantam, 1971), p. 13; Anna Chennault, *A Thousand Springs,* pp. 263–64.
13 Bernard Fall, *Hell in a Very Small Place* (Philadelphia: Lippincott, 1967), p. 24.
14 *New York Times,* 19 June 1954, p. 3.

pilots being occupied with CIA-supported insurgencies in Indonesia, Burma and Tibet. At the same time it continued to train large number of Chinese mechanics at its huge Taiwan facility. As a right-wing eulogist observed in 1955, they were thus ready for service "if the Communists thrust at Formosa or Thailand or Southern Indochina. . . . CAT has become a symbol of hope to all Free Asia. Tomorrow the Far Eastern skies may redden with a new war and its loaded cargo carrier may roll down the runways once more."[15]

Alsop's "Invasion": Air America Enters into Laos

The Quemoy crises of 1954 and 1958 were generated in large part by a build-up of Chiang's troops on the offshore islands, from which battalion-strength commando raids had been launched. While this build-up was encouraged by local military "advisers" and CIA personnel, it was officially disapproved by Washington. The crises generated new pressures in the Pentagon for bombing the mainland, but with their passage the likelihood of a US-backed offensive seemed to recede decisively. United States intelligence officials later confirmed that the Soviet Union had disappointed China during the 1958 crisis by promising only defensive support. Some US officials concluded that the US could therefore risk confrontation with impunity below China's southern border, since any response by China would only intensify the Sino-Soviet split. The fallacy of this reasoning was soon to be made apparent.

After Quemoy, Laos appeared to present the greatest likelihood of war in the Far East, though hardly because of any inherent aggressiveness in the Laotian people themselves. In 1958, the nonaligned government which had been established in Laos under Prince Souvanna Phouma appeared to be close to a neutralist reconciliation with the pro-Communist Pathet Lao. Fearful that this would lead to the absorption of Laos into the Communist bloc, the United States decided to intervene, and Souvanna Phouma was forced out of office on 23 July 1958 by a timely withholding of US aid. Egged on by its American advisers, the succeeding government of Phoui Sananikone declared itself no longer bound by the provisions of the 1954 Geneva agreements and moved swiftly toward a covert build-up of US military aid, including nonuniformed advisers. Even so, the CIA and the military were not satisfied with the new government, which the State Department had approved. As Hilsman and Schlesinger have re-

---

15 Corey Ford, *Saturday Evening Post,* 12 February 1955, p. 102. For CAT in other countries, see *The Pentagon Papers,* p. 137.

vealed, the CIA organized a right-wing power base under General Phoumi Nosavan and made him a key figure in its subsequent scenarios.

CIA and Pentagon officials were now set upon a course, often opposed to that of the US ambassador in Vientiane, which led to the further destabilization of Laos and hastened the growth of the Pathet Lao. The CIA's plotting on behalf of General Phoumi has therefore frequently been derided as self-defeating. This assumes, however, that the CIA's interest was confined to the rather amorphous internal politics of Laos; in fact the scope of its strategy was far wider.

In December 1958 both North Vietnam and Yunnan province in southern China began to complain of overflights by American or "Laotian" planes. These charges, Arthur J. Dommen intimates, may refer in fact to "flights of American reconnaissance aircraft"; this is corroborated by the revelation in the *Pentagon Papers* that Civil Air Transport was active in supporting the Tibetan operations of this period.[16] (Dommen's informative book, *Conflict in Laos,* was prepared with the aid of the Council on Foreign Relations, published by Praeger, and dedicated to one of the most notorious CIA agents in Taiwan and later in Laos, Robert Campbell James.) Soon afterwards, Peking began to complain of US-supplied Nationalist Chinese Special Forces camps in Yunnan province.

By March 1959, according to Bernard Fall, "Some of the Nationalist Chinese guerrillas operating in the Shan states of neighboring Burma had crossed over into Laotian territory and were being supplied by an airlift of 'unknown planes.' "[17] Laos was already beginning to be what it has since clearly become: a cockpit for international confrontation.

In 1959, following a government crackdown against the leaders and military forces of the Pathet Lao, the country saw an outbreak of sporadic fighting which General Phoumi quickly labeled a North Vietnamese "invasion." On 23 August the *New York Times* reported the arrival of two CAT transports in the Laotian capital, Vientiane. More transports arrived soon thereafter. On 30 August a "crisis" occurred that was to be used as a pretext for a permanent paramilitary airlift operation. (Meanwhile, on 31 March 1959, CAT, Inc., the American management corporation operating the Taiwan company, changed its name to Air America, Inc.)

---

16 Arthur J. Dommen, *Conflict in Laos: The Politics of Neutralization* (New York: Praeger, 1964), p. 115; *Pentagon Papers,* p. 137.
17 Bernard Fall, *Anatomy of a Crisis* (Garden City, N.Y.: Doubleday, 1969), p. 99.

All through August, reports from three of Phoumi's generals created a minor war hysteria in the US press, which depicted an invasion of Laos by five or more North Vietnamese battalions. At one point, when August rains washed out a bridge, the *New York Times* reported "Laos Insurgents Take Army Post Close to Capital," and speculated that they were trying to cut off Vientiane from the south. As for the "crisis" of 30 August, the *Washington Post* wrote that 3,500 Communist rebels, "including regular Viet-minh troops, have captured eighty villages in a new attack in northern Laos." Much later, it was learned that in fact not eighty but three villages had been evacuated, after two of them had been briefly blanketed by 81-mm mortar fire at dawn on 30 August. No infantry attack had been observed: the defending garrisons, as so often happened in Laos, had simply fled.

After it was all over, the Laotian government claimed only that it had lost ninety-two men during the period of the "invasion" crisis from 16 July to 7 October 1959; more than half of these deaths ("estimated at fifty killed") took place on 30 August. A UN investigating team, after personal interviews, reduced the latter estimate from fifty to five. No North Vietnamese invaders were ever discovered. Though the Laotians claimed at one point to have seven North Vietnamese prisoners, it was later admitted that these were deserters who had crossed over from North Vietnam in order to surrender.

Joseph Alsop, however, who had arrived in Laos just in time to report the events of 30 August, wrote immediately of a "massive new attack on Laos" by "at least three and perhaps five new battalions of enemy troops from North Vietnam." In the next few days he would write of "aggression, as naked, as flagrant as a Soviet-East German attack on West Germany," noting that "the age-old process of Chinese expansion has begun again with a new explosive force." Unlike most reporters, Alsop could claim to have first-hand reports: on 1 September at the town of Sam Neua, he had seen the arrival on foot of survivors (one of whom had a "severe leg wound") from the mortared outposts. Bernard Fall, who was also in Laos and knew the area well, later called all of this "just so much nonsense," specifying that "a villager with a severe leg wound does not cover 45 miles in two days of march in the Laotian jungle."[18] Alsop, by Fall's ac-

---

18 Bernard Fall, *Street Without Joy* (Harrisburg, Pa.: Stackpole, 1964), pp. 334–35; cf. *Anatomy*, p. 136.

count, had been a willing witness to a charade staged for his benefit by two of Phoumi's generals.[19]

As on many occasions between 1949 and 1964, Alsop's reports were to play an important role in shaping the Asian developments he described. The London *Times* drew attention to the stir his story created in Washington. Senator Dodd and others clamored vainly that in the light of the "invasion" Khrushchev's impending visit to America should be put off. Though this did not happen, there were three lasting consequences of the "great Laos fraud" of August 1959.

First, on 26 August, the State Department announced that additional US aid and personnel would be sent to Laos: thus the military support program was stepped up at a time when a congressional exposure of its scandal and futility had threatened to terminate it altogether. Second, reportedly under a presidential order dated 4 September, CINCPAC Commander Harry D. Felt moved US ground, sea, and air forces into a more forward posture for possible action in Laos. (A signal corps unit is supposed to have been put in Laos at this time, the first US field unit in Southeast Asia.)[20] Third, the planes of CAT (i.e., Air America) were moved into Laos to handle the stepped-up aid, and additional transports (over the approved 1954 levels) were given to the Laotian government. At the same time a Chennault-type "volunteer air force" of US active and reserve officers ("American Fliers for Laos") was said by the *Times* to be negotiating a contract for an operation "like that of the Flying Tigers."[21]

The timing of these germinal decisions is intriguing. On the day of the aid announcement, 26 August, Eisenhower had left for Europe at 3:20 in the morning to visit western leaders before receiving Khrushchev in Washington. At a press conference on the eve of his departure, he professed ignorance about the details of the Laotian aid request, which had just been received that morning. He did, however, specify that the State Department had not yet declared the existence of an "invasion" (something it would do during his absence).[22] The date of the "Presidential Order" on Laos, 4 September,

19 Denis Warner, another anti-Communist journalist, heard some of the same witnesses, and reported that the local general "accepted as fact what the most junior western staff officer would have rejected as fiction (*The Last Confucian*. New York: Macmillan, 1963, p. 210). This seems to be a barb directed at Alsop, a former US staff officer in Chungking under Chennault.

20 *Bangkok Post,* 12 September 1959.

21 *New York Times,* 25 September 1959, p. 4; 27 September 1959, p. 16.

22 The State Department's announcement of 26 August caused some congressmen to complain that they had heard nothing about increased assistance in a secret briefing two days before (*New York Times,* 31 August 1959, p. 10).

was the day allotted in Eisenhower's itinerary for a golf holiday at the secluded Culzean Castle in Scotland. According to his memoirs, which corroborate earlier press reports, "our stolen holiday was interrupted *the following morning* [i.e., 5 September] by bad news from Laos." Eisenhower added, "My action *on return to the United States* was to approve increased aid to the pro-United States government" (emphasis added). He is silent about the troop movements he reportedly authorized.[23]

Knowing this, one would like to learn why a US response to an artificially inflated "emergency" on 30 August was delayed until Eisenhower's virtual isolation five days later, even though it could not await his return to Washington three days after that. Once again it is the knowledgeable Joseph Alsop who supplies the corroborating details: "Communications are non-existent in little Laos. Hence word of the new 'invasion' took more than 48 hours to reach the commander of the Laotian Army, General Ouane Rathikone. There was, of course, a further delay before the grave news reached Washington. Time also was needed to assess its significance."[24]

Bernard Fall rejects this explanation: "The Laotian Army command . . . *did* know what went on in the border posts since it had radio communications with them."[25] The Senate Foreign Relations Committee would do well to investigate the resulting possibility that the first US field unit in Southeast Asia was put in by a combination of deliberate misrepresentation and evasion of proper presidential review. Washington columnist Marquis Childs reported soon after the "invasion" that: "A powerful drive is on within the upper bureaucracy of Defense and Intelligence to persuade President Eisenhower that he must send American troops into Laos. . . . They will consist of two Marine regiments of the Third Marine Division now stationed on Okinawa and components of the 1st Marine Air Wing, also on Okinawa [having been moved up in the course of the crisis]. Notice would be served on the Communists—Red China and North Vietnam—that if they did not withdraw in one week, they would be attacked. According to one source, they would use the tactical atomic weapons with which they are in part at least already equipped."[26]

Senator Mansfield asked in the Senate on 7 September whether

23 Dwight D. Eisenhower: *Waging Peace: 1956–1961* (Garden City, N.Y.: Doubleday, 1965), p. 431. These memoirs complicate the picture by the erroneous statement that Eisenhower flew to Scotland on the morning of 3 September, rather than 4.
24 Joseph Alsop, *Washington Post,* 4 October 1959, A25.
25 *Street Without Joy,* p. 334; cf. *Anatomy,* p. 136.
26 *Washington Post,* 11 September 1959, A14.

the President and Secretary of State Herter still made foreign policy, or whether the various executive agencies, like Defense and CIA, had taken over. Today, with Air America deep in Laotian war business, Congress should surely learn more about the arrival of CAT's planes in Vientiane on 22 August, before the 30 August crisis and the US government's two critical policy decisions. The "American Fliers for Laos" would violate the provisions of the Neutrality Act quite as clearly as had the Flying Tigers: was there then an authorization from Eisenhower to parallel that granted by Roosevelt? One witness who might be called to testify is Joseph Alsop, who, like some of the China hands in the CIA and the Pentagon, had himself worked for Chennault in China during World War II.

Air America Helps to Overthrow a Government

Although the CIA's General Phoumi was largely responsible for the intrigues of the August "invasion," the State Department's Phoui Sananikone was still in office. On 30 December, according to Schlesinger, the CIA "moved in" and toppled Phoui.[27]

A few months later, in April 1960, the CIA helped to rig an election for their man Phoumi. Dommen reports that "CIA agents participated in the election rigging, with or without the authority of the American ambassador. A Foreign Service officer . . . had seen CIA agents distribute bagfuls of money to village headmen."[28] But this maneuver was so flagrant that it discredited the government and (according to Denis Warner) "precipitated" a coup in August, restoring the old neutralist premier, Souvanna Phouma.[29]

Over the next few weeks, Souvanna Phouma's new government succeeded in winning the approval of the king, American ambassador Winthrop Brown, and the new right-wing, but pliant, national assembly. In due course his pro-neutralist government was officially recognized by the United States. Nevertheless General Phoumi, after consulting with his cousin Marshal Sarit in Thailand, decided to move against Souvanna, proclaiming a rival "Revolutionary Committee" in southern Laos. Phoumi's first announcement of his opposition took the form of leaflets dropped from a C-47 over the Laotian capital. Presumably the pilot was an American mercenary, as the Laotians were not known to have been trained to handle these planes.

In the next three months, according to Schlesinger, "A united

---

27 Arthur J. Schlesinger, Jr., *A Thousand Days* (Boston: Houghton Mifflin, 1965), p. 326.
28 Dommen, p. 133.
29 Denis Warner, *Reporting Southeast Asia* (Sydney: Angus and Robertson, 1966), p. 167.

embassy, including CIA [i.e., CIA station chief Gordon L. Jorgensen] followed Brown in recommending that Washington accept Souvanna's coalition. . . . As for the Defense Department, it was all for Phoumi. *Possibly* with encouragement from Defense and CIA men *in the field,* Phoumi . . . proclaimed a new government and denounced Souvanna. The Phoumi regime became the recipient of American military aid, while the Souvanna government in Vientiane continued to receive economic aid. Ambassador Brown still worked to bring them together, but the military *support* convinced Phoumi that, if he only held out, Washington would put him in power."[30] The words which I have italicized are inexcusably misleading: Phoumi, from the beginning of his formal insurgency in September, had high-level CIA and Pentagon encouragement to oust Souvanna's supporters in Vientiane. The proof of this was that while Sarit's forces in Thailand blockaded Vientiane, Air America was stepping up its military airlift to Phoumi's base at Savannakhet.

"It was plain," writes Dommen, "that General Phoumi was rapidly building up his matériel and manpower for a march on Vientiane. From mid-September, Savannakhet was the scene of an increased number of landings and take-offs by unmarked C-46 and C-47 transports, manned by American crews. These planes belonged to Air America, Inc., a civilian charter company with US Air Force organizational support and under contract to the US Government."[31]

In October, Hilsman reports, Ambassador Brown was telling Souvanna that the United States "had Phoumi's promise not to use the aid against . . . the neutralist forces" in Vientiane. Yet even as he did so, two men "flew to Savannakhet and gave Phoumi the green light to retake Vientiane."[32] The two men were not some CIA spooks "in the field," but John N. Irwin II, Assistant Secretary of Defense for International Security Affairs, and Vice-Admiral Herbert D. Riley, chief of staff of the US Pacific Command. Meanwhile the Meo tribesmen, encouraged by the CIA, defected from Souvanna in mid-October, at which point Air America began supplying them with

---

30 Schlesinger, pp. 326–37.

31 Dommen, p. 154. A. Schlesinger, so scathing about "CIA spooks" in Laos, is discreetly silent on the subject of Air America. Even Hilsman, while attacking the "tragedy" of inter-agency rivalry and the CIA's "attempt to 'play God' in Lao political life," says merely that "air transports of a civilian American airline began a steady shuttle to Phoumi's base in Savannakhet (*To Move a Nation*, p. 124). It is important to remember that Schlesinger and Hilsman (both ex-OSS) were intimately involved with covert CIA operations during the Kennedy administration.

32 Keyes Beech, "How Uncle Sam Fumbled in Laos," *Saturday Evening Post,* 22 April 1961, p. 89.

matériel and US Special Forces cadres from Savannakhet. Despite the 1962 Geneva agreements, this airlift has continued up to the present.

December 1960: Eisenhower O.K.s Air America in Laos

Why did top US officials deliberately foment a conflict between non-Communist forces in Laos, a conflict that led to rapid increases in the territory held by the Pathet Lao? According to *Time* magazine (17 March 1961), "the aim, explained the CIA, who called Phoumi 'our boy,' was to 'polarize' the communist and anti-communist factions in Laos." If so, the aim was achieved: the country is today a battle-field where US bombings, with between four and five hundred sorties a day in 1970, have generated six hundred thousand refugees. "Polar-ization," as sanctioned by the Thai blockade of Vientiane and a US refusal of supplies, forced Souvanna Phouma to request an airlift of rice and oil (and later guns) from the Soviet Union, and in the end to invite in North Vietnamese and Chinese "technicians." The first So-viet transport planes arrived in Vientiane on 4 December 1960, and the Russians were careful to send civilian pilots. As Dommen notes, they were "following the precedent set by the United States."[33]

In late December an American transport was actually fired on by a Soviet Ilyushin 14, and a major international conflict seemed pos-sible. Of course there were some in CIA and Defense who thought that a showdown with "communism" in Asia was inevitable, and better sooner than later. Many more, including most of the Joint Chiefs, believed that America's first priority in Laos was interna-tional, to maintain a militant "forward strategy" against an imagined Chinese expansionism. Thus the actual thrust of American policy, if not its avowed intention, was toward the Chennault-Air America vision of "rollback" in Asia.

The last weeks of 1960 were to see ominous indications that anti-Communist forces were only too willing to internationalize the conflict, especially with the first reports in the *Times* and *Le Monde* that General Phoumi's forces were being bolstered by Thai combat troops in Laotian uniforms and by Thai helicopters.[34] The expulsion of Souvanna from Vientiane in mid-December ended nothing; for the next eighteen months Laos would have two "governments," each rec-ognized and supplied by a major power.

Did Eisenhower authorize this race to the brink? Years later, in 1966, an article in the *New York Times* claimed that the President

---

33 Dommen, p. 164.
34 *New York Times*, 21 December 1960, p. 30; *Le Monde*, 6 December 1960, p. 4.

"had specifically approved" the CIA's backing of Phoumi against Ambassador Brown's advice; the article, however, said nothing about the Pentagon and Air America's airlift.[35] Eisenhower's own memoirs, in an extraordinary passage, state quite clearly that it was after 13 December (*after* the crisis posed by the new Soviet airlift) that he approved the use of "United States aircraft" to "transport supplies into the area." Air America's planes are clearly referred to, since the use of Air Force transports was not authorized until 26 April 1961: "As Phoumi proceeded to retake Vientiane, General Goodpaster reported the events to me. . . . He then posed several questions: 'First, should we seek to have Thai aircraft transport supplies into the area? Second, if the Thais can't do the job, should we use United States aircraft?' . . . I approved the use of Thai transport aircraft and United States aircraft as well!"[36]

These last pages of Eisenhower's memoirs reveal how little he was briefed by bureaucrats as they prepared for a changeover to the incoming Kennedy administration. Just as he knew nothing of the detailed plans for an invasion of Cuba which had been approved by the CIA's "Special Group" on 4 November, so he apparently did not know that Thai helicopters were already being used in a combat support role, nor that Air America had been flying missions for Laos for over a year.

This would help explain why a story reporting the crash of an Air America plane in November on the Plaine des Jarres was not carried in any American newspaper, though it was printed abroad in the *Bangkok Post* of 28 November 1960. (The plane's American pilot was wounded seriously; the Chinese co-pilot, son of Nationalist Chinese ambassador to Washington Hollington Tong, was killed.)

It also fits in with the fact that US officials announced on 7 December (six days before Eisenhower authorized the flights) that they had "interrupted military air shipments" to Phoumi.[37] After the interruption, Eisenhower was asked to authorize what was in fact a *resumption* of the airlift to Phoumi while apparently under the impression that he was *initiating* it. Thus Air America was "legalized"

35 *New York Times,* 28 April 1966, p. 28.

36 Eisenhower, pp. 608–09.

37 *New York Times,* 8 December 1960, p. 7. "At the same time, they added, the United States has accelerated delivery to South Vietnam of military equipment needed to fight Communist guerrillas [and] also has recast military training of the Vietnamese Army to emphasize anti-guerrilla operations." The story shows how (as on many later occasions) de-escalation in Laos was balanced by escalation in Vietnam; and also how critical military decisions attributed to the Kennedy administration in 1961 had in fact been made by the Pentagon during the lame-duck Eisenhower administration.

just in time for the incoming Kennedy administration. For the purposes of this legalization the Soviet airlift—which Pentagon machinations had done so much to induce—was not a disaster but a godsend: the airlift could now be justified to the President (as it was to the people) by the formula that (in Sulzberger's words) "we are starting to match" the Soviet airlift.[38]

As in the case of the September 1959 Executive Order, so once again Eisenhower's *ex post facto* authorization of Air America in December 1960 may have been strategically timed to coincide with his seclusion. General Phoumi's troops, after pausing for many weeks in their drive up the Mekong River, bestirred themselves in December, and finally entered Vientiane at the equivalent of 5:00 A.M. Eastern Standard Time, 16 December. Eisenhower's memoirs indicate that General Goodpaster asked him about a US airlift sometime before Phoumi's entry in Vientiane, but after 13 December.[39] If so the Goodpaster interview probably took place in Walter Reed Army Hospital, rather than in the White House, for Eisenhower entered hospital as planned for his annual physical examination on the evening of 13 December, and left it at 10:20 A.M. 15 December. Once again, by coincidence or not, a crucial presidential decision about Air America was implemented, as an "emergency," at a time of Eisenhower's scheduled isolation.

Perhaps some student of White House contingency procedures can confirm whether the Vice-President of the United States, Richard Nixon, played any part in these two dubious decisions.

A final indication of constitutional chicanery about the authorization of Air America's airlift is the energy expended by right-wing CIA elements in rewriting Laotian history for the December 1960 period. We can see this in the CIA-inspired attack by Charles Murphy on the role of Eisenhower and Kennedy in the Bay of Pigs fiasco, an attack for which the CIA had the gall to seek an official State Department clearance:

> Phoumi eventually took the capital, Vientiane, early in December, *but at this point* the Russians intervened openly. . . . In concert with a large-scale push by well-trained troops from North Vietnam, they introduced a substantial airlift into northern Laos (an operation that is still continuing). The collapse of the Royal Laotian Army then became inevitable unless the U.S. came in *with at least equal weight* on

38 *New York Times,* 21 December 1960, p. 30. This is the earliest allusion I have been able to find in any American paper to Air America's stepped-up activities after August 1960.
39 Eisenhower, p. 609.

Phoumi's side. One obvious measure was to put the airlift out of business. The job could have been done by "volunteer" pilots and the challenge would at least have established, at not too high an initial risk for the U.S., how far the Russians were prepared to go. Another measure would have been to bring SEATO forces into the battle, as the SEATO treaty provided. In the end, Eisenhower decided to sheer away from both measures. . . . Even the *modest additional support* that the Defense Department tried to extend to Phoumi's battalions in the field during the last weeks of the Eisenhower Administration was diluted by reason of the conflict between Defense and State.[40]

Phoumi did not secure Vientiane until 16 December; the Soviet airlift had begun on 4 December. By thus reversing the order of events, the article implies that the US was sending aid to a legal government, the USSR to rebels; but the genesis of the conflict was in fact the other way round. One should not be surprised to learn that, once again, this rewritten version of history was first published in the column of Joseph Alsop.[41]

The Murphy article, though misleading in its historical facts, correctly shows the magnitude of the choice Eisenhower faced that December. The Laotian crisis of the election year 1960, like the Tonkin Gulf crisis of the election year 1964 and the *Pueblo* crisis of the election year 1968, placed the President under great pressure to put more US troops into Asia. In all three cases, the military wanted a vastly escalated response to a crisis for which they, along with our intelligence community, were largely responsible. The Soviet airlift was apparently presented to Eisenhower as being so reprehensible that the "volunteers" should shoot the planes down; yet it was Air America that set a precedent for this, apparently without presidential authorization.

Air America's actions were in fact leading our country into war in Southeast Asia. And it is hard to believe that Air America's directors were unconscious of this. Retired Admiral Felix B. Stump, until 1958 US Commander-in-Chief, Pacific, and Air America's board chairman since 1959, had told a Los Angeles audience in April 1960, "World War III has already started, and we are deeply involved in it." Later he declared it was "high time" the nation won over commu-

40 Charles J. V. Murphy, "Cuba: The Record Set Straight," *Fortune,* September 1961, p. 94, emphasis added; article discussed in Paul W. Blackstock, *The Strategy of Subversion* (Chicago: Quadrangle, 1964), p. 250.

41 *Washington Post,* 6 January 1961, A19: "The success of Phoumi and Boun Oum produced a result which Washington had not foreseen. The Soviets and North Vietnamese quite flagrantly intervened in Laos, to restore their pawns [i.e., Souvanna Phouma!] to power."

nism in the Far East, and he called for the use of tactical nuclear weapons if necessary. Containment was not enough: we must "move beyond this limited objective."[42]

The admiral was not speaking in a vacuum. Now in one country, now in another, the tempo of US operations in Southeast Asia did indeed increase steadily over the next few years. After a disastrous experiment in the latest counterinsurgency techniques in Laos, for example (with Air America planes and pilots transporting the Laotian army), the Kennedy administration agreed in May 1961 to a Laotian cease-fire and negotiations. One day later, Rusk announced the first of a series of steps to increase the involvement of US forces, including Air America, in Vietnam. A year later the United States signed the July 1962 Geneva agreements to neutralize Laos. Unfortunately, as in 1954 and 1961, the price for US agreement to this apparent de-escalation was a further build-up of US (and Air America) commitments in Vietnam and also Thailand. No diplomatic agreements have ever interrupted this slow but inexorable American build-up in Southeast Asia. Hence it is not surprising that in the Paris talks the other side has been intransigent about the principle of US troop withdrawal, nor that Nixon's public "Vietnamizing" of the war should be balanced by a secret expansion of Air America's role in it.

Despite the 1962 Geneva agreements, Air America has never dismantled its private war enterprise in Laos. Although the agreements providently called for the withdrawal of "foreign civilians connected with the supply, maintenance, storing, and utilization of war materials," Air America continued to fly into northeastern Laos, and it appears that some of the uniformed US military "advisers" simply reverted to their pre-Kennedy civilian disguise. The first military incident in the resumption of fighting was the shooting down of an Air America plane in November 1962, three days after the Pathet Lao had warned that they would do so.

What made the Air America coterie, with its influential backers in the Pentagon and CIA and its dependent Nationalist Chinese remnants from Burma, hang on in Laos with such tenacity? Hilsman tells us that, at least as late as 1962, there were those in the Pentagon and CIA "who believed that a direct confrontation with Communist China was inevitable."[43] In his judgment, the basic assumption underlying the CIA's programs in Laos, and particularly the airlift to the

---

42 Fred J. Cook, *The Warfare State* (New York: Macmillan, 1962), p. 265; *Los Angeles Times*, 6 April 1960, III, p. 2.
43 Hilsman, p. 311.

Meos, "seemed to be that Laos was sooner or later to become a major battleground in a military sense between the East and West."[44]

In 1962, says Hilsman, a CIA proposal for a " 'covert' but large-scale landing" on the Chinese mainland itself was turned down; and in June 1962, on the eve of the Laos Geneva Conference, the Chinese ambassador in Warsaw was informed (for the first time) "that no United States support would be given to any Nationalist attempt to invade the mainland." This apparent rejection of Chennault's old "rollback" proposals did not, however, put an end to covert operations in Southeast Asia—quite the opposite.

Now that a US attack on China seemed less likely, first Vietnam and later Thailand threatened to move toward "neutralism" and a rapprochement with their Communist neighbors. Many observers now agree with Tom Wicker of the *New York Times* that one important reason for Diem's removal in November 1963 was "Washington's apprehension that Diem's unstable brother, Nhu, was trying to make a 'neutralist' settlement with the Viet Cong and North Vietnam through French intermediaries."[45]

In 1964 the increasing Vietnamese drift toward neutralism became an even greater argument for a US escalation, but President Johnson proved unwilling to authorize any dramatic public steps in an election year. Once again, as in the election year 1960, covert war proved to be the easiest answer to the dilemma between democracy and imperialism: how to appear peaceful at home while intervening abroad.

Once again Laos was the perfect terrain: as in 1960, a CIA-linked right-wing coup, followed by a left-wing reaction, was the moving cause for a major outbreak of fighting. Once again Air America's planes were involved in continuous warfare, as they have been with incremental escalations ever since. They were now joined by jets of the USAF and Navy (on 5 August 1964, the latter were diverted from their Laotian targets for the Tonkin Gulf retaliation). As in 1960, this activity in Laos supplied the infrastructure and air capability for a subsequent build-up in Vietnam.

To an extraordinary extent the history of Air America *is* the history of America's recent involvement in Southeast Asia. The airline

---

44 *Ibid.*, p. 115.

45 Tom Wicker, *JFK and LBJ: The Influence of Personality upon Politics* (New York: William Morrow, 1968), pp. 187–88; cf. *Washington Post*, 1 July 1971, A18; *Pentagon Papers*, p. 204.

has grown with this involvement, so that by 1968 it had amassed a fleet of nearly two hundred planes and employed an estimated eleven thousand people. (By comparison, its "competitor," the Flying Tiger Line, which was the largest all-cargo carrier in the world when Air America was set up, had only twenty-two planes and 2,089 employees by 1968.)

It is a striking index of the real war strategy of the current administration that Air America's operations, far from being phased out, are on the increase. The main problem Washington sees in Southeast Asian policy is that the war has become too public; the idea now is to hang on by reemphasizing the covert while publicly "Vietnamizing" the war to dull popular concern. Nixon is again stepping up our undercover involvements in Southeast Asia, with special focus in Laos and Cambodia, battlefields rarely penetrated by nosy TV camera teams.

As the *New York Times* reported on 18 September 1969, authoritative sources confirmed that "United States B-52 strikes along the Laotian sections of the [Ho Chi Minh] trail have increased greatly in the last two weeks . . . as many as 500 sorties a day were being flown over Laos, and . . . the increase in bombing in Laos was part of the reason for the lull in the air war in South Vietnam. . . . United States planes—of Air America, Continental Air Services and the United States Air Force—were flying reinforcements, supplies, and arms to advanced areas, while American Army officers and agents of the Central Intelligence Agency were advising local commanders."

There are clear indications that this upsurge in covert warfare is slated to be an enduring rather than a momentary phenomenon. In October 1969 Air America was making job offers to pilots who had been processed and given security clearances as much as three years earlier, but never employed. One prospective flyer—who was told he would be based in Saigon but could expect to operate throughout Southeast Asia—asked why positions had suddenly become available after such a long interval. The explanation was that Air America's operations had been at a steady level for the last four or five years—including the peak period of the Vietnam escalation—but that they were now expected to increase!

And in the wake of the Tonkin escalation, one Washington faction held, as Bernard Fall has written: "That the Vietnam affair could be transformed into a 'golden opportunity' to 'solve' the Red Chinese problem as well, possibly by a pan-Asian 'crusade' involving

Chinese Nationalist, Korean and Japanese troops, backed by United States power as needed."[46]

These strange lusts for conflagration, which do not yet seem to have been sated, have never quite achieved official dominance in Washington. But the old fantasies of rollback were nourished by Chennault and his successor, Retired Admiral Felix Stump, while each was serving as board chairman of CAT and Air America. And the combination of Air America and the CIA did manage to advance the fantasy in Laos—under Kennedy, it seems, as well as Eisenhower—by strengthening the intransigence of General Phoumi while "official" US policy was to induce him into a neutral coalition.

What is the source of the quasi-independent political power that has fueled Air America in such efforts? Later in this book we will take a look at Air America's influential private backers and directors, representing the Rockefellers and other respectable New York financial interests. Why should such pillars of America's "external establishment" involve themselves in such a shady enterprise, and why choose such a fustian spokesman for rollback as Stump to be its chairman? To answer such questions will take us deep into the intricate involvements that will be seen to prevail between Wall Street, the CIA, and the Kuomintang.

46 Bernard Fall, *Vietnam Witness 1953–1966* (New York: Praeger, 1966), p. 103.

During the spring of 1961, when President Kennedy made his first series of Vietnam decisions, Laos—not Vietnam—was the dominant issue and largely determined how Vietnam should be handled, according to the Pentagon account. . . . President Kennedy chose to seek a political compromise and military cease-fire rather than continue to support the Laotian rightists. Because of this shift in strategy in Laos, the Pentagon study says, the Kennedy administration felt impelled to show strength in Vietnam to reassure America's allies in Asia.

On May 17 [1964], when the Pathet Lao launched an offensive on the Plaine des Jarres . . . , the study declares, this "deliberate, cautious approach" to escalation planning [in Vietnam] was suddenly thrown into "crisis management."

The Pentagon Papers

Chapter Two
Laos: 1960–70

 The key to President Nixon's program of overt troop withdrawal in Vietnam has been covert escalation in Laos. His Key Biscayne statement on Laos of 6 March 1970 itself drew attention to the connection between the two conflicts, which was soon underlined by Vice-President Agnew. In reality the so-called Vietnamization in 1969 of the ground war in South Vietnam was balanced by a sharp escalation of the US air war in Laos, where it could not be observed by western newsmen. This escalation was then rationalized (though not admitted) by the President's statement on Laos, which put forth a grossly misleading history of North Vietnamese "persistent subversion" and "invasion."

This story was put together long before the

27

Nixon administration. Many of its allegations were supplied years ago by US intelligence sources, who had a stake in misrepresenting the Laotian war which they had themselves largely helped to create. The statement must, however, be answered, since it is at least as misleading as the intelligence reports of North Vietnamese and Chinese aggression in South Vietnam that preceded our air war in that country. Of course the escalation in the long run will involve two sides, and some day historians can analyze the whole involvement in Laos of Thailand, the Philippines, South Vietnam, North Vietnam, the United States, Taiwan, and China.

It is important, however, to see that it has been not North Vietnam but the United States, and more particularly its apparatus of civil and military intelligence agencies, that has been consistently guilty of the *initial* subversion of whatever order has been established in Laos through international agreements. Thus the President's statement should be examined in the light of indubitable CIA and US Air Force activities that he wholly leaves out.

Although the present war in Laos dates back to 1959, the President's statement was totally silent about the 1959–61 period. This is understandable, since virtually every independent observer has condemned the subversive activities in Laos of the CIA and other US agencies during the period when Mr. Nixon was Vice-President. A Rand Corporation report on Laos concluded, for example, that in 1959 it was not the pro-Communist Pathet Lao but the right-wing Sananikone government (which had been installed by US intrigue and was counseled by US advisers) that "precipitated the final crisis which led to war in Laos."[1]

This "final crisis" followed a probe by a government patrol into the small but sensitive disputed area of Huong Lap on the North Vietnamese border, which had been governed as part of Vietnam in the days of the French. When the patrol was, predictably, fired upon, the government charged the North Vietnamese with frontier incursions and claimed that this was related to a planned insurrection by the Pathet Lao. It then obtained a vote of emergency powers from the assembly, and soon ordered the two remaining battalions of the Pathet Lao to be integrated forthwith into the national army.

The Pathet Lao had previously (in November 1957) agreed to this integration, as part of a political settlement in which they received

---

1 A. M. Halpern and H. B. Friedman, *Communist Strategy in Laos,* Rand, RM–2561, p. 51; cited and amplified in Bernard Fall, *Anatomy of a Crisis* (Garden City, N.Y.: Doubleday, 1969), p. 108.

two cabinet posts and were permitted to participate in elections for specially created seats in the national assembly. In this election the Pathet Lao and their allies (the party of left-leaning neutralist Quinim Pholsena) obtained 32 percent of the votes and thirteen of the twenty-one contested seats, showing that they had grown considerably in popularity in the four years since the 1954 Geneva agreements. (Prince Souphanouvong, the Pathet Lao leader and half-brother of the then premier Prince Souvanna Phouma, received more votes than any other candidate.)

Arthur Schlesinger, Jr., has recorded the response of the US to the election:

> Washington decided to install a reliably pro-Western regime. CIA spooks put in their appearance, set up a Committee for the Defense of National Interest (CDNI) and brought back from France as its chief an energetic, ambitious and devious officer named Phoumi Nosavan. Prince Souvanna, who had shown himself an honest and respected if impulsive leader, was forced out of office [by a withholding of US aid and CIA encouragement of a parliamentary crisis, allegedly through the use of bribes] . . . a veteran politician named Phoumi Sananikone took his place.[2]

The Pathet Lao were then excluded from the new cabinet approved on 18 August 1958.

In May 1959 one Pathet Lao battalion refused, understandably, to be assimilated under the new right-wing government, and it decamped to a valley on the North Vietnamese border. The Sananikone government then declared that the Pathet Lao had committed an act of open rebellion and that only a military solution appeared possible. It thus by its own actions deflected the Pathet Lao from the role of political opposition into a military insurgency for which it was poorly prepared, so that it was forced increasingly to depend on North Vietnamese support.

In August 1959 the government itself received a large increase in US military support by claiming, falsely, that it had been "invaded" by a North Vietnamese force of as many as eleven battalions. (In February the government had given itself the right to receive this support by declaring unilaterally, with US approval, that it would no longer be bound by the limitations on foreign military aid that it had accepted at Geneva in 1954.) Bernard Fall and the British historian Hugh Toye linked the phony invasion scare to a US congressional

---

2 Arthur Schlesinger, Jr., *A Thousand Days* (Boston: Houghton Mifflin, 1965), pp. 325–26.

exposé at this time of major scandals in the Laos aid program, and to the very real risk that US military aid would be curtailed.[3]

It is frequently claimed that the Pathet Lao was never more than a front for North Vietnamese ambitions in Laos; but this is contradicted by the election results of 1958 (the last honest elections in Laos). Though before 1954 Souphanouvong and his cadres had fought with the Vietminh against the French, the indubitable growth in popularity of the Pathet Lao between 1954 and 1958, by which time it had established a country-wide network of cells at the village level, must be attributed to its own talent for organization, particularly in exploiting the resentment of the many hill tribes against the dominant Lao population in the lowlands and cities.

Let us examine the President's statement itself.

1) "By 1961 North Vietnamese involvement became marked, the communist forces made great advances, and a serious situation confronted the Kennedy administration."

Comment: The crisis facing President Kennedy in early 1961 was the armed conflict following the successful displacement from the capital city of Vientiane of Souvanna Phouma's neutralist government (which we officially recognized) by the CIA-supported right-wing insurrectionary forces of General Phoumi Nosavan. His rebellion against Souvanna had from the outset received logistical support from the CIA's proprietary airline, Air America. With its help, Phoumi's royal Laotian army drove the neutralist troops of General Kong Le, Souvanna's military chief, to the north and into a temporary alliance with the pro-Communist Pathet Lao. After Kong Le captured the Plaine des Jarres from Phoumi's troops, the Pathet Lao moved south to join him. Souvanna Phouma and Kong Le, genuine neutralists who feared North Vietnamese influence, nevertheless had been forced to seek communist support in order to survive Phoumi's attack. Thus CIA-sponsored subversion was itself directly responsible for the Communists' "great advances."[4]

3 Hugh Toye, *Laos: Buffer State or Battleground* (Oxford: OUP, 1968), pp. 113–31; US Congress, House, Committee on Government Operations, *United States Aid Operations in Laos: Seventh Report*, 86th Cong., 1st Sess., 15 June 1969.

4 Text of the President's statement as printed in the *San Francisco Chronicle*, 6 March 1970, p. 9. The late Bernard Fall observed of the CIA's policy of deliberate "polarization" in Laos in this period that "it had thrown into communism's arms a great many people who essentially were *not* communists (just as in 1946 many Vietnamese who at first merely wanted the French to get out as colonial masters in Vietnam were finally pushed into Ho Chi Minh's Vietminh) but who, by deliberate action on our side, were left with no alternative." (Fall, *Anatomy of a Crisis*, p. 199; cf. p. 189.)

Cf. also Arthur Schlesinger, Jr., *A Thousand Days*, p. 328. "The Eisenhower Administration, by rejecting the neutralist alternative, had driven the neutralists into reluctant alli-

It is true that in late 1960 Souvanna Phouma's government, faced with US encouragement of a rebellion against it, did in response invite in Russian, North Vietnamese, and Chinese "advisers," thus creating the first known North Vietnamese presence in Laos since the 1954 Geneva agreements. However, A. J. Dommen dates the presence of North Vietnamese combat troops (along "the Laos-Vietnam border") from July/August 1962, and contrasts them with "the technical experts and cadres that North Vietnam had maintained in Laos since the end of 1960."[5] Bernard Fall estimated that: "The fighting in Laos in 1960–62 involved relatively small forces from the [North Vietnamese] 335th and 316th divisions, many of whose men were of the same Thai *montagnard* stock as the tribesmen on the Laotian side."[6] The British observer Hugh Toye writes that "On balance, participation by Vietminh infantry, as opposed to cadres and support detachments, in the skirmishes of 1961–2 is unlikely." But by early 1961 the US had brought in AT-6s armed with bombs and rockets, US pilots to fly them, and Special Forces "White Star" teams to encourage guerrilla activity by Meo tribesmen behind the Pathet Lao lines. Furthermore, Air America was using American helicopters and American pilots to move Phoumi's troops into battle. At this time the Joint Chiefs of Staff pressed for a military showdown over Laos, including the possible use of tactical nuclear weapons, while Richard Nixon himself, in a meeting with Kennedy, urged "a commitment of American air power."[7]

2) *"[In 1962]   During the course of those long negotiations [at Geneva for a Laotian settlement] fighting continued and the communists made further advances."*

Comment: This is misleading, since both the delays and the renewal of fighting in 1962 were again clearly attributable to Phoumi

---

ance with the communists and provoked (and in many eyes legitimized) open Soviet aid to the Pathet Lao. All this was done without serious consultation with the incoming administration which would shortly inherit the problem." For further details, see Toye, *Laos*, pp. 145–65.

5 Arthur J. Dommen, *Conflict in Laos: The Politics of Neutralization* (New York: Praeger, 1964), p. 238. Even though he conceded that North Vietnam in 1962 was "very probably" moved by fear of the five thousand US troops airlifted into Thailand, Dommen was no apologist for the North Vietnamese presence in Laos. On the contrary, his book (prepared with assistance from the Council on Foreign Relations staff) urged "the sudden encirclement of one of the Vietnamese border patrol battalions . . . and its noiseless liquidation by a determined and highly trained [US] Special Forces unit." This, he argued, "would have a tremendous shock effect in Hanoi" (p. 301).

6 Bernard Fall, *Vietnam Witness 1953–66* (New York: Praeger, 1966), p. 249.

7 Toye, *Laos* (Garden City, N.Y.: Doubleday, 1969), p. 178; Roger Hilsman, *To Move a Nation* (Garden City, N.Y.: Doubleday, 1967), p. 127; *New York Times*, 25 March 1961, p. 2; Fall, *Anatomy of a Crisis*, p. 206; *Fortune*, September 1961, p. 94; Schlesinger, pp. 336–37.

Nosavan, not to the communists. For months President Kennedy and his special envoy Averell Harriman had been attempting to restore Laotian neutrality and bring about the withdrawal of foreign military elements, by working to establish a tripartite coalition government (Phoumist, neutralist, and Pathet Lao). Phoumi continued to resist Harriman's efforts to involve him in such a coalition for months after Kennedy attempted to coerce him by cutting off his subsidy of $3 million a month. In contravention of the May 1961 cease-fire, and against US official advice, Phoumi also built up a garrison at Nam Tha (only fifteen miles from the Chinese border) to a strength of five thousand and began to probe into enemy territory.

When the Pathet Lao, after giving repeated warnings, fired on Nam Tha in May, Phoumi's troops withdrew precipitously into Thailand. Thus the "further advances" of the Pathet Lao were achieved "after a flurry of firefights but no Pathet Lao attack."[8] The Thai government now requested SEATO aid, and the United States responded by sending troops in accordance with the Thanat-Rusk memorandum, signed just two months before, which provided for unilateral US assistance to Thailand. By all accounts "the Royal Lao Army ran from Nam Tha as soon as the first shells started to fall," claiming falsely (as they had done and continued to do in other crises) that they had been attacked by North Vietnamese and Chinese troops.[9]

This deliberate flight was what President Nixon now calls "a potential threat to Thailand." Phoumi's purposes at Nam Tha were by most accounts not military but political, to thwart the Geneva negotiations and further involve the United States. According to the London *Times,* the CIA had again encouraged Phoumi to resist the establishment of a neutral government in Laos; made up out of its own funds the subsidy which Kennedy had withheld; and urged Phoumi to build up the Nam Tha garrison in spite of contrary US official advice.[10] A State Department spokesman denied the story, and others suggest that the subsidy may have been paid by Phoumi's kinsman, Sarit Thanarat of Thailand, or by Ngo Dinh Diem.

There are, however, disturbing similarities between the Nam Tha build-up and the CIA's "Quemoy ploy" of 1954, when without doubt it encouraged Chiang to build up offensive forces on the offshore island, again in spite of official US advice. One such common feature

8 Toye, *Laos,* p. 182; cf. Hilsman, *To Move a Nation,* p. 140.

9 Denis Warner, *The Last Confucian* (New York: Macmillan, 1963), pp. 217–18.

10 London *Times,* 24 May 1962; 31 May 1962. A story in the *Saturday Evening Post,* 7 April 1962, pp. 87–88, also identified a "handful" of CIA and MAAG members as working "industriously to undermine our present policy in Laos."

was the activity of Chinese Nationalist Kuomintang troops, apparently armed and supplied by the CIA and Air America, in the Nam Tha area.[11]

3) *"In approving the 1962 [Geneva agreements] the Kennedy Administration in effect accepted the basic formulation which had been advanced by North Vietnam and the Soviet Union for a Laotian political settlement. . . . The 666 Americans who had been assisting the Royal Lao Government withdrew under ICC supervision. In contrast, the North Vietnamese passed only a token forty men through ICC checkpoints and left over 6,000 troops in the country."*

Comment: As part of the 1962 Geneva agreements, the government of Laos declared that it would "not allow any foreign interference in the internal affairs of the Kingdom of Laos"; while the other signing governments agreed to the prohibition of all foreign troops and "paramilitary formations" in Laos, including "advisers" (except for "a precisely limited number of French military instructors"). President Nixon's picture of North Vietnamese violations is created by referring to intelligence reports of six thousand North Vietnamese troops in Laos, which (as we have seen) objective scholars such as Toye do not accept.

It does appear that at about this time North Vietnamese border patrol battalions began to move into positions on the Laotian side of the frontier passes; but Dommen and Toye suggest that this action was primarily defensive, in reaction to the five thousand US troops which had been flown into Thailand. Meanwhile Kennedy's acceptance of the 1962 agreements was violated by the US in Laos in at least two respects:

a) Roger Hilsman, then State Department intelligence chief, records that the president and national security council agreed with Harriman's contention that "the United States should comply with both the letter and the spirit of the agreements in every detail . . . and thereafter there should be no . . . 'black' [covert] reconnaissance flights to confirm whether the North Vietnamese had actually withdrawn."[12]

Yet within one or two weeks after the agreements were signed such reconnaissance was carried out at low levels over Pathet Lao camps by USAF intelligence using RF-101 Voodoo jets. According to Dommen this was part of "regular aerial surveillance of northern

---

11 President Kennedy made another effort to have the KMT troops removed from the area in the spring of 1961, but some four thousand were reported to have insisted on remaining in Laos and Thailand (*Washington Post*, 16 March 1970, A10).

12 Hilsman, *To Move a Nation*, pp. 152–53.

Laos in connection with contingency planning related to the deployment of American troops in Thailand."[13] One RF-101 was hit over
the Plaine des Jarres on 13 August 1964 but made it back to its base
in Bangkok. The reconnaissance flights continued until May 1964,
when they were belatedly authorized by the new administrations
which had come to power in both the United States and Laos.

These overflights seem from the outset to have been concerned
less with the Ho Chi Minh trail in southern Laos than with the Plaine
des Jarres some two hundred miles to the northwest. This was the
area in which the CIA and Air America had since 1960–61 armed,
trained, and supplied Meo guerrillas.

b) Inasmuch as the Pathet Lao objected vigorously to the support
by the CIA and Special Forces of the Meo guerrilla tribesmen inside
the Pathet Lao area of northeast Laos, the agreements called for the
withdrawal of "foreign military advisers, experts, instructors . . . and
foreign civilians connected with the supply . . . of war materials."[14]
Yet Air America continued its airlift into northeast Laos, if only
because (as Roger Hilsman observes) "arming the tribesmen en-
gendered an obligation not only to feed them . . . but also to protect
them from vengeance."[15] The Pathet Lao and some neutralists objected violently to Air America's airlift in support of their recent
enemies; they objected even more violently to Air America's overt
airlift of October 1962 to Kong Le.

The first military incident in the breakdown of the 1962 agreements was the shooting down on 27 November 1962 of an Air
America C-123 plane over the Plaine des Jarres. The plane, it soon
developed, had not been shot down by the Pathet Lao, but by a new
left-leaning neutralist faction under Colonel Deuane, which now opposed Kong Le and his increasing dependency on the Americans.[16]

So far as Air America's airlift is concerned, the President's asser-
tion that "our assistance has always been at the request of the legitimate government of Prime Minister Souvanna Phouma" is false. The
government (which was a tripartite coalition) had not been consulted;
Souvanna himself, as Dommen writes, "had neither endorsed the Air
America airlift (the contract was a carryover from [Phoumi's right-

13 Dommen, *Conflict in Laos*, p. 238; Grant Wolfkill, *Reported to Be Alive* (London: W. H. Allen, 1966), pp. 273–74.

14 *Protocol to the Declaration on the Neutrality of Laos;* Articles 1(a), 2, 4; in Dommen, pp. 314–15.

15 Hilsman, *To Move a Nation*, p. 115; cf. Bernard Fall, *Street Without Joy* (Harrisburg, Pa.: Stackpole, 1967), p. 340; Dommen, *Conflict in Laos*, p. 233.

16 The *New York Times*, 5 December 1962, p. 3; Dommen, *Conflict in Laos*, p. 243.

wing] government, and had merely been initialed for the coalition by Keo Vithakone, Secretary of State for Social Welfare, a Phoumist) nor prohibited it."[17] Nor apparently was Souvanna consulted about reconnaissance overflights until May 1964.

These US violations of the 1962 agreements were not in response to North Vietnamese activity; they date back to the signing of the agreements themselves, one month before the date set for the withdrawal of foreign troops. (In this respect the President's claim that "our assistance . . . is directly related to North Vietnamese violations of the agreements" suggests a time sequence of causality which is the reverse of the truth.) In effect, in August 1962 our military and civilian intelligence services invited the other side to violate the newly signed agreements by proving conspicuously to them (though not of course to the US public) that the agreements would be violated on our side.

In addition, it appears that the "withdrawal" of US military advisers was illusory. It has just been revealed that for "several years" several hundred members of the "civilian" US AID mission (working out of the mission's "rural development annex") have been former Special Forces and US Army servicemen responsible to the CIA station chief and working in northeast Laos with the CIA-supported Meo guerrillas of General Vang Pao. Vang Pao's *Armée Clandestine* is reportedly not even answerable to the Royal Lao government or army, being entirely financed and supported by the CIA.

Dommen's carefully qualified description of US compliance with the 1962 agreements ("Not a single American military man was left in Laos *in uniform*") says nothing to refute the Pathet Lao charge which has now been confirmed by American reporters in Laos: that the Meos' Special Forces "advisers" simply remained, or soon returned, to work for the CIA in the guise of civilian AID officials.[18]

One country embarrassed by these provocations was the Soviet Union. In 1962, as in 1954, Moscow had helped to persuade its Asian allies to accept a negotiated settlement which the Americans would not honor. The Soviet Union soon moved to extricate itself from its

17 Dommen, *Conflict in Laos*, p. 244.

18 Jack Foisie, *San Francisco Chronicle*, 10 March 1970, p. 16; Dommen, *Conflict in Laos*, p. 239, italics added. According to Foisie, "There is the possibility that some [annex] men have gained temporary leave from the Armed Forces and can return to the military after their contract expires." Some of the US "civilian" pilots working in Laos are also reported to have been recruited from the USAF on this basis.

On 13 March 1970 Senator Fulbright reported that Richard Helms, Director of Central Intelligence, had "generally confirmed" the accuracy of news dispatches from Laos reporting the CIA activity (New York Times, 14 March 1970, p. 11).

Laotian involvement, since its support of Souvanna now caused it to lose favor not only in Peking but also in Hanoi.

4) "The political arrangements for a three-way government survived only until April 1963, when the Pathet Lao communist leaders departed from the capital and left their cabinet posts vacant. Fighting soon resumed."

Comment: The Pathet Lao leaders did not resign their cabinet posts in the coalition government; two of their four ministers withdrew from Vientiane, giving the very good reason that, on 1 April and 12 April, two of their allies in Colonel Deuane's left-neutralist faction (one of them Quinim Pholsena, the Laotian foreign minister) had been assassinated. The Pathet Lao has since attributed these murders to a CIA assassination team recruited by the Laotian Military Police Chief Siho. It is known not only that the CIA was using such teams in Vietnam but that in 1963 it was responsible for collaborating with Siho in training his cadres. But the murders can also be attributed to the growing factionalism between Kong Le and Deuane in the neutralist forces. (One of Deuane's men on 12 February killed Kong Le's deputy commander, a few weeks after the murder of a left-oriented Chinese merchant.)

It seems clear that the resumed fighting on the Plaine des Jarres in April 1963 was chiefly, if not entirely, between the two neutralist factions, rather than with the Pathet Lao. Moreover, Kong Le's faction, with the support of his old enemy Phoumi, was able to capture certain key outposts, such as Tha Thom, controlling a road north into the Plaine des Jarres.[19] But the negotiations between Souvanna Phouma and Souphanouvong in April and May 1964 (after the opening of a new French peace initiative) suggest that the 1962 political arrangements did not break down irrevocably for almost two years.

5) "In mid-May 1964 the Pathet Lao supported by the North Vietnamese attacked Prime Minister Souvanna Phouma's neutralist military forces on the Plain of Jars."

Comment: Dommen confirms that in May 1964, Kong Le's men were attacked by the left-neutralist followers of Colonel Deuane. The

---

19 As late as 4 May 1964, William Bundy could tell a House Committee that the power change since July 1962 in the Plaine des Jarres area had "been favorable . . . to the noncommunist elements of the Government"; House Committee on Appropriations, *Foreign Operations Appropriations for 1965, Hearings Before a Subcommittee*, 88th Congress, 2nd Sess., p. 414.

Pathet Lao shelled the positions of Phoumist troops flown in since 1962, while the North Vietnamese may have played a supporting role, as did the United States with Kong Le. The result of Deuane's initial attacks was roughly to restore the *status quo ante* April 1963: the town of Tha Thom in particular was recaptured by his men. By the end of May, Deuane's men and the Pathet Lao held virtually all the territory occupied by the neutralists and the Pathet Lao in June 1962, but no more.[20] It is essential to understand these specific events, inasmuch as they were used as a pretext for launching the US bombing of Laos in May, a new policy which soon was extended to both North and South Vietnam.

What Nixon omits to say is that the fighting in May was, once again, preceded not by a left-wing but by a right-wing initiative. On 19 April a right-wing faction headed by Police Chief Siho staged a coup against Souvanna Phouma—a coup that caused the final collapse of the tripartite coalition government, a restructuring of the cabinet to shift it to the right, the disappearance of an independent neutralist faction, and the eventual decline and fall of the former right-wing leader Phoumi Nosavan. Thus it is not true, as the President's statement claims, that "the present government of Laos . . . has been the one originally proposed by the communists": the 1962 political settlement broke down altogether when the cabinet was reconstituted without Pathet Lao permission or participation. It is thus not unreasonable for the Pathet Lao to ask (as it did in early 1970) for a conference of all parties to establish a new coalition government (*New York Times,* 10 March 1970).

The day before Chief Siho's coup, on 18 April, Souvanna and Phoumi had met with Pathet Lao leader Prince Souphanouvong on the Plaine des Jarres, reportedly to work out details of a new agreement to neutralize the royal capital of Luang Prabang and reunite the coalition government there.

Though the details are unclear, it seems that the coup was at least in part designed to prevent the restoration of the neutralist coalition. No one has denied Denis Warner's report that Siho "used the aquiescence of Souvanna Phouma and Phoumi Nosavan in the neutralization of the royal capital of Luang Prabang as the excuse" for the

---

20 Dommen, *Conflict in Laos,* p. 256: "On May 16, the dissident followers of Colonel Deuane Siphaseuth, with Pathet Lao and North Vietnamese support, compelled Kong Le to abandon a number of positions on the Plain and to evacuate his Muong Phanh command post. . . . By the end of May, the Pathet Lao and the 'true neutralists' [under Deuane] occupied virtually all the ground that had been held jointly by themselves and Kong Le . . . in June 1962"; cf. Toye, *Laos,* p. 193.

coup.[21] Ambassador Unger and William Bundy of the State Department personally persuaded Siho to release Souvanna and restore him as prime minister; but the reconstitution of the Laotian army under a new general staff consisting of nine rightist generals and only one neutralist indicated the real shift of power to the right.[22] The new command then ordered the neutralist troops on the Plaine des Jarres to be integrated with the right under its authority.

This order was too much for many of Kong Le's men on the Plaine des Jarres and, instead of complying, six battalions of troops defected, some of them to Deuane's left-neutralist faction. Warner confirms that "the resulting mass defections . . . led [in May] to the rout of Kong Le's troops and the fall of the Plain of Jars."[23] Again, as at Nam Tha in 1962, many troops withdrew, amid charges of a North Vietnamese and Chinese Communist invasion, without ever having been directly attacked.[24]

These right-wing maneuvers in Laos, whether or not they were directly encouraged by American advisers on-the-scene, cannot but have been indirectly encouraged by the highly publicized debate in Washington over Vietnam. It was known that in early 1964 many generals were calling for US air strikes against "Communist bases" in the north, including the bombing of the Ho Chi Minh trail in Laos. The result of Siho's April coup, if not the intention, was to make way for the initiation of this bombing policy.

One striking feature about the 19 April coup is that it was announced in Bangkok one day before it occurred (*Bangkok Post,* 18 April 1964), and over Taiwan Radio the day before that.

6) *"In May 1964, as North Vietnamese presence increased, the United States, at royal Lao government request, began flying certain interdictory missions against invaders who were violating Lao neutrality."*

Comment: By this important admission it is now for the first time conceded that the US assumed a combat role in Laos in May 1964, at a time when the North Vietnamese army was still engaged in a

21 Denis Warner, *Reporting Southeast Asia* (Sydney: Angus and Robertson, 1966), p. 190. Wilfred Burchett (*The Second Indochina War* [New York: International Publishers, 1970], pp. 162–63) says that although the 18 April tripartite meeting was in fact fruitless, fear of its success caused the CIA to proceed with the 19 April coup.

22 *New York Times,* 14 May 1964, p. 11; 19 May 1964, p. 5; Fall, *Street Without Joy,* p. 341.

23 Warner, *Reporting Southeast Asia,* p. 191. The integration order recalled a similar rightist order in 1959 to the Pathet Lao, an order that was instrumental in triggering the Laotian war.

24 *New York Times,* 16 May 1964, p. 2; 28 May 1964, p. 10.

support role comparable to that of Air America. (North Vietnam was not formally accused by the US of violating the Geneva agreements until 29 June 1964.) The air attacks were first carried out by US "civilian" pilots from Air America, in T-28 fighter-bombers based in Thailand but carrying Laotian markings. On 11 June 1964, one of these T-28s attacked the Chinese cultural and economic mission at the Pathet Lao capital on the Plaine des Jarres, killing at least one Chinese. The United States at that time denied responsibility, though the State Department revealed that Thai pilots also flew the T-28s and had been involved.[25]

On 21 May 1964, the United States admitted for the first time that "unarmed United States jets" were flying reconnaissance missions over Laos. Dean Rusk later explained that this was in response to Souvanna Phouma's general request for assistance; but Souvanna Phouma refused to comment on the matter of reconnaissance flights for the next three weeks. In fact these flights had been conducted regularly since at least as early as August 1962. What was new was that in mid-May President Johnson ordered the planes to switch from high-altitude to provocative low-altitude reconnaissance. At the insistence of the chief of naval operations, he also authorized accompanying escorts of armed jet fighters. These were ordered not to bomb or strafe Laotian installations until and unless United States planes were damaged.[26] When a Navy RF-8 was shot down on 6 June, President Johnson ordered retaliatory strikes.

At this point Souvanna Phouma finally commented publicly on the reconnaissance flights: he reportedly asked that they cease altogether forthwith. (The *New York Times* on 10 June published a report that he had not agreed to the use of armed escorts.) On 12 June Souvanna announced that the reconnaissance flights would continue; this suggested to some observers that since the 19 April coup and the collapse of the neutralists Souvanna was no longer his own master.[27] His reluctant *ex post facto* acquiescence in the use of jet

25 *Pentagon Papers*, p. 239; Dommen, *Conflict in Laos*, p. 259; Toye, *Laos*, p. 194. The first substantial reports of North Vietnamese infiltration followed the new US bombing policy. Cf. T. D. Allman (*Far Eastern Economic Review*, 1 January 1970, p. 21): "When the Vientiane government permitted the Americans to start the bombing, the North Vietnamese committed increasing amounts of troops in an effort to discredit that government."

26 *Pentagon Papers*, p. 239; Dommen, p. 238; Joseph C. Goulden, *Truth Is the First Casualty: The Gulf of Tonkin Affair—Illusion and Reality* (New York: Rand McNally, 1969), p. 97.

27 Toye, *Laos*, p. 194; Dommen, *Conflict in Laos*, p. 258: "Souvanna . . . became daily more of a figurehead in a situation over which he had little control." In response to the news of Souvanna's objections, the United States announced that it was suspending the reconnaisance flights "for at least 48 hours"; but at the same time the State Department

fighter escorts for reconnaissance is the closest approximation in the public record to what President Nixon now calls a "Royal Lao Government request" for interdictory missions one month earlier.

It has never been explained why the US reconnaissance pilots were ordered to conduct their flights over Laos at low altitudes and slow speeds, when (as they informed their superiors) with their modern equipment they could obtain photographs of equal quality if they were permitted to fly higher.[28] The orders seem to reflect the determination of certain Air Force and Navy officials either to coerce the other side by a US air presence, or alternatively to obtain a suitable provocation, as was finally supplied by the Tonkin Gulf incidents, for the bombing of North Vietnam.

The withdrawals from the Plaine des Jarres in 1964 produced what Phoumi had failed to obtain by his withdrawal from Nam Tha in 1962—a direct armed US intervention in Laos and the frustration of a new initiative (this time by the French) to restore peace in that country. The similarities between the two withdrawals—the gratuitous right-wing provocations, the flight before being attacked, and the incredible stories of Chinese Communist invasion—have been attributed by some to Laotian lack of discipline.

Toye, however, will not accept this explanation for 1962[29] and there are disturbing indications that in 1964 Laotian and US hawks were still intriguing together to bring about a further Americanization of the war. Perhaps the chief indication was the dispatch in May of US Navy aircraft carriers into the Tonkin Gulf area for the purpose of conducting "reconnaissance" flights and air strikes against Laos (even the new armed flights could easily have been initiated, as in the past, by the USAF in Thailand).

By the time the US jet air strikes got under way in June, the rainy season in Laos had begun, the panic was over, and there was no prospect of ground military activity in Laos for the next several

---

announced that the flights would continue "subject to consultation." This was by no means the first time that the United States had treated Souvanna in so humiliating a fashion; cf. Fall, *Anatomy of a Crisis*, pp. 193ff., 223.

28 Goulden, *Truth Is the First Casualty*, p. 97. Grant Wolfkill, then a prisoner of the Pathet Lao, testifies to the lowness of the flights in 1962 (*Reported to Be Alive*, pp. 273–74): "Flying at a thousand feet, it [an unmarked jet F-101] whipped through the valley and swung around leisurely at one end. I could see the pilot's head as the plane turned. . . . Three days later the F-101 returned. . . . Every gun in the camp blazed away at it this time. With arrogant indifference the jet maintained its course." Statement of Secretary Rusk, 30 July 1964, in US Department of State, *American Foreign Policy, 1964*, p. 943; see also Dommen, *Conflict in Laos*, p. 258.

29 Toye, *Laos*, p. 182: "After a flurry of fire fights but no Pathet Lao attack, Nam Tha was abandoned. This time there could be no doubt about it; General Boun Leut is no poltroon; he had obeyed Phoumi's orders."

months. Yet many observers (including Melvin Laird, who had his own Pentagon channels) predicted accurately that the aircraft carriers moved in against Laos might soon be used against North Vietnam. As *Aviation Week* reported on 22 June 1964, President Johnson appeared to be awaiting reactions to the Laotian air strikes ("the first US offensive military action since Korea") before taking "the next big step on the escalation scale." On 3 June 1964 a *New York Times* correspondent reported "a sense of crisis and foreboding" in Southeast Asia, attributed "more to the statements of US Government officials than to any immediate emergency in Laos, South Vietnam or Cambodia."

Congress would do well to investigate the crucial decisions made during the period preceding the Tonkin Gulf incident, for the 1970 period, as we shall see, offers disturbing parallels to the withdrawals of 1962 and 1964.

7) "Since this administration has been in office, North Vietnamese pressure has continued. Last spring, the North Vietnamese mounted a campaign which threatened the royal capital and moved beyond the areas previously occupied by communists. A counterattack by the Lao government forces, intended to relieve this military pressure and cut off supply lines, caught the enemy by surprise and succeeded beyond expectations in pushing them off the . . . Plain of Jars."

Comment: Though it is too early to analyze authoritatively the events of 1969 in Laos, it is clear that this statement leaves out the biggest recent development of all. Shortly after November 1968 (when it halted the bombing of North Vietnam) the US began to apply to combat zones in Laos the tactic of massive bombardment which hitherto had been reserved for Vietnam and the region of the Ho Chi Minh trail in the Laotian panhandle. According to Senator Cranston, air strikes against Laos increased from 4,500 sorties a month (before the November 1968 halt to the bombing of North Vietnam) to between 12,500 and 15,000 sorties a month in 1970. (Other sources suggest a much more dramatic increase.)[30]

This new policy has led to the total annihilation of many Laotian towns (at first briefly, but falsely, attributed to a North Vietnamese "scorched earth" policy). It has also been accompanied by the

---

30 T. D. Allman reported in the *Far Eastern Economic Review* (1 January 1970), p. 21, that "the US now flies as many as 20,000 bombing sorties a month in Laos"; Richard Dudman (*St. Louis Post-Dispatch,* 23 December 1969) put the level one year earlier at 1,000 a month.

evacuation and resettlement (apparently sometimes by coercion) of between five and six hundred thousand Laotians, or about a quarter of the total population. (See the *Nation,* 26 January 1970; *New York Times,* 12 March 1970, p. 3.)

With this new tactic, General Vang Pao's CIA-advised Meo guerrillas have been ordered to withdraw rather than suffer serious casualties in attempting to hold forward positions: their function is rather to engage the enemy and thus expose them to heavy losses through air strikes. These are the tactics once alleged by our generals to be succeeding in South Vietnam: attrition of the enemy by massive bombardment, rather than serious attempts to hold territory. The new tactics (like the original covert US military involvements eight years earlier) were inaugurated during the "lame-duck" period of a change-over in administrations. In December 1968 the Pathet Lao protested to the International Control Commission that US planes were dropping four or five times as many bombs in Laos as they had done two months earlier.[31]

In accordance with their orders to engage the enemy while avoiding heavy casualties, Vang Pao's guerrillas have twice in the last year made spectacular advances into the enemy Plaine des Jarres area (on one occasion to about thirty miles from the North Vietnamese border) and then withdrawn from key outposts like Xieng Khouang and Ban Ban without waiting for the enemy to attack in strength. Just as with General Phoumi in 1962, these withdrawals from isolated advance positions in the face of enemy probes have been widely publicized and used as arguments for US escalation. The Kennedy administration did not take this bait; apparently the Nixon administration (with its 1970 B-52 strikes) did.

In the wake of the reported bombing increase, there has also been a reported rise in Pathet Lao and North Vietnamese ground activity. Apparently none of this activity has violated the 1961–62 cease-fire line as seriously as Vang Pao's unprecedented forays of April–May and August–September into the Xieng Khouang–Ban Ban area. Most of the Pathet Lao activity in the northeast has been directed against Meo outposts within their base area, notably the forward communications post of Na Khang, which was used for the all-weather bombing of North Vietnam, and the US-Thai base at Muong Soui, which was used to support the Meo outposts. On 25 August 1969 the *New York Times* said that "If Vang Vieng falls . . . the Laotian

31 *New York Times,* 31 December 1968, p. 6.

government will have been pushed behind the cease-fire line of 1961";
but even Vang Vieng was still on the Pathet Lao side of the line.

There are disturbing indications that in 1969 (as in 1962 and 1964) right-wing provocations and escalations were deliberately intended to frustrate Souvanna Phouma's continuing efforts to restore peace and a neutralist coalition government. In May 1969, Souvanna Phouma saw the North Vietnamese ambassador to Laos (at the latter's invitation) for the first time in over four years. On 15 May he announced he was hopeful that the Laotian problem could be solved even before the end of the Vietnam war. It was later revealed that he had offered a formula for the termination of US bombing comparable to that used in Vietnam: a gradual reduction in the bombing in return for a gradual withdrawal of North Vietnamese troops. Souvanna said that he would accept the continued use of the Ho Chi Minh trail by the North Vietnamese troops "with the condition that those troops withdrew" elsewhere.[32] (I have been informed that in September, four months after this proposal by Souvanna, the North Vietnamese withdrew altogether from the Plaine des Jarres.)

Four days later, on 19 May, the *New York Times* reported that with the advent of the rainy season, Laos was "suddenly quiet." Pathet Lao pressure had tapered off: "Where there is any action government forces appear to be taking the initiative." Only one day later "fierce fighting" was reported from the Plaine des Jarres: Vang Pao's CIA-supported guerrillas had clashed with the enemy thirteen miles from Xieng Khouang. On 27 May Vang Pao was reported to have withdrawn from Xieng Khouang (which he had held for one month) "following orders . . . not to risk heavy casualties." The next day his troops seized Ban Ban, about thirty miles from North Vietnam, "as Laotian and American bombers continued devastating attacks on North Vietnamese soldiers and supply lines all over northeastern Laos."[33]

This chronology recalls the depressing sequence of occasions in the Vietnam war when a new diplomatic initiative was followed by a new escalation or an intensification of the bombing, instead of a hoped-for reduction.[34] This pattern of a "politics of escalation"

32 *New York Times*, 15 May 1969, p. 13; 17 May, p. 3; *Far Eastern Economic Review*, 5 June 1969, p. 569; *San Francisco Chronicle*, 6 March 1970, p. 26.

33 *New York Times*, 19 May 1969, p. 6; 20 May, p. 3; 27 May, p. 5; 28 May, p. 9.

34 Franz Schurmann, Peter Dale Scott, Reginald Zelnik, *The Politics of Escalation in Vietnam* (Boston: Beacon Press, 1966); David Kraslow and Stuart H. Loory, *The Secret Search for Peace in Vietnam* (New York: Random House, 1968), pp. 3–74; *Ramparts*, March 1968, pp. 56–58; *New York Times*, 6 January 1968, p. 28.

appeared to repeat itself in February of 1970. In early February

> Souvanna Phouma startled the diplomatic community by publicly
> offering to go to Hanoi to negotiate an end to the conflict. . . . Sou-
> vanna was ready, so he said, to agree to the neutralization of the
> Plain of Jars . . . and . . . promised that his government would "close
> its eyes" to what goes along the Ho Chi Minh Trail.[35]

On 17 February the Associated Press reported "some of the heaviest
air raids ever flown in Southeast Asia" and, on 19 February, the first
"massive air strikes by US B-52 bombers in the Plain of Jars region." On 22 February the AP fed the American public the typical
kind of panic story that has been emanating from northeast Laos
ever since the phony "offensive" of August 1959. Vang Pao's guerrillas, it said, had been "swept from the Plain of Jars by an overwhelming North Vietnamese blow . . . with a third of its force dead
or missing. . . . The government garrison of 1,500 men based at
Xieng Khouang was hit by 6,000 North Vietnamese supported by
tanks."

On the next day came the typical corrective story: the attack
had been made by 400 troops, not 6,000; the defenders (who had
falsely inflated their strength "for payday purposes") had withdrawn
with "very little close-in action." It would appear that once again
wildly exaggerated tales from remote areas had resulted in the frustration of a peace initiative, by what was (as Senator Mansfield
warned) a significant escalation of the bombing.[36]

> 8) "We are trying above all to save American and Allied lives
> in South Vietnam which are threatened by the continual infiltration
> of North Vietnamese troops and supplies along the Ho Chi Minh
> trail. . . . Today there are 67,000 North Vietnamese troops in [Laos].
> There are no American troops there. Hanoi is not threatened by
> Laos; it runs risks only when it moves its forces across borders."

Comment: The CIA's persistent support, guidance, and encouragement of Meo guerrilla activities in northeast Laos cannot be
rationalized by references to the Ho Chi Minh trail. As anyone can

35 *Newsweek,* 16 February 1970, p. 37.

36 *San Francisco Chronicle,* 17 February 1970; 19 February; 22 February; 23 February.

In August 1969 there was also the mysterious episode of the tribal double-agent who, on Vang Pao's instruction, sold a map of the secret Meo headquarters at Long Cheng to six members of the North Vietnamese Embassy. According to T. D. Allman, "The affair . . . appeared to be at least in part a right-wing effort to reduce the Prime Minister's room to maneuver and perhaps even force a break in diplomatic relations between the two countries." *Far Eastern Economic Review* (11 September 1969), p. 648.

see by looking at a map, the Ho Chi Minh trail runs south from the Mu Gia pass in the southern portion of the Laotian panhandle, 200 miles to the southeast of the Plaine des Jarres. These Meo tribesmen were first trained by the French for paramilitary activities inside what is now North Vietnam, where some of them continued to operate for years after the 1954 Geneva agreements, almost to the time when their French officers were replaced by CIA "Special Forces."[37] Veterans of the Special Forces, now "civilians" working for the CIA, are still working with the Meos behind enemy lines; Air America, and more recently Continental Air Services, have never ceased to airlift and supply them.

Hanoi is indeed directly threatened by these CIA activities just across the Laotian border. Heavily fortified Meo outposts at Pa Thi and Na Khang were developed as forward communications centers for the all-weather pinpoint bombing of North Vietnam.[38] On 21 November 1968 the *Far Eastern Economic Review* reported "evidence that American aircraft, including jets, were flying from a secret base in northern Laos . . . about fifty miles from the North Vietnam border."

It is difficult to explain the tenacity of the CIA's ground operations behind enemy lines in northeast Laos, or the recent conversion of the Plaine des Jarres into an evacuated "free strike" zone for F-4s, F-105s, and B-52s, except as part of a "forward strategy," to remind North Vietnam of the threat that the United States might resume bombing it. The President's statement indeed suggests that the US hopes to use its escalation in Laos as a means of imposing its peace formula on Vietnam. ("What we do in Laos has thus as its aim to bring about the conditions for progress toward peace in the entire Indochinese Peninsula.")

One cannot confirm or refute the 1970 intelligence estimates of 67,000 North Vietnamese in Laos. What is clear is that the intelligence estimates have themselves sharply "escalated" from the figure of 50,000 that was used by the Pentagon up until one month earlier. One is reminded of the similar "escalation" of infiltration estimates for South Vietnam in January 1965. The claims then put forward as to the presence of regular North Vietnamese army units in South Vietnam, including at least a battalion if not a division, were tacitly refuted only six months later by no less an authority than McNa-

---

37 Fall, *Street Without Joy*, p. 341.
38 Robert Shaplen, *Time Out of Hand* (New York: Harper & Row, 1969), p. 346; *New York Times*, 26 October 1969, p. 24.

mara.[39] Six months later it was of course too late. The regular bombing of North and South Vietnam had been initiated; the full "Americanization" of the Vietnam war had been achieved.

The President's statement on Laos was an alarming document, alarming above all not because of what it misrepresented, but because of what it might portend. In its skillful retelling of events known only to a few, it resembled the State Department's White Paper of February 1965 on Vietnam. The White Paper, which also relied heavily on intelligence "estimates," was not really an effort to understand the true developments of the past. It was instead the ominous harbinger for a new strategy of victory through American air power, a document aimed not at serious students of Southeast Asia (who swiftly saw through it) but at the "silent majority" of that era.

The publication of the Pentagon Papers has confirmed the double roles of the intelligence documents that were finally published as the State Department's White Papers of 1961 and 1965 on Vietnam. In both cases the documents first strengthened a particular case for escalation being debated within the bureaucracy, and later were published as part of a carefully concatenated escalation scenario.[40] Not only public opinion but the bureaucratic decision-making process itself was distorted by the dubiously inflated claims of external North Vietnamese intervention contained in both documents. The 1965 White Paper in particular doubled the US intelligence estimates of infiltration from North Vietnam which had been publicly released only six months before, on 29 July 1964; these increased infiltration estimates actually followed the emergence of secret bureaucratic planning to carry the war north, rather than giving rise to it.[41]

The escalated infiltration statistics in the Key Biscayne statement appear to have played the same controversial double role:

Hanoi's most recent military build-up in Laos has been particularly

---

39 Secretary McNamara on 17 June 1965, Department of State *Bulletin*, 5 July 1965, p. 18; cf. Department of State *Bulletin*, 22 March 1965, p. 414; 17 May 1965, pp. 750, 753; Theodore Draper, "How Not to Negotiate," *New York Review of Books*, 4 May 1967, p. 27n; Theodore Draper, *Abuse of Power* (New York: Viking, 1967), pp. 76–77; Schurmann, Scott, and Zelnik, *Politics of Escalation,* p. 47n.

With respect to the current estimate of 67,000 North Vietnamese troops in Laos, one needs to know how many of these are involved in the Ho Chi Minh trail and how many are border guards sent in defensively (as in the past) to occupy the Laotian side of the border passes. One also needs to know the sources and reliability of the information. The months of January and February have repeatedly seen highly questionable US escalations of infiltration estimates followed by escalations of the bombing. One is reminded not only of the 1965 White Paper but also of the bombing escalation in February 1967.

40 *Pentagon Papers*, pp. 107, 152–53, 338, 422. The 1965 White Paper was drafted by Chester Cooper, a former CIA officer attached to the White House staff.

41 *New York Times*, 27 January 1965, p. 2; cf. *Pentagon Papers*.

escalatory. They have poured over 13,000 additional troops into Laos during the past few months, raising their total in Laos to over 67,000. Thirty North Vietnamese battalions from regular division units participated in the current campaign in the Plain of Jars with tanks, armored cars, and long-range artillery.

But thirty North Vietnamese battalions (or about 9,000 men) are unlikely to have participated in a campaign which (as we have seen) involved only 400 combat troops, who were mostly indigenous Pathet Lao. This figure of 400, a typical number for a Pathet Lao operation, was later confirmed by US Embassy sources in Vientiane. French and Laotian officials in Vientiane put the total North Vietnamese presence at 30,000 or 35,000 in mid-1970, of which at least 60 percent were involved in maintaining the Ho Chi Minh and Sihanouk trails and 5 to 10 percent remained in the rear. Inasmuch as at least half of the remainder (75 percent, according to the British military attaché) were engaged in support functions, this would only leave about 5,000 or so North Vietnamese troops available for actual combat.[42]

In other words, the North Vietnamese combat presence in Laos is at most roughly equal to the 4,800 or so Thai irregular troops which Senator Fulbright has estimated to be fighting in Laos under CIA auspices. It is vastly outnumbered by the CIA's whole mercenary force of 30,000 in Laos, said by a Senate Foreign Relations Committee staff report to provide the "cutting edge" of the Vientiane armed forces.[43] In this context the Key Biscayne statistics, compiled at the time of the Pathet Lao's important 5-point peace proposals in early 1970, would appear to be special pleading for the continuation of America's largest covert war effort, from the very intelligence sources responsible for the prosecution of that war. In Laos, as soon after in Cambodia, the manipulation of intelligence has been the key to the manipulation of policy.

---

42 These statistics are taken from the valuable appendix to Fred Branfman, "Presidential War in Laos, 1964–1970," in Nina Adams and Alfred W. McCoy (eds.), *Laos: War and Revolution* (New York: Harper & Row, 1970), pp. 278–80.

43 *San Francisco Chronicle,* 3 August 1971, pp. 1, 18.

On August 26 [1964] . . . the Joint Chiefs of Staff . . . said that . . . an air war against the North was now "essential to prevent a complete collapse of the US position in Southeast Asia." The Joint Chiefs' memorandum was the first appearance, the account says, of a "provocation strategy" that was to be discussed at the Sept. 7 White House session—in the words of the narrative, "deliberate attempts to provoke the DRV into taking actions which could then be answered by a systematic US air campaign."

Chapter Three
The Tonkin Gulf Incidents: 1964

Seaman Patrick N. Park, on the night of 4 August 1964, was directing the gun-control radar of the USS *Maddox*. For three hours he had heard torpedo reports from the ship's sonarman, and he had seen, two or three times, the flash of the *Turner Joy*'s guns in the rainy darkness. But his radar could find no targets, "only the occasional roll of a wave as it breaks into a whitecap." At last, just before midnight, a target: "a damned big one, right on us . . . about fifteen hundred yards off the side, a nice fat blip." He was ordered to open fire; luckily, however, not all seamen blindly follow orders.

> Just before I pushed the trigger I suddenly realized, That's the *Turner Joy* . . . . There was a lot of yelling of "Goddamn" back and forth,

51

with the bridge telling me to "fire before we lose the contact," and me yelling right back at them . . . . I finally told them, "I'm not opening fire until I know where the *Turner Joy* is." The bridge got on the phone and said, "Turn on your lights, *Turner Joy."* Sure enough, there she was, right in the cross hairs . . . fifteen hundred yards away. If I had fired, it would have blown it clean out of the water. In fact, I could have been shot for *not* squeezing the trigger. Then people started asking, "What are we shooting at . . . ?" We all began calming down. The whole thing seemed to end then.[1]

Joseph Goulden's fascinating book, which has gathered much new information about the Tonkin Gulf incidents, sees the experience of Patrick Park as, with one exception, a microcosm of the entire Tonkin affair:

> illustrating the confusion between illusion and reality and the inclination of man to act upon facts as he anticipates they *should be,* rather than what rational examination shows them *to be.* The exception is that Park refused to squeeze the firing pin, while Washington acted on the basis of assumption, not fact—hastily, precipitously, perhaps even unnecessarily—firing at an unseen enemy lurking behind the blackness of misinformation (p. 14).

Not all will accept the analogy between Washington and a confused young seaman, but this hardly lessens the importance of Goulden's patient researches. He has not really written a "thesis" book; his method is to stick closely to official documents (above all the neglected Fulbright Committee *Hearing* of 1968)[2] and first-hand interviews. At times he can be faulted for believing so much of what was told him in the Pentagon. Even so, the result is devastating. It is now even more clear that the Tonkin Gulf Resolution (in his words) "contains the fatal taint of deception": the administration knew much more than the simple story of "unprovoked attack" by which the resolution was pushed through Congress.

The *Maddox,* according to McNamara in 1964, was on a "routine patrol in international waters": in fact it was on an electronics intelligence (ELINT) or spy mission for the NSA and CIA. One of its many intelligence requirements orders was "to stimulate Chicom-

---

1 Joseph C. Goulden, *Truth Is the First Casualty* (New York: Rand McNally, 1969), p. 12. This chapter originally appeared as a review of Goulden's book. Two further valuable studies of the Tonkin Gulf incidents have since appeared: Anthony Austin, *The President's War* (Philadelphia: J. B. Lippincott, 1971); and Eugene Windchy, *Tonkin Gulf* (Garden City, N.Y.: Doubleday, 1971).

2 US Congress, Senate, Committee on Foreign Relations, *The Gulf of Tonkin, the 1964 Incidents,* 90th Cong., 2nd Sess. (Washington: GPO, 1968). Cited hereafter as *Hearing.*

North Vietnamese electronic reaction," i.e., to provoke them into turning on their defensive radars so that the frequencies could be measured. To this end the *Maddox,* between 1 and 4 August, repeatedly simulated attacks by jabbing in toward the shore with its fire-control radars turned on (as if preparing to shoot on target). In so doing it frequently violated the twelve-mile limit which Pentagon officials thought North Vietnam claimed for her territorial waters.[3] Far from being "routine," this was only the third such patrol in the Tonkin Gulf in thirty-two months; and the North Vietnamese had to assess it in the context of a recent US build-up, South Vietnamese threats to carry the war north, and actual attacks.

On 1 and 2 August, we learn from the Pentagon Papers, the North Vietnamese must indeed have thought that a US invasion of North Vietnam was beginning. A State Department memo of 7 November 1964, written three months after the event, concluded that American T-28s from Laos "probably" bombed and strafed North Vietnamese border villages on 1 and 2 August, the latter at the same time and in the same latitude as the first Tonkin Gulf incident near the island of Hon Me. The key word "probably" indicates that the State Department itself, even three months later, was not properly informed of these covert CIA air operations in Laos. The *New York Times* suggests that "Thai pilots" ("under the control of [Vientiane] Ambassador Leonard Unger") were responsible for the provocative raids, but without any corroborating evidence. Elsewhere it notes that some of the T-28s were "manned by pilots of Air America (a pseudo-private airline run by the CIA)"[4] The Pentagon Papers also disclose (p. 258) that sometime between 25 and 30 July "the Joint Chiefs proposed air strikes by unmarked planes" against North Vietnam.

This "coincidence" of secret bombing in the Hon Me latitude was matched by covert naval attacks by South Vietnamese and Chinese Nationalist sea commandos (in the so-called 34-A Marine

---

3 Against McNamara's professed ignorance of any formal claim before September 1964, Goulden cites Deputy Secretary Cyrus Vance's statement on 8 August 1964 ("I think that they do claim a 12-mile limit"), and a Navy intelligence message of May 1963. According to the *New York Times* (11 August 1964, p. 15) the *Ticonderoga*'s task force commander Rear Admiral Robert B. Moore "indicated that the destroyer . . . might have been 2 or 3 miles inside the 12-mile limit set by Hanoi for territorial waters."

McNamara told the committee that the *Maddox* could simulate an attack on the coast by turning on special transmitters, but the Pentagon later said the ship carried passive equipment and could only listen.

4 *The Pentagon Papers,* as published by the *New York Times* (New York: Bantam, 1971), pp. 239, 306. On p. 261 the *Times* summary seems to imply that the State Department memo itself refers to Thai pilots, rather than Air America pilots; but this is not the case (cf. p. 306).

Operations) against the island of Hon Me itself. On 31 July, just before the *Maddox* patrol, South Vietnamese units under American direction had for the first time used American "swift boats" to bombard the North Vietnamese coast, attacking the islands of Hon Ngu and Hon Me. McNamara had claimed that the US Navy and the *Maddox* were "not aware of any South Vietnamese actions, if there were any"; but the ship's cable traffic reveals frequent references to the 34-A Operations, and there were even plans for the SOG (Studies and Operations Group) liaison officer to board the *Maddox* in Taiwan. On 25 July in Taiwan the *Maddox* had taken aboard an NSA "Communications Van" (COMVAN) with its special complement of intelligence personnel and communications technicians; and some of the COMVAN team were able to intercept and interpret North Vietnamese ship-to-shore messages. Goulden reports that they heard North Vietnamese orders to position a defensive ring of PT-boats around Hon Me after the first incident, and also speculations about the possible link between the *Maddox* and the raids.

Near Hon Me on the morning of 2 August they intercepted orders for PT-boats to attack the *Maddox;* the *Maddox* cabled that "continuance of patrol presents an unacceptable risk," but was ordered to resume its itinerary. The *Maddox* returned to a point eleven miles from Hon Me island, and then heard a North Vietnamese order for its attack. This was the prelude for the first incident of 2 August—an undisputed incident in which it is also conceded that the *Maddox* fired the first shots. A North Vietnamese patrol boat was left "dead in the water," and another probably damaged. The *Maddox* then withdrew, having been dented by a single machine-gun bullet.

At this point the *Maddox* might have broken off the patrol permanently (after all, the original orders of the Joint Chiefs had warned about the risks from the stepped-up 34-A operations). Alternatively, it might have resumed the patrol as originally planned, along the entire six-hundred-mile coastline of the Tonkin Gulf. The President's decision was, without bombing North Vietnam, to send "that ship back up there" together with a second destroyer, the *Turner Joy;* but the admirals of the Pacific command in Honolulu translated this general order into a third, much more dangerous course of action. The destroyers were ordered to modify the original patrol plan and to spend the next two days in a single forty-five-mile stretch (between Navy checkpoints "Charlie" and "Delta") around the obviously sensitive island of Hon Me which had just been shelled by the South Vietnamese.

On 2 August Herrick suggested termination of the patrol altogether, and Admiral Johnson (Seventh Fleet commander) reported his intention to end it on the evening of 4 August. (*Hearing,* p. 32; in this case the disputed second incident would never have arisen.) The on-scene commanders were, however, overruled by a second cable from Honolulu, which restricted the ships even more closely to the Hon Me area. It specified that "the above patrol will . . . (b) possibly draw NVN PGMS (North Vietnamese patrol boats) to northward away from area of 34-A ops."

The Pacific command, in other words, hoped the destroyers might serve as decoys and distract North Vietnam's pitifully small fleet of PT-boats, leaving unimpeded the 34-A operations to the south. (McNamara claimed that "every possible effort was made to keep these two operations separate," and this may hold true for the efforts of Washington and the ship commanders, but not for Honolulu's preoccupation with Hon Me.)[5] After listening to further intercepts (which strictly speaking he may not have been authorized to do) Captain Herrick aboard the *Maddox* spelled out more clearly the dangers of the Hon Me area:

A. Evaluation of info from various sources indicates that DRV [Democratic Republic of Vietnam, i.e., North Vietnam] considers patrol directly involved with 34-A ops. DRV considers United States ships present as enemies . . . and have already indicated readiness to treat us in that category . . .
B. DRV are very sensitive about Hon Me. Believe this is PT operating base, and the cove there presently contains numerous patrol and PT craft which have been repositioned from northerly bases.

Meanwhile the South Vietnamese had already (at 12:30 A.M., 4 August) conducted a second series of 34-A raids some seventy miles southwest of the destroyers. McNamara reported in 1968 that he was not informed of these second raids until *after* he and the President authorized the air strikes against North Vietnam. Nevertheless the facts were known to "some senior commanders above the level of the commanders of the task force"—a line of command consisting of Admirals Johnson, Moorer, and Sharp. Goulden asks why this essential information did not reach McNamara, who consulted Admiral Sharp about the air strikes by telephone.

Despite the raids, and the mounting nervousness on both sides,

5 As evidence for his proposition, McNamara cited two cables from Admiral Johnson envisaging withdrawal, while he overlooked the cables from Honolulu which promptly overruled them (*Hearing,* pp. 31–32).

the daylight hours of 4 August were uneventful. The night was pitch dark from a cover of black storm clouds, and the sea and atmospheric conditions (as McNamara conceded) were such as to cause both radar and sonar to function erratically. It was in these murky circumstances that the alleged second incident (or "unprovoked attack") took place. Unexplained radar blips at thirty-six miles northeast and an enemy intercept caused Captain Herrick to fear an imminent ambush at 7:40 P.M.; two hours later (if we accept a problematic Pentagon chronology), the ships opened fire at fresh radar contacts moving in from the west and south. A "torpedo wake" was then seen from the *Turner Joy* (or more specifically a track in the fluorescent water that in the words of a viewer "wasn't no porpoise").

In 1964 McNamara told the Fulbright committee how the ships then reported "that they were under continuous torpedo attack." His account suppressed a later cable from Herrick saying that "all subsequent *Maddox* torpedo reports [after the first] are doubtful in that it is suspected that sonarman was hearing ship's own propeller beat." (For some reason this cable from Herrick took three or more hours to reach Washington, arriving nineteen minutes after the planes had been launched against North Vietnam.) Soon after, the *Turner Joy* cabled that *its* sonar had received *no* indications of torpedo noises, "even that which passed down side." A reverse paradox occurred with the fire-control radars. The *Turner Joy* radar fixed on several targets. The *Maddox* nearby locked on only one; and that, as we have seen, was the *Turner Joy*.

There are other grounds for doubting the reality of the alleged 4 August attack. No radar or electronic activity was ever detected from the alleged attackers, raising doubts that they could have tracked the destroyers on such a dark night. The North Vietnamese promptly disclaimed any role in the second incident, while identifying certain South Vietnamese craft which they claimed had slipped out that evening from Danang. (Their denial was later sustained by an important North Vietnamese prisoner-of-war, the second-in-command of the PT squadron in question, who supplied much other useful information to his American interrogators.) Normally an incident of this sort involving so many uncertainties would be followed by a naval board of inquiry. Such a review followed the so-called "third" Tonkin Gulf incident of 18 September 1964. The board found that although two other US destroyers had held numerous radar "contacts," had reported attack, had seen "tracer bullets" and "light flashes," and in the end had fired some three hundred rounds of ammunition, there had in fact been no North Vietnamese attack. The lack of any such inquiry into the 4 August incident is itself one further ground for suspicion.

Washington was not unaware of all this confusion when it ordered the retaliatory air strike. On the contrary Captain Herrick's first expression of doubt had been relayed to Washington by the Naval Communications Station, Philippines, as early as 1:27 P.M. EDT, 4 August (or 1:27 A.M., 5 August, in the Tonkin Gulf):

> Review of action makes many reported contacts and torpedoes fired appear doubtful . . . . Freak weather effects and over-eager sonarman may have accounted for many reports. No actual visual sightings by *Maddox*. Suggest complete evaluation before any further action.[6]

It was about this time that President Johnson had agreed in principle to an American reprisal, making it clear that he wanted more positive information before the reprisal attack was launched. McNamara's testimony showed that for the next four and a half hours there was confusion and debate over whether to proceed: "I personally called Admiral Sharp and . . . said we obviously do not want to carry out retaliatory action unless we are 'damned sure what happened.' "[7] Certainty was restored, according to his account, by two corroborating sources. The first was Admiral Sharp (Commander-in-Chief, Pacific, or CINCPAC), who communicated many times with subordinate commanders, then phoned in at 5:23 "stating that he was convinced the attack had occurred and that all were satisfied it had."

If Sharp really said this, it was a gross misrepresentation. Herrick, according to the cables seen by the committee staff, had merely confirmed the "apparent attempted ambush," not the alleged attack two hours later. Sometime after the strike order had been released, after 8:00 P.M. EDT, Herrick sent another cable which itemized his con-

---

6 *Hearing*, p. 54; cf. p. 55.

7 McNamara explained he could report his exact words because "I have a transcript of that telephone conversation" *(Hearing, p. 56)*. Two hours later Fulbright asked for the transcript, since the Defense Department had agreed to supply all relevant communications. McNamara first replied that he would be happy to make it available, but soon qualified this promise by saying he did "not know how much of this will be recorded." Forgetting what he had said earlier, he now stated that "the source of my statement is my memory of what I myself said and did" (pp. 60–61). This important discrepancy is unfortunately overlooked by Goulden (pp. 152–53). The transcript has apparently never been supplied.

The *New York Times* abstract of the Pentagon Papers says (p. 262) that McNamara learned of the confusion about the attack from Sharp at 4:00 P.M. But McNamara testified at the *Hearing* that the message "came in to us" at 1:27 P.M. (p. 55), though he was not sure he "saw the cable or whether it was brought to my attention" (p. 56).

tinuing doubts: for some reason this cable was not received in Washington until 10:59 P.M., when the retaliating airplanes were already airborne. At 11:00 the ship *Turner Joy* was again asked in an "urgent" cable for witnesses and evidence: their reply indicated still further grounds for doubt.

McNamara's second source of corroboration, the allegedly "unimpeachable" intercepts of North Vietnamese communications, deserve far more scrutiny than Goulden gives them. There were four groups of intercepts concerning the events of 4 August, all of them supplied by the intelligence personnel aboard the *Maddox* to Herrick, to CINCPAC, and to Washington. The first two are credible, but do not prove an attack. The latter two, which if true would clearly confirm an attack, are both highly dubious, and not just because they both contain false information. McNamara himself chose to summarize the intercept groups for the record:[8]

No. 1. Located the position of the *Maddox* and the *Turner Joy*.

No. 2. (Received Washington 9:20 A.M.) Directed three vessels "to make ready for military operations."

(It is unfortunate that Goulden twice (pp. 147, 207) echoes McNamara's original characterization of this intercept as "North Vietnamese orders . . . to initiate the attack." Senator Gore, who had just acquired the text, successfully challenged McNamara on precisely this point, and forced him to accept the more moderate phrasing.)

No. 3. (Received Washington about 11:00 A.M.) Reported an American plane falling and ship wounded.

No. 4. (Received Washington "immediately after the attack ended," i.e., just after 1:30 P.M.) Reported "that they had shot down two planes and sacrificed two ships."

The third and fourth groups, in other words, came in after the first highly excited flurry of cables from the American destroyers reporting attack. What made them so credible at the time is that in part they also echoed the cables: the *Maddox* had reported the disappearance of an unidentified aircraft from its screen, and the *Turner Joy* had reported sinking two enemy boats. Intercept group no. 4, which arrived in Washington in the crucial minutes right after Herrick's expression of doubts, must have seemed like a clincher. As Herrick himself told Goulden in an interview, "We heard . . . their

8 *Hearing*, p. 92.

damage report confirm our assessment that two of the boats had been sunk." It must have had an equal impact on McNamara, who has stated that his own decision at 6:07 P.M. to go ahead with the strike order was based particularly on "the communications intelligence."

Nevertheless, as Goulden points out, Herrick at the time was not completely convinced by the last intercept, and for four and a half hours McNamara was not either. What is more important: by evening (Washington time) the *Turner Joy* was no longer certain it had sunk two vessels; and in retrospect the grounds for believing so seem suspect. The *Turner Joy* had seen a "target" disappear from its radars, supposedly accounting for one ship, and some personnel thought they had seen a column of black smoke, supposedly accounting for another. But the radars were disturbed by atmospheric conditions that night and it was "dark as hell." Goulden himself doubts that these bits of evidence prove anything and he quotes without challenging it the conclusion of a high-level Pentagon informant that "the so-called second attack of August 4 never took place."

If this informant is correct, the similarity between the destroyer's cables and the last intercepts is no longer corroborative but highly suspicious. It is made all the more suspicious by the absence thus far of any credible evidence that US aircraft were damaged or missing.[9] How, then, are we to explain the strange circumstance that a North Vietnamese "intercept" reported information which echoed the cables sent by the *Maddox* and the *Turner Joy* but which later turned out to have no convincing basis in fact? One possible explanation is that the North Vietnamese did, in fact, radio the news that two of their ships were lost, but somehow did so in error. It is also possible that the shots fired by the *Turner Joy* somehow struck two North Vietnamese ships. Both possibilities seem remote ones, however, and in any case neither accounts for the reports about downed aircraft. A third possibility is that American technicians were subconsciously influenced by the destroyer's cable traffic in their hearing or interpretation of the North Vietnamese messages; but it is difficult to imagine how such errors could have been consistently made in the case of both groups of intercepts. A fourth possibility should therefore be considered: that the intercept may deliberately have been fed in—or distorted in the process of translation or summary—by American intelligence personnel

---

9 All of the published official reports about the second incident confirm the original in the *New York Times* that the United States suffered no hits, damage, or casualties (*New York Times*, 5 August 1964, p. 1). Thus the report of two downed US aircraft would indeed seem to be, as Goulden concludes, a "total untruth" (p. 153).

in order to end the fateful and unexpected indecision in Washington.

This possibility is increased by another undisputed anomaly: the failure of either one of the destroyers to detect any electronic activity from North Vietnamese ships—whether radar or radio communication—after about 2:30 P.M. Tonkin time, or some six hours before the alleged incident. Under these circumstances it is not only hard to imagine how the North Vietnamese could have conducted an attack out at sea in the darkness, it is also hard to imagine the origins of the information in the third and fourth "intercepts." Herrick confirmed to Goulden what the Fulbright committee had already learned, that "We had no radio contact, or heard no communications going on between the PT boats" (p. 153). As Goulden quite properly asks:

> The communication van's ability to intercept North Vietnamese messages had been amply demonstrated during the preceding four days; why, then, no intercepts from the PT boats during the August 4 incident? Messages from director ships, or a headquarters on Hon Me, which were audible to the North Vietnamese would also have been audible to the *Maddox*'s monitors—yet Herrick avows none were heard during the engagement. What, then, was the origin of the damage report?[10]

If such grave suspicions about the performance of our intelligence network are unfounded, there is much that can be done to put them at rest. The intercepts should be made public, both in their original form and as characterized at the time in intelligence reports. Investi-

---

10 If the third and fourth intercepts are valid, how are we to account for the conflicting testimony of the North Vietnamese prisoner-of-war? US naval intelligence officers who interviewed him for more than a hundred hours in 1966 reported that he was "co-operative and reliable. . . . Yet he specifically and strongly denies that [on 4 August] any attack took place." (*Hearing*, p. 75; Goulden, p. 213.) McNamara anticipated the Fulbright committee's questions about the prisoner with a new piece of evidence.

His [the prisoner's] disclaimer of PT participation is contradicted by information received by a later captive. A North Vietnamese naval officer captured in July 1967 provided the name of the commander of the PT squadron. In intelligence reports received immediately after the August 4 attack, this commander and his squadron were identified by name and number *as participants*. [*Hearing*, p. 18, emphasis added; cf. p. 74.]

But the committee staff subsequently established that the second testimony, insofar as it was relevant, corroborated rather than contradicted the first. The Pentagon, it developed, had attached importance to the second prisoner's testimony, not because he confirmed or denied the second incident (he was not involved and had no information on this point) but *solely* because he corroborated the name mentioned in the "intelligence reports." Goulden identifies these reports as "radio intercepts," and McNamara stated that intercept group no. 4 came "immediately after the attack ended." (The Pentagon's interest in the second prisoner itself suggests official concern as to the intercepts' reliability.) Unfortunately for McNamara's case, the second-in-command to the PT squadron commander named in the intercepts was none other than the first prisoner, who had stated "definitely and emphatically that no PTs could have been involved." (US Congress, Senate, Committee on Foreign Relations, *The Gulf of Tonkin, the 1964 Incidents: Part II, Supplementary Documents*, p. 13; Goulden, p. 214.)

gation should be made to determine whether anything happened to US aircraft on that day that would have led the North Vietnamese to think they had shot down two planes. Even the disclosure of an honest error would serve, at this point, to clear the air rather than to poison it.[11]

In January 1968 Ambassador Goldberg, in presenting the American version of the *Pueblo* incident to the UN Security Council, did not hesitate to quote directly from intercepts of North Korean PT-boat communications that were only three days old. Yet one month later McNamara would not even discuss the North Vietnamese intercepts with the Fulbright committee until its staff adviser (who had received the appropriate clearance when in the Navy) had been sent out of the room. Such furtiveness, until it has been explained, only deepens the credibility gap.

McNamara's dilemma of 1964 must be grasped: to doubt the existence of an attack on 4 August is to doubt the credibility of the intelligence network which "proved" there was one. And if one does not choose with McNamara to believe the "proof," then there is much more to question in the lower echelons of our national security bureaucracy than Admiral Sharp's evident eagerness to bomb North Vietnam. Sharp might well have been restrained by McNamara, had it not been for the performance of the intelligence community's technicians who handled the intercepts.

Sooner or later, most discussions of the Tonkin Gulf incidents (including McNamara's) return, if only to dismiss it, to the possibility of conspiracy. In fact two kinds of conspiracy have been hinted at, a conspiracy *by* the administration, and a conspiracy *against* it. (Failure to distinguish between these has led to confused accounts in which McNamara appears simultaneously as villain and victim.) On the first point, there have been charges of deliberate provocation of the North Vietnamese, as when I. F. Stone neatly characterized the Tonkin Gulf incidents as a "question not just of decision-making in a crisis but of crisis-making to support a secretly prearranged decision."[12]

We have already seen how America's and South Vietnam's first bombardment raids against North Vietnam (at or near Hon Me Island) were followed by the *Maddox*'s persistent feints toward Hon

---

11 The North Vietnamese PT squadron commander should also be interrogated, unless (as has been rumored) he has since been returned to North Vietnam in an exchange of prisoners.

12 I. F. Stone, "McNamara and Tonkin Bay: The Unanswered Questions," *New York Review of Books,* 28 March 1968, p. 11.

Me Island two days later. In the preceding weeks Hanoi had been subjected to other new pressures. On 19 July General Khanh had made a major public appeal for a *bac thien* or march to the north, and on 22 July Marshal Ky revealed that CIA-trained commando operations inside North Vietnam had been stepped up 40 percent since 10 July.[13] Goulden reveals that every one of these escalations (including Khanh's calls for invasion) had been suggested and finally approved as parts of a "measured pressure" plan prepared by the inter-agency Vietnam Working Group, which Johnson had appointed one month after Kennedy's death. The group was headed by William Sullivan of the State Department, who later became US ambassador to Laos. (One of the Sullivan group's working papers specifically mentioned the patrol boat base and radar station on Hon Me Island.)

Another proposal of the Sullivan group was the setting up of the Navy's Yankee Station, which was first used for naval air strikes against Laos in early June. In June the well-informed *Aviation Week* had underlined the importance of this "first US offensive military action since Korea." It added ominously: "President Johnson apparently is awaiting public reaction to the Laos air strikes in this country and abroad *before taking the next big step on the escalation scale.*"[14]

All of these escalations were not conspiratorial in any legal sense but were duly authorized, as part of a secret policy approved by the President, to increase the pressure on North Vietnam. But the Tonkin Gulf incidents also suggest a concerted campaign of deception, not *by* those in power around the President, but *of* them by their subordinates. Goulden argues that the commanders in Honolulu should now explain why they did not, until too late, tell Washington of the 4 August 34-A raids; and why Herrick's obvious doubts about the incidents were transformed along the line into a report that he was "satisfied" an attack had taken place.

Goulden also asks whether Washington was kept informed by CINCPAC of the various North Vietnamese threats against the *Maddox,* and of Herrick's warnings of danger: he was told (but could not confirm) that the White House did not hear of the intercepted North Vietnamese threats on 1–2 August until after the 2 August incident. Finally he asks about Honolulu's alteration of Washington's orders, to provide for repeated runs in toward the Hon

---

13 *Saigon Post,* 23 July 1964; *I. F. Stone's Weekly,* 12 September 1966, p. 3.
14 *Aviation Week,* 15 June 1964, p. 21; 22 June 1964, p. 15, emphasis added.

Me area, and whether Washington was consulted about this. The Foreign Relations Committee should pursue these questions, especially since the 4 August air strike decision was made, it is now known, "on the basis of CINCPAC recommendations."[15]

There are many other questions for Admiral Sharp and the US Pacific commanders. Who authorized the first T-28 air strikes against North Vietnam? Why did Sharp not consult Washington before ordering the much larger aircraft carrier *Constellation* to join the *Ticonderoga* in the Tonkin Gulf, barely in time to make the large-scale retaliation of 4 August possible?[16] (In like manner the Navy ordered the *Enterprise* north without consultation after the *Pueblo* incident; but President Johnson, now more experienced, kept the ship out at sea.)[17] Why were the President's instructions after the first incident, calling in his own words for "a combat patrol over the destroyers," not carried out? On 4 August Herrick complained specifically that near Hon Me a fifteen-minute reaction time for operating air cover was unacceptable: "Cover must be overhead and controlled by destroyers at all times." Yet this request for what the President had already ordered was rejected by Admiral Moore of the *Ticonderoga,* who, however, promised his aircraft were ready for "launch and support on short notice." Why then (according to the official Pentagon chronology), when Herrick cabled at 7:40 P.M. 4 August that an attack appeared "imminent," were fighter aircraft not launched from the *Ticonderoga* until fifty-six minutes later, arriving at 9:08 P.M.?[18]

Such questions (there are still others) suggest there may be more to the Tonkin Gulf affair than confusion and precipitous reaction. Goulden criticizes the naval commanders severely; he does not, however, call for disclosure of the intercepts and the intelligence reports about them. One can understand his caution—there is little precedent for outside review of intelligence activities—but a review that stops short with Admiral Sharp and his colleagues is likely to prove frustrating. An inquiry will not accomplish much if it reveals that the admirals violated only the spirit of Washington's cautionary directives, and never the letter of them. More important, there are many

15 Admiral U. S. G. Sharp and General William C. Westmoreland, *Report on the War in Vietnam (as of 30 June 1968)* (US GPO, 1969), p. 85; cf. p. 12. At the time Sharp told a *Time* reporter that on 4 August "he made about 100 calls to Washington."

16 As it was, the *Constellation,* delayed by storms, was still some two hundred miles out from Yankee Station when her striking planes took off.

17 On both occasions Sharp was aboard a plane returning from Vietnam; as a result he was unusually difficult to reach from Washington.

18 The apparent delay of ninety minutes contrasts strangely with the five or so minutes it took aircraft to arrive during the first incident, before the President's orders.

signs that the intelligence community, rather than Honolulu or the White House, was the prime source of the many "coincidences" which together led to Tonkin.

McNamara, in the 1968 hearings, admitted at one point that US military personnel in Vietnam had the power to "suggest" and "work out adjustments" to the "South Vietnamese" 34-A attacks.[19] These personnel were members of the so-called SOG or "Studies and Operations Group," reporting in theory to General Westmoreland, but in fact to the CIA. The CIA was likewise deeply involved in the counter-guerrilla activities against North Vietnam, expanded after the arrival in Saigon on 1 May of Brigadier General William DePuy, ex-CIA deputy division chief. Finally, the CIA's cover operation in Taiwan, the US Naval Auxiliary Communications Center (NACC), worked hand-in-glove with the NSA in communications and electronics intelligence missions such as that of the *Maddox*.

This is not said to launch a blanket attack against the CIA, some of whose civilian personnel voiced in 1964 what were probably the administration's strongest internal warnings against an escalation in Vietnam.[20] But of all Johnson's civilian advisers, the CIA's John McCone was in early 1964 the most important advocate of expanding the war against North Vietnam. Here as elsewhere McCone, the proponent of a "forward" or "rollback" strategy against Communist territory, was pitted against McNamara, the spokesman of a militant strategy of "containment." In 1963 the two men had divided bitterly over the issue of whether or not to mount a second Bay of Pigs against Cuba. As for the Far East, McNamara had in 1962 passionately opposed "McCone's somewhat apocalyptic view that sooner or later a showdown with the Chinese Communists was inevitable."[21] Hilsman assures us that Rusk also was opposed to the CIA's proposal in that year (supported by Ray Cline, the station chief in Taiwan) for a large-scale landing by Chiang on the Chinese mainland—"a sort of even grander Bay of Pigs."[22]

In early 1964 the proposal to bomb North Vietnam was seen,

---

19 *Hearing*, p. 31. Cf. *Pentagon Papers* (p. 239): "The 34-A attacks were a military effort under the control in Saigon of Gen. Paul D. Harkins. . . . The Studies and Operations Group . . . drew up the advance monthly schedules for approval in Washington."

20 *Pentagon Papers*, p. 254. Right after the Tonkin Gulf incidents, someone leaked a study prepared by Willard Matthias for the CIA Board of Estimates, which foresaw a "prolonged stalemate" in Vietnam, and the possibility of "some kind of negotiated settlement based on neutralization" (*New York Times*, 23 August 1964; Dommen, *Conflict in Laos: The Politics of Neutralization* (New York: Praeger, 1964), p. 298).

21 Roger Hilsman, *To Move a Nation* (Garden City, N.Y.: Doubleday, 1967), p. 318.

22 *Ibid.*, p. 314. Ironically Nixon has now promoted Cline to Hilsman's old post as Director of Intelligence and Research in the State Department, reportedly on the recommendation of Anna Chennault.

even by its supporters in the Johnson administration, to raise the risk of a showdown with Communist China. Here Johnson and McNamara found themselves in a difficult position that was rapidly becoming a dilemma. On the one hand the two men had agreed (at a crucial emergency meeting held only two days after Kennedy's assassination) to an unconditional pledge of military support to South Vietnam.[23] On the other hand neither man had shown any appetite for a major expanded air war: McNamara still wanted to prove the ability of the US Army advisers to win a limited war without escalating it beyond recognition, and Johnson also showed grave reluctance to escalate until after his campaign and election as a "peace candidate." Yet nothing in South Vietnam seemed to be going right; and William Sullivan, who had worked closely with Harriman to achieve the 1962 "neutralization" of Laos, was slowly converted to the view that the Johnson policy of doing "whatever is necessary" might lead in the end to bombing North Vietnam.

After a joint survey mission to Vietnam in March, McNamara still believed that the war must be won within South Vietnam itself; McCone on the other hand recommended "that North Vietnam be bombed immediately and that the Nationalist Chinese Army be invited to enter the war."[24] Johnson wanted the two men to rethink their positions toward a consensus, but the gap was too great. The Sullivan working group had been set up in December as a compromise between the two positions (to develop a list of bombing targets —thus postponing the decision on bombing, but also increasing its likelihood); and the plan of gradually increasing pressures against North Vietnam which it now produced represented a similar effort to steer a "middle" course. The multistage scenario began with hints and warnings, such as sending unmarked jets to create sonic booms over Hanoi, to be followed by the establishment of the Navy's Yankee Station, frequent feints at the shore by destroyers, and South Vietnamese torpedo boat raids. It would climax with a policy of selected "tit-for-tat" or "punch-for-punch" bombing reprisals[25] which would in the end hit against Hanoi and Haiphong proper.

This was the consensus "package," but it failed to resolve the debate. On the one hand, the Joint Chiefs of Staff had recommended

---

23 Tom Wicker, *JFK and LBJ: The Influence of Personality upon Politics* (New York: William Morrow, 1968), p. 205.

24 Edward Weintal and Charles Bartlett, *Facing the Brink: An Intimate Study of Crisis Diplomacy* (New York: Scribners, 1967), p. 72.

25 The less euphemistic phrase "punch-for-punch" seems more appropriate: the Sullivan group contemplated bombing a North Vietnamese factory if the Viet Cong killed a village official, which is hardly "tit-for-tat." Needless to say, the air strikes against PT-boat bases and petroleum installations on 5 August were hardly "tit-for-tat" either.

unanimously by March that America (in the words of a well-informed right-wing source) "attempt to force the Communists to desist from their aggression by punishing their homeland."[26] On the other hand Goulden (p. 91) agrees with other reports that from March through May Johnson was unwilling to buy the Sullivan compromise: "Persons who watched him that spring concluded that he was stalling; that when suddenly brought against the hard decisions required to implement his broad policy goal, he was not so confident it was worth the effort." As a result the tension within the administration began to increase. Elaborate contingency plans for rollback were planned, and discussed with allies; US Navy personnel and the CIA began to train South Vietnamese for the 34-A marine operations; but *none of these plans had yet been authorized by the President*. Meanwhile, this uncertainty about American intentions was seen within the administration as a prime cause of the growing political instability and neutralist sentiment in Saigon. This instability was increased by the many calls in July for a new Geneva conference (U Thant was to report on such matters to Johnson on 6 August), and led to reports of a possible *coup* in Saigon at the time of the second Tonkin Gulf incident.[27] Within the administration, the growing risk of neutralism in Saigon became a prime argument for carrying the war north.[28]

Frustrated in early 1964, the advocates of bombing looked outside the administration to spokesmen like Dodd and Goldwater for public support: in April (long before Khanh had joined the cry) Richard Nixon called for US intervention, proclaiming that "the goal of the South Vietnamese army must be a free North Vietnam, and that the war must be carried north to achieve that goal."[29]

The "freeing" of North Vietnam has never become a US policy objective. Nor was it contemplated by the Sullivan scenario, which specified that the United States should make it abundantly clear it had no intention of destroying or occupying North Vietnam. (Failure to make this clear, it was understood, would not only increase North Vietnamese resistance but might well provoke that direct confrontation with China which McCone thought was inevitable. US Ambas-

26 American Security Council, *Washington Report,* 22 June 1964, p. 3; cf. *Washington Post,* 1 July 1971, A18.

27 London *Times,* 6 August 1969, p. 8; Franz Schurmann, Peter Dale Scott, and Reginald Zelnik, *The Politics of Escalation* (Boston and New York: Beacon Press and Fawcett, 1966), pp. 35–43.

28 Fred Greene, *U.S. Policy and the Security of Asia* (New York: McGraw-Hill, 1968), p. 237: "One reason for the American reaction on August 4 was the need to stabilize a deteriorating political situation in Saigon, and in this regard the bombings proved to be of some, though limited, value."

29 *New York Times,* 17 April 1964, p. 1; 19 April 1964, p. 82.

sador Kenneth Todd Young has written that recently one of the principal US themes in the Warsaw ambassadorial talks with China has been that "the United States has no . . . intention of seeking to overthrow the Democratic Republic of North Vietnam.")[30] Nevertheless, former CIA hand William Bundy told a secret House committee session in May that "rollback"—hitherto the slogan of rightwing propagandists like the American Security Council—was in fact a US strategic goal: "The objectives of our Far East policy are clear. They are, as they have been for many years under both parties, to preserve and strengthen the will and capacity of the peoples of the area to resist Communist aggression, and thus to produce a situation of strength from which we may in time see a rollback of Communist power."[31] He allegedly told the Committee that the United States would drive the Communists from South Vietnam, even if it meant "attacking the countries [*sic*] to the north."[32] In the same month an article leaked to *Fortune* named China as "the true war base of the Communist offensive against South Vietnam," and warned that the US might soon have to extend the war north. It cited "Western intelligence" as believing Russia had already told Hanoi it would stay out if a more forthright US intervention provoked the Chinese into a Korea-type response. ("Left to themselves, the Chinese could not cope with the totality of US forces.")[33]

The important top-level Honolulu Conference of 1–2 June 1964 (Rusk, McNamara, Taylor, McCone, Lodge, Sharp, and William Bundy) marked the beginning of the end of the "limited war" strategy so dear to Kennedy and McNamara. Reportedly this conference agreed to a "forward strategy" for CINCPAC against China (another slogan emanating from the right, in this case from the CIA-subsidized Foreign Policy Research Institute of Dr. Strausz-Hupé) in the whole of Southeast Asia.[34]

30 Kenneth Todd Young, *Negotiating with the Chinese Communists: The United States Experience, 1953–1967* (New York: McGraw-Hill, 1968), p. 269. This may have been first stated at the meeting of 29 July 1969.

31 House Committee on Appropriations, *Foreign Operations Appropriations for 1965, Hearings Before a Subcommittee,* 88th Cong., 2nd Sess. (Washington: GPO, 1964), p. 310.

32 *New York Times,* 19 June 1964, p. 5.

33 Charles J. V. Murphy, "Vietnam Hangs on U.S. Determination," *Fortune,* May 1964, pp. 159, 162, 227. In 1961 an article under Murphy's name attempted to vindicate the CIA for its role in the Bay of Pigs by blaming Eisenhower and Kennedy; cf. *supra,* p. 20.

34 In 1966 it was revealed that CINCPAC's (Admiral Sharp's) formal mission was to maintain a "forward strategy on the periphery of the Sino-Soviet bloc in the Western Pacific" (*New York Times,* 27 March 1966, IV, p. 10). As early as 22 June 1964 the *Times* wrote of America's new "forward strategic position to face Communist China," of "an anti-Communist strategy that is far broader than the present war effort within South Vietnam."

Soon after this conference Johnson ratified for Laos the "punch-for-punch military policy" which he had previously refused to ratify for Vietnam. This included authorization for air strikes against Laos, and the readying of US bombers "to hit targets in North Vietnam and elsewhere if Washington gives the word."[35] He also authorized the various covert proposals of Sullivan which began in July, but he *still* postponed decision on the issue of bombing North Vietnam.

Laos, in other words, was the target offered, as a compromise, to the proponents of air strikes against North Vietnam. And it was the aircraft carriers that had been moved in for the purpose of striking Laos which made the strikes against North Vietnam, not yet authorized, possible at any moment. (In addition, the airfield at Danang had been secretly lengthened to handle jet F-100s—despite their prohibition under the 1954 Geneva agreements—and F-100s had been brought in to fly strikes against Laos by 21 June.) Goulden fails to see how intimately events in Laos were linked to internal pressures on Johnson to escalate, for he unfortunately swallows the CIA version which presents the right-wing Laotian coup of 19 April 1964 as a *response* to stepped-up Pathet Lao activity ("In mid-April the Communist Pathet Lao mounted battalion-sized attacks against government positions, prompting a brief rightist overthrow of Premier Souvanna Phouma [a neutralist]."). In fact the chronology, and the causality, was the other way round: the fighting in the Plaine des Jarres was resumed in mid-May, after the coup had been followed by a new Army command of rightist generals who assumed command over the hitherto separate neutralist troops. As the pro-American correspondent Denis Warner confirms, the resulting "mass defections from the ranks of the neutralists . . . led to the rout of Kong Le's troops and the fall of the Plain of Jars."[36]

In other words, the right wing, not the Pathet Lao, provided by their coup the impetus that led to American escalation. The importance of Laos as a "trigger" to the Vietnam war is confirmed by the *New York Times* account of the Pentagon Papers study:

> On May 17, when the Pathet Lao launched an offensive on the Plaine des Jarres that threatened to collapse the pro-American Government of Premier Souvanna Phouma, . . . the study declares, [a] "deliberate, cautious approach" to escalation planning was suddenly thrown into "crisis management." The Administration immediately

35 *Aviation Week,* 22 June 1964, p. 15.
36 Denis Warner, *Reporting Southeast Asia* (Sydney: Angus and Robertson, 1966) p. 191; cf. *supra,* p. 38.

turned the Laotian air operations up a notch by intensifying the T-28 strikes.[37]

The 19 April anti-neutralist coup in Vientiane, like Khanh's anti-neutralist coup of 30 January in Saigon, was officially disapproved of in Washington. But both coups were spearheaded by pro-American figures (security chief Siho in Vientiane, Special Forces Chief Nghiem in Saigon) whose officers and cadres had been set up by the CIA.[38] It can be shown that Kennedy's original escalations in Vietnam, like Johnson's, followed US escalations in Laos which were presented as responses to Communist provocations, but which in fact were originally triggered by actions of CIA personnel and their Asian cohorts. The air strikes after Tonkin, in other words, cannot be written off as an isolated instance of ill-advised judgment reached "hastily" and "precipitously" by Washington.

Goulden concludes with a review of the "mistakes seen in Tonkin." Assuredly Washington made mistakes, and, as Goulden demonstrates, they do "recur all too frequently." One of his most telling chapters is a review of the command-and-control snafus surrounding other ill-fated electronics intelligence missions—the USS *Liberty* in the 1967 Israeli-Arab War, and more recently the *Pueblo*. The Israelis, he reveals, attacked the *Liberty* after the US military attaché, in good faith, had denied there were any US ships in the area. The attaché had seen a JCS cable ordering all US craft in the area a hundred miles out to sea; the *Liberty*, however, had not received the order. The original message had been despatched, in error, to the Philippines and then to Fort Mead in Maryland; a follow-up, confirming order was likewise deflected in error to Morocco. Again Washington was thrown into a crisis of which it had no good intelligence. As McNamara later admitted, "I thought the *Liberty* had been attacked by Soviet forces. Thank goodness, our carrier commanders did not launch directly against the Soviet forces who were operating in the Mediterranean." A warning message about the dangers inherent in the *Pueblo*'s mission was similarly misdirected. Goulden's review

37 *Pentagon Papers,* p. 246.

38 It has frequently been charged that Khanh seized power on 30 January "after the CIA had decided on him as the new ruler" (Alfred Steinberg, *Sam Johnson's Boy.* New York: Macmillan, 1968, p. 762). Robert Shaplen, whose book is written largely from CIA sources, denies this; but he admits that "some of the high-ranking Americans in town knew what was going on" (*The Lost Revolution.* New York: Harper & Row, 1965, p. 232). According to the *Washington Post* (1 July 1971, A18), "Gen. Khanh personally discussed with [McNamara's enemy] Lodge his intended coup, two days in advance." If so, how was it that "the swift coup put the U.S. Secretary of Defense in the humiliating position of having had no inkling from his intelligence sources of the imminent downfall of an allied government?" (*Newsweek,* 10 February 1964, p. 19.)

underlines the dangers in thus shadowing the territorial waters of the world: at least 225 US personnel have been killed or captured in ELINT and other "ferret" missions since January 1950; and some of these incidents, like the *Pueblo*'s, have led not only to increased tension but to international crises.

But it can be misleading to compare the *Liberty* to the *Maddox*. No one in the administration wanted to strike against Israel, and we did not do so; but for years elements in CINCPAC and the CIA have wanted to strike against communism in Asia. On 4 August we did. The most important revelations about the Tonkin Gulf incidents are not the mistakes—delayed cables, the inadequate procedures for review. The most important revelation is of another recurring pattern —the readiness of our national security bureaucracy to escalate in Southeast Asia for the attainment of bureaucratic objectives, *with or without a provocation.*

At one level the objectives may appear to have been relatively finite—the passage of the Tonkin Gulf Resolution (which Johnson had decided upon after the first Tonkin incident), the forestalling of international pressures for a Geneva conference, the revival of Saigon's interest in an ill-starred war, or the quiet deployment of aircraft for a "forward strategic position" against China. But for some at least the long-range objective seems to have been "a rollback of communist power" in the area. Although such fantasies may not have been widely shared in Washington, the air strikes and troop deployments of 5 August fitted into a long-continuing build-up of US strike forces around China's periphery. (Even America's apparent disengagements, as in 1954 and 1962, have always been balanced by new and strengthened commitments to the region.)

The Tonkin Gulf Resolution led not only to a major war in Asia, but to the credibility gap at home. The young in particular have lost respect for those who accepted, without criticism, a clearcut story which no serious student has since found credible. Senator Fulbright himself has said he regrets his own role in the Tonkin Gulf affair "more than anything I have ever done in my life."[39] It is still in his power to reopen the Tonkin Gulf hearings, to question Admiral Sharp and other relevant witnesses, and to demand publication of the intercepts on which the strike decision was based. To do so may cause trouble between Congress and the military but will hardly increase public disaffection. The truth (and the search for it) will more likely allay the worst apprehensions of the anti-war movement. Congress

39 *Hearing,* p. 80.

is now implicated in the deception of Tonkin; its own credibility is at stake. Many believe our political system is now so militarized that congressional powers are irrelevant, or subservient, or somehow actually collusive.

On 26 August 1964, the Joint Chiefs of Staff in a secret memorandum to McNamara recommended bombing North Vietnam as a "psychological boost" for "the requisite governmental stability and viability" in Saigon.[40] Working only with the available bureaucratic documents, the Pentagon study leaked by Daniel Ellsberg called this document "the first appearance . . . of a 'provocation strategy' that was to be discussed at the Sept. 7 White House session—in the words of the narrative, 'deliberate attempts to provoke the D.R.V. into taking actions which could then be answered by a systematic U.S. air campaign.' "[41] The phrase and the description in the Pentagon study are accurate; the date, however, is wrong. The sordid story of the Tonkin Gulf incidents suggests that, long before the US bureaucracy was willing officially to consider a "provocation strategy," such a strategy was already being put into practice by a bureaucratic faction with a strong base in the intelligence communities. Thus to seek the origins of the Indochina war one must go behind the Pentagon Papers, to the covert US operations, and parapolitics, which gave rise to them. And if that faction resorted not only to secrecy and verbal deception, but the deliberate fraudulent alteration of intelligence intercepts, then one can challenge it on legal as well as moral grounds. For the US Criminal Code, which does not prevent the government from lying to its people, states clearly (Section 1001) that no people shall make misrepresentations to the government.

The Pentagon Papers reveal systematic collusion and deception, and these vices should be condemned. But where collusion resorts to fraud, it should be prosecuted as a crime and a conspiracy.

Appendix: The Tonkin Gulf Intercepts Once More

A recent book by Anthony Austin, an Assistant Editor of the *New York Times,* has thrown fresh light on Tonkin Gulf Intercept Groups 3 and 4, which "proved" the existence of an attack on 4 August by echoing our own cable traffic, but which are now difficult to credit. Austin argues persuasively that Groups 3 and 4 consist in fact of North Vietnamese messages picked up at the time of the first Tonkin Gulf incident on 2 August. Less persuasively, he suggests that

40 *Pentagon Papers,* p. 354.
41 *Ibid.,* pp. 312–13.

71

intercepts played little or no role in the decision-making of 4 August, and that the false record that included Groups 3 and 4 arose some time later as the result of an *ex post facto* "clerical error."

Let us first recall McNamara's account (Tonkin Gulf *Hearing,* p. 92) of Intercept Groups 3 and 4:

3. "The Swatow boats reported an enemy [US] aircraft falling and enemy vessel wounded, and that message coming 12 minutes after our ships reported that they were being attacked."

4. ". . . reporting that they had shot down two planes and sacrificed two ships and adding further details of the engagement."

Austin, who has interviewed "present and former officials of the government," has published three valuable additional pieces of information, drawn from "new and reliable evidence," in support of his hypothesis. He points out that Intercept Groups 3 and 4, reporting an attack, which conform not at all with the realities of 4 August, conform exactly with North Vietnamese perceptions of the undisputed first incident on 2 August. (A Hanoi radio broadcast of 12 August claimed that, on 2 August during the first incident, one US plane was destroyed and two others hit; it is likely, moreover, that on that day at least two, perhaps three, DRV torpedo boats were lost.) He reports also that the so-called intelligence community "participated in the normal fashion in the evaluation of the evidence" on 2 August, but *not* on 4 August: "the usual interdepartmental consultation among experts on the middle level of officialdom was dispensed with. The evaluation was done by the Pentagon alone."[42] And he reports that "Some weeks later, with the Tonkin Gulf incidents consigned to history, the contents of the intercepted North Vietnamese messages were put together in a wrap-up for inclusion in the government records. . . . But the records of at least one government agency contained a jumbled wrap-up of the messages of those days." Therein, he adds, "may lie the explanation."[43]

From his investigation, Austin concludes with Fulbright that on 4 August "there was no attack at all." But he also rejects the possi-

---

42 Austin, *The President's War*, p. 341. This surprising fact is confirmed by Lyndon Johnson, who writes that "several experts in technical intelligence" were called to the White House on 2 August, but not, apparently, on 4 August (Lyndon Baines Johnson, *The Vantage Point*. New York: Holt, Rinehart and Winston, 1971, pp. 112, 114).

43 Austin, pp. 342–43.

bility of "forged intercepts" or the "idea of a conspiracy to trick the President and Secretary of Defense into retaliating." The possible explanation which he presents is that of an *ex post facto* "bureaucratic muddle . . . a clerical error":

> The North Vietnamese messages that came in on August 4 were Intercepts 1 and 2 . . . giving the location of the destroyers and instructing the Swatows to prepare for military action. . . . These intercepts were not regarded on that day as any weightier than Herrick's reports of radar contacts, sonar soundings and the sighting of a torpedo wake . . . nor could they have been, since they did not say anything about attacking. What clinched the decision to retaliate . . . was the confirmation of an attack that was obtained from Admiral Sharp. . . . Some weeks later . . . whoever wrote the summary made a clerical error, confusing the sequence of some of the messages, with the result that the August 2 messages that spoke of damaging an enemy vessel, downing planes and sacrificing two boats (the messages we have called Intercepts 3 and 4) were recorded mistakenly as having been intercepted on August 4.[44]

The US story of "unprovoked attack" on the *Pueblo* turns out to be based in part on a similar *ex post facto* rearrangement of questionable intercept records: thus the information he reports deserves our interest. But "errors" that thus recur do not dispel our suspicions of conspiracy: they increase them. The facts, moreover, indicate that Intercept 2, at least (received at 9:20 A.M., E.S.T.), *did* figure prominently in the retaliation decision of 4 August; as McNamara revealed, "consideration" of that retaliation began in the Pentagon "at about 10 o'clock" on the basis of Intercept 2 ("indicating that the North Vietnamese had issued orders to initiate the attack").[45] This was about an hour before the first flash report of the attack, possibly thirty minutes before the "attack" had occurred even in the minds of the destroyers' crews.[46] Johnson in his memoirs likewise indicates that a phone call to him from McNamara "a few minutes after nine" about Intercept 2 ("our intelligence people had intercepted a message that strongly indicated the North Vietnamese were preparing another attack") preceded the first warning from the *Maddox*.[47] This telephone call appears

44 *Ibid.* p. 342.
45 *Hearing*, pp. 70–71.
46 This possibility is obscured by the demonstrable confusion in the Pentagon chronology of the second incident, where certain cables appeared to be listed twice and the true relationship to Washington time is unclear.
47 Lyndon Johnson, *The Vantage Point*, p. 114.

to have been important in securing congressional support for the retaliation: this support was first assured that morning at Johnson's "regular Tuesday breakfast meeting with the Democratic Congressional leadership."[48]

There is at least one piece of evidence suggesting that, *pace* Mr. Austin, the intercepts (or summaries of them) were important on 4 August: Herrick's unexplained telegram of 7:46 or 8:46 local time, "Received info indicating attack by PGM P-4 imminent." Later investigators who knew radars doubted that Herrick could have reached this conclusion from the alleged radar reports of patrol boats thirty-six miles away below the horizon, even on a night of unusual "ducting." As Austin reports, this cable "seemed to be a guarded reference to one of the intercepts" (No. 2).[49] The independent recurrence of the word "attack" in Herrick's cable, as in McNamara's and Johnson's accounts, strongly suggests that the word "attack" was used on 4 August in an intelligence report of Intercept 2, even if this use was unjustified.

Thus from different informed sources we have strong indications that intercepts inspired not only the perception of an imminent attack, but the retaliation against it, perhaps before the attack had occurred. Yet, while Johnson and McNamara relied on this highly technical and highly debatable intelligence as a basis for war, the customary evaluation of it by the intelligence community was dispensed with before the retaliation, just as the normal court of inquiry by the Navy was dispensed with afterwards. Inasmuch as Congress was deceived on 4 August, so Congress today should learn by whom, and why, that normal evaluation was deemed to be unnecessary.

The hypothesis of an *ex post facto* "clerical error" about Intercepts 3 and 4 does not address itself to the timing of these intercepts in McNamara's chronology so as to coincide with moments of decision in Washington, and also with details in the destroyers' cable traffic. Intercept Group 3, reporting an "aircraft falling," was said by McNamara to have been received in Washington twelve minutes after the destroyers' first flash report of the same attack (*Hearing,* pp. 17, 92). (This was after the *Maddox* reported that "unidentified aircraft had disappeared from its radar screen" at 9:08 P.M. Tonkin Gulf time.) Intercept Group 4, reporting the loss of two North Vietnamese ships, was said by McNamara to have been received in Washington "immediately after the attack ended," or just after the crucial cable

48 Austin, p. 29.
49 *Ibid.,* pp. 178–79.

from Herrick expressing doubts and suggesting a "complete evaluation before any further action" (*Hearing*, pp. 92, 57).

McNamara and Johnson agree as to the importance of these intercepts in the former's determination on that day that the attack had taken place; and Johnson adds actual details, not revealed by McNamara, from the text of the intercepts themselves.[50] In thus breaking the taboo on direct quotation from the intercepts, Johnson would seem to have finally nullified the DIA's arguments against their publication.[51] They should now be published, *verbatim*, as first translated, and as first summarized. If a former President has the liberty to quote from the text of these intercepts (presumably kept in his library), it would seem contemptuous indeed to deny the documents any longer to the American Congress, to their qualified staff with top secret clearance, and indeed to the American people.

50 *Hearing*, p. 59; Johnson, p. 114: "During the afternoon additional intelligence reports flowed in. We intercepted a message from one of the attacking North Vietnamese boats in which it boasted of having fired at two 'enemy airplanes' and claimed to have damaged one. The North Vietnamese skipper reported that his unit had 'sacrificed two comrades.' Our experts said this meant either two enemy boats or two men in the attack group. Another message to North Vietnamese PT boat headquarters boasted: 'Enemy vessel perhaps wounded.' Clearly the North Vietnamese knew they were attacking us."

51 According to Austin (pp. 170–71), Deputy Secretary of Defense Paul Nitze refused to give a copy of the text to Senator Fulbright, on the ground that "it would reveal to the North Vietnamese that we had broken their code." William Bader, the Fulbright committee staff member and State Department veteran with top secret clearance, was not allowed to remain in the room when McNamara discussed the intercepts with the Fulbright committee. Now Lyndon Johnson proceeds with impunity to quote from them in a private memoir.

One notes with some cynicism that former officials John P. Roche (*New York Times Magazine*, 24 January 1971) and William Bundy (Austin, p. 332) have stated that the intercepts were transmitted not in code but in clear text.

At Haiphong, avoid damage to merchant shipping. No attacks authorized on craft unless US aircraft are first fired on and then only if clearly North Vietnamese.

Cable from Joint Chiefs of Staff to
Admiral Sharp, authorizing first strikes against
oil facilities in Hanoi and Haiphong, 22 June 1966
The Pentagon Papers

Chapter Four
Provoking China
and the USSR: 1966-68

The Court-Martial of Colonel Broughton

Historians may well come to regard 1967 as a turning-point in the Vietnam war. The second half of 1967 saw the beginnings of a public dialogue, recorded in the statements of US and North Vietnamese officals, which led finally to President Johnson's suspension in March 1968 of the bombing over part of North Vietnam. Many factors, military, political, and fiscal, contributed to this difficult turnabout. One of these factors would be the growing split between the President and his hawkish Commander-in-Chief, Pacific, Admiral Ulysses S. Grant Sharp (CINCPAC), who in August 1967 argued vainly, through the forum of Senator Stennis' Senate Preparedness Investigating Subcommittee, for permission to close the North Vietnamese port facilities of Haiphong, Campha, and Honggai. In analyzing the reasons for this split, future historians may come to look much more closely at the mysterious events of 2 June 1967, when, for the first time, US planes attacked a Soviet ship in a North Vietnamese harbor. As yet little is known about the attack, but from this little it is clear that much remains to be told.

It was not until April 1969 that the US government gave any indication that something improper had happened two years before. In that month the *Washington Star* published an interview with former USAF Colonel Jacksel M. N. Broughton, now retired and living in Santa Barbara. Colonel Broughton's story was plausible on the face of it: on 2 June two of his pilots in the 355th Tactical Air Fighter Wing, based at Takhli in Thailand, had accidentally strafed the 341-foot Soviet freighter *Turkestan* in Campha harbor; and as their acting commander, he had tried to cover up for them. "Two of my majors got trapped," Broughton told the *Star*. "They were strafing some anti-aircraft guns when another battery opened up on them." The pilots fired at the second battery and hit the ship by mistake.

So plausible is this account, indeed, that Colonel Broughton's own behavior becomes difficult to account for. As a Pentagon statement of 10 April was to confirm, the colonel chose to conceal the incident rather than report it. Having made this decision, Colonel Broughton was faced with the problem of the film contained in the cameras attached to the fighter's guns. Either on his own initiative or after having been ordered to produce the telltale film, he personally removed the film from the gun-cameras, processed it to determine its contents, and finally destroyed it (*San Francisco Chronicle,* 11 April 1969, p. 13). Thus, faced with the "accidental" violation of presidential orders by two of his subordinates, the colonel apparently chose to aggravate their guilt, and voluntarily implicated himself, by a deliberate conspiracy (in violation of Article 81 of the Uniform Code of Military Justice) to suppress and destroy the evidence. Or so it might appear to civilian eyes; the Air Force, apparently, took a more lenient view. The two pilots, Majors Alonzo L. Ferguson and Frederick G. Tolman,[1] were found not guilty in a court-martial and were still (as of April 1969) on active duty. It is not yet clear what the pilots were charged with: though by their unauthorized action they had killed a Soviet seaman, it is more likely that the court-martial

1 Names as printed in the *San Francisco Chronicle*. The USAF *Register* for 1967, while listing Colonel Broughton and Major Ferguson, has no record of a Major Tolman.

was interested in their violation of Air Force discipline. Broughton "was convicted of destroying government property and processing the film in an unauthorized manner": he was fined $600. In July 1968, however, an Air Force review board set aside the court-martial conviction. No more might ever have been heard of the affair had Colonel Broughton himself not chosen to talk.

The usual concern of the armed services for discipline is proverbial: one thinks of the San Francisco Presidio "mutiny," when US Army privates received sentences of up to sixteen years for sitting down and singing, "We Shall Overcome." Only one day after the *Turkestan* affair, on 3 June 1967, Colonel Levy was to receive a sentence of three years' hard labor for having refused to teach medicine to the Green Berets. In this context the USAF court-martial and review board might be said to have exhibited a lack of concern for propriety which begins to approach that of Colonel Broughton himself. The strafing of a Soviet ship, whether accidental or otherwise, was clearly an event with the gravest political implications. The mere risk of such an event had for months overshadowed the debate then raging as to whether political or strategic priorities, civilian or military controls, were to determine the pattern of US bombing over North Vietnam. This was precisely the issue over which Johnson and Sharp were divided at the time: the President's reluctance to authorize raids on or near port facilities because of his fear that a Soviet vessel might be accidentally hit. It explains why, when the bombing was curtailed on 31 March 1968, two key military targets (and only two) remained unscathed: Gialam International Airport near Hanoi and the actual port facilities of Haiphong harbor. Though willing to escalate the war in countless other respects, the President was notorious for his fears of a direct military confrontation with the USSR.[2]

To have attacked a Soviet ship on 2 June 1967 was a particularly serious action, even if accidental. For at that very moment the United States and the Soviet Union were faced with what was generally

2 It was common knowledge that, on the night of the first Hanoi-Haiphong raids, 29 June 1966, he had gone to a Catholic Dominican chapel and prayed. "For months afterward President Johnson would tell occasional visitors how he worried that night that the raids would somehow go wrong and an errant bomb would strike a Soviet ship in Haiphong harbor and start World War III." (Kraslow and Loory, *The Secret Search for Peace in Vietnam*. New York: Random House, 1968, p. 13.) Unfortunately, there is no indication that the President's worries were shared by his commanders in the Pacific. One of them, Admiral Roy L. Johnson, Commander-in-Chief, Pacific Fleet, was asked about the risk of hitting Soviet ships within two miles of Haiphong targets just authorized. "I have enough confidence in the professional skills of our aviators," the former Navy pilot replied, "that the possibility never really worried me." (*New York Times,* 22 April 1967, p. 2.) Only four days later, for the first time, a UK ship in Haiphong harbor was rocketed.

recognized to be the gravest risk of a direct confrontation since the 1962 Cuban missile crisis. Nasser had just blocked the Straits of Tiran, Israel was threatening retaliation, Soviet and American ships had just converged on the area. On 5 June the six-day Middle East war was to break out. In this context, how are we to understand the court-martial's cavalier exoneration of those responsible for an attack that was clearly unauthorized, belligerent, homicidal, and dangerous?

The failure of the armed services to discipline a conspiracy with international political consequences would seem strange under any circumstances. It seems even more strange when we consider the reported details of the *Turkestan* incident itself, the political context in which the incident occurred, and finally the recurring pattern of unauthorized attacks against the ships of North Vietnam's Communist allies in North Vietnamese harbors. *We shall see that every one of these unauthorized attacks occurred when the Communist nation in question appeared to be moving toward some kind of political understanding with the United States.*

The Bombing of the *Turkestan*: 2 June 1967

The US government has now issued three different accounts of the *Turkestan* attack: on 3 June (when it denied the attack occurred), on 18 June (when it reversed itself), and on 10 April 1969 (when it supplied further details). Its two subsequent statements are inconsistent with each other as well as with the first. The Soviet account, in contrast, has been precise and substantially consistent since the outset. Now that its major contention has been confirmed, its details (which have never been challenged) should be replied to by the US government as well. Until they are refuted, the details of the Soviet account suggest that the attack was deliberate and premeditated. Furthermore, other apparently insignificant details supplied by the Pentagon corroborate the notion that the attack could not have been accidental.

According to the Soviet accounts, the 341-foot Motor Vessel *Turkestan* was anchored four hundred meters (about one quarter of a mile) offshore in the roadstead of Campha harbor, where it had been taking on coal for Japan. Except for the Cypriot ship *Asma* tied up at dockside, there was no other ship in the harbor. At 4:40 P.M. local time (11:40 A.M. Moscow time):

> Four American fighter-bombers appeared from the direction of the mainland, in the northwest, flying at a low altitude. Two planes separated from this group, *dived on the Soviet ship, and dropped a*

bomb. . . . "Visibility was excellent," the captain said, "and there could be no question of an attack by mistake. The American pilots *trained their machine-guns on the central superstructure of the ship* where the crew lives and works." (*Tass,* 5 June 1967; FBIS *Daily Report,* 5 June 1967, BB14, emphasis added.)

As a result of the attack, one crewman was killed and six others were wounded, one of them so critically that he required an operation lasting three hours. According to an earlier account, the two American aircraft "attacked *from different directions* [a third account said 'from two sides'] to bomb the *Turkestan.* A bomb fell about 100 meters from the vessel [i.e., about 300 meters offshore], after which both bombers strafed the ship with large-caliber machine-guns firing explosive bullets." (*Tass,* 3 June 1967; *New York Times,* 4 June 1967, p. 6.) The dead man, Rybachuk, had been machine-gunned after going to an outside door in response to the ship's alarm (suggesting more than a single accidental overflight). An unexploded 20-mm explosive shell was found on the *Turkestan,* along with numerous shell splinters. (The US statement of two weeks later was to admit the use of "20-mm suppressive fire.")

The various Soviet accounts of the incident seem on the whole not only plausible but relatively restrained. For example, the charge that *one* bomb was dropped corrects an earlier reference by Tass in English to "bombs" being dropped—the only apparent inconsistency in the Soviet version. Although the captain was quoted on 3 June as saying the attack was deliberate, this charge was not leveled formally by the Soviet Union until its second note of 5 June, after the United States had denied the incident occurred. Given the claims of Soviet eyewitnesses that the planes dived on the central portion of the ship *from different directions* after dropping a bomb three hundred meters offshore, one begins to see just how significant would have been the testimony of the film which Colonel Broughton destroyed. If the attack was indeed accidental, then he unfortunately eliminated the best possible evidence for showing this.

On 3 June, after an investigation lasting less than twenty-four hours, the United States denied that the attack had occurred. As supporting evidence the Pentagon released the findings of Admiral Sharp that only two targets had been attacked in the Campha area— a road and an anti-aircraft site—and that these were both "more than three miles from the Soviet ship." (*New York Times,* 4 June 1967, p. 7.) Even at the high speeds of modern supersonic jet fighter aircraft —F-105s can fly up to 650 miles an hour—at least eighteen seconds would have had to have elapsed between the strafing of one of these targets and of the *Turkestan* more than three miles away. This would seem to exclude the possibility of an accident. The United States in its 18 June statement explained that yet another anti-aircraft site had later been attacked by a third flight of aircraft, a claim echoed by Colonel Broughton's statement that his majors "got trapped." But if it is true that planes were diverted to a new anti-aircraft target, the pilots would have had to be flying at lower speeds to execute such maneuvers. Assuming that the pilots were flying at 200 miles per hour, and that the anti-aircraft site was situated by coincidence at precisely the closest onshore approach to the *Turkestan,* the latter's distance of four hundred meters offshore would still represent a significant time lapse in the order of five or more seconds. Let us not forget the concentration of fire on the *Turkestan* (as evidenced by the seven casualties), nor the words of the US Note on 3 June that: "U.S. military pilots are under strict instructions to avoid engagements with any vessels which are not identified as hostile." (*New York Times,* 4 June, 1967, p. 7.) Admiral Sharp's inquiry confirmed on the same day that "The fact that the *Turkestan* was at Campha was known by the aircraft crews, who were cautioned to avoid the ship." (*Ibid.*)

But the Pentagon statement of denial, taken in context with other US statements, is even more interesting for other reasons. As a glance at the accompanying chart (see pp. 98–99) will show, the US official response to the *Turkestan* incident was unlike that to any other incident involving an alleged attack against a Soviet-bloc ship. In 1966 the United States tended publicly to ignore or reject such charges (even when privately conceded), just as by 1968 the US response had become one of publicly expressing regrets in advance of an investigation. The response of the United States on 2 June was unique. Although some US officials claimed there were "reasons to doubt" the Soviet charges, the Defense Department announced that CINCPAC in Honolulu had been asked to supply the flight plans of US aircraft in the area, and that an American reply would be deferred until his investigation had been completed.

This response was diplomatically significant in two respects: Washington was professing its own ignorance of what had actually happened in Campha harbor, and it was taking the unusual step of identifying one of its own officials, Admiral Sharp, as the man who would be responsible for the forthcoming US reply. It is clear that Moscow was not deaf to these subtleties. Tass responded that by thus passing the buck "the Pentagon generals made it seem that they were not in on the secret"; and Tass particularly objected to the choice of Admiral Sharp as investigator (US officials, it claimed, thus "seek to whitewash those responsible"—FBIS *Daily Report,* 6 June BB10; 5 June, BB14).

The next day, 3 June, the US government published a Note to the USSR government, concluding that on the basis of pilots' reports, it *appeared* that any damage to the ship was "in all probability the result of [North Vietnamese] anti-aircraft fire" (*New York Times,* 4 June 1967, p. 7). This Note, if read closely, fell short of being a strict "denial" as the *New York Times* then called it. However, Washington also took the unusual step of releasing the results of Admiral Sharp's investigation, which had been concluded in less than twenty-four hours. The statement is worth reading closely, in the light of what we now know:

> Admiral Ulysses S. G. Sharp, commander-in-chief, U.S. Pacific Command, has completed his investigation into the allegations by the Soviet Union that U.S. aircraft bombed the Soviet ship *Turkestan,* in the port of Campha in North Vietnam. *The conclusion of the investigation is that no U.S. aircraft bombed or strafed the Soviet ship. There is absolutely no evidence to confirm the Soviet allegation.*

The statement noted that two flights of F-105s had attacked two military targets in the Campha area (a "segment of road" and "an anti-aircraft site") and that each of these two targets was "more than three miles from the Soviet ships." It then made a curiously elaborate distinction:

> The pilots of the aircraft which attacked the road *reported* that they observed the bombs impacting on the road segment. *Flight film taken by the aircraft* attacking the anti-aircraft *sites* (*sic*) confirmed that the ordnance from that flight detonated on target. The fact that the *Turkestan* was at Campha was known by the aircraft crews, who were cautioned to avoid the ship. There was no strafing by aircraft of either flight at any time. . . . It is probable that the heavy North Vietnamese anti-aircraft fire was responsible for any damage to the Soviet ship.

Finally it reported that the attacks had occurred between 4:35 and 4:50 P.M., or until ten minutes *after* the time announced by the Soviets for when the incident began.

Two separate and telling details indicate that CINCPAC, in drafting this language, already knew more than he was letting on.

The unexplained second reference to "the anti-aircraft sites" (after claiming that "*an* anti-aircraft site" had been attacked, as one of only two targets) suggests that CINCPAC had already encountered the excuse of the second anti-aircraft site which was closer to the *Turkestan*. If so, CINCPAC's false conclusion, and the claim that the only targets attacked were "more than three miles away," were not simply errors made in good faith on insufficient evidence, but conscious and deliberate lies made with the intention of concealing from someone (not the Russians, obviously!) the truth of the Soviet claim. The curiously elaborate distinction between the verbal assurances of the first flight of aircraft, and the flight film of the second, also suggests that the anomaly of the missing flight film had already come to light, since in June 1967 all F-105s were equipped with gun-cameras. Yet CINCPAC concluded its investigation within twenty-four hours, with the statement that "there is absolutely no evidence to confirm the Soviet allegation." On both of these grounds, we are justified in concluding that the CINCPAC denial was not drafted in good faith.

Both of these details, moreover, cast grave doubts on the Pentagon claim of 18 June, that a *third* flight of F-105s, previously uninvestigated, was responsible for the attack (and hence indirectly for the confusion). The story of a third flight is also contradicted by the Pentagon statement of April 1969, which made it clear that the erroneous denial of 3 June was made, not because of a third and unknown flight in the area, but because of Colonel Broughton's destruction of evidence. Indeed, it is hard to believe that whoever drafted CINCPAC's "investigation" report of 3 June intended it to be published; for it must have given Soviet officials a chance to refute errors of fact, and even to ask such elementary questions as *why* all of the flight film had not been consulted.

The 3 June document, in conclusion, arrives at a totally false conclusion chiefly by means of an elaborate tissue of truths, some of which can tell us important facts about other truths that are being suppressed. This bureaucratic phenomenon is familiar to students of the Vietnam war. The slow painful road to the truth about the Tonkin Gulf incidents is, as we have seen, littered with such documents. Thus it is important to ask, in this case, whom the 3 June denial was intended to deceive—the American people, or the American government.

As has been amply illustrated in the last ten years, it is not considered a crime for US officials to give outright lies to their public.

Those who are elected risk the sanction of not being returned to office, but no one has ever overruled Arthur Sylvester's defense of the US government's right to deceive others. Only five days later, on 8 June 1967, the Pentagon was to issue a false cover story about the mission and offshore location of the NSA spy-ship *Liberty,* just as in 1960 it had released a fictitious flight-plan for the U-2 shot down by the Soviet Union. A completely fictitious falsehood would have then been more persuasive, in the *Turkestan* incident, than CINCPAC's inadequate and almost pathetic effort to arrive at a falsehood by means of half-truths. The document's inhibitions suggest that the author wished to misrepresent matters to his superiors, not to his countrymen: thus he felt constrained to arrive at the desired conclusion by means of deliberate omissions, rather than by invented lies.

The inadequacies of this "investigation" seem to have been apparent to the US State Department, for the US government Note of 3 June, in its expression of regrets for any possible damages and injuries, carefully avoided a specific endorsement of Admiral Sharp's "conclusion." It is likely, however, that the incident might have disappeared into Pentagon files, and the irregularity of the destroyed flight film never made public, but for a rapid and dramatic change of circumstances which no one could have foreseen. On 5 June the Israeli-Arab war erupted. By 10 June the hostilities were largely over, in part because of US and Soviet insistence on a cease-fire and the convening of an emergency session of the UN General Assembly. On 17 June Premier Kosygin arrived in the United States, and on the same day the Chinese exploded their first hydrogen bomb. The US press reported that President Johnson was seeking a personal summit meeting with Premier Kosygin (the first such meeting since Kennedy met Khrushchev in 1961), but that the US government was encountering difficulties in arranging this. These difficulties were resolved, however, in time for the Glassboro summit talks of 23 and 25 June, preceded by Rusk's meeting with Gromyko on 19 June. One difficulty was eliminated by the Pentagon's disclosure, on 18 June, that it had on that day received "new information" which contradicted its earlier denial of the *Turkestan* incident:

> New information disclosed that . . . a third flight of F-105 aircraft passed through the area at the general time of the incident [that is to say, between 4:35 and 4:50 P.M.]. As previously reported, there was no strafing by the aircraft of the first two flights. However, it now appears that there was 20-mm suppressive fire against a North Viet-

namese anti-aircraft site at Campha by aircraft of the third flight and that some of this fire may have struck the *Turkestan* (quoted in the *New York Times,* 19 June 1967, p. 19.)[3]

This explanation, on the face of it, is as hard to accept as the statement it refutes. It is simply inconceivable that the first two flights of F-105s could have been unaware that a third flight was also attacking anti-aircraft sites in the same town in the same fifteen-minute period. Thus the "third flight" explanation, if believed in, would indicate the presence of a still wider conspiracy to conceal information from the US Secretary of Defense. What mattered at the time, however, was the unprecedented admission by the United States that it had bombed a Soviet ship, and had been wrong in seeking to deny this.

Admiral Sharp, it is interesting to note, played no public role in this correction of his earlier false report. The Pentagon spokesman specified that the "new information" had been supplied in "a report from General John D. Ryan of the U.S. Air Force Pacific" (CINC-PACAF)—one of Admiral Sharp's subordinate commanders (*Washington Post,* 19 June 1967, A1). According to Soviet sources (to whom we must turn for the only adequate account of this important statement): "The Pentagon spokesman also announced that General Ryan's report has been brought to the notice of the Soviet government and that the investigation continued." (Tass, 19 June 1967, in FBIS *Daily Report,* 19 June 1967, BB1.) Two days later, the US government delivered a Note to the Soviet embassy in Washington which expressed regret over the incident and assured "that US authorities will make every effort to insure that such incidents do not occur" in the future (*New York Times,* 21 June 1967, p. 3; FBIS *Daily Report,* 28 June 1968, BB1).

In the context of US-Soviet cooperation over the Middle East and in holding the Glassboro talks, it seems clear that Washington had moved much closer to Moscow's version of the *Turkestan* incident and away from Admiral Sharp's. Whatever Washington's degree of contrition and regret over the *Turkestan* attack, it was not shared in CINCPAC headquarters. On 18 June, the day of the retraction, the

---

3 According to *Le Monde* (20 June 1967, p. 8), the third flight was one of three en route to bomb locomotive shops in Bacgiang, sixty-five miles inland, when they were attacked over Campha. I have not seen this information reported in the US press. On the surface it seems difficult to reconcile with the Soviet claim that the F-105s "appeared from the direction of the mainland, in the northwest."

The Pentagon's confusion of responsibility and error was made by an unusual and curious procedure. The admission came in telephone calls from Pentagon officials to newsmen (*New York Times,* 19 June 1967, p. 19).

USAF and Navy bunched all of their outstanding authorizations to fly one hundred and sixty-six missions against North Vietnam. This was the largest number of missions in eight months—since 2 November 1966—and was only shy by nine of the previous all-time daily record. One of the targets was the railway yard at Kep, close to one of the four MIG bases where it was feared that Soviet maintenance crews were stationed.

This is only one of the many depressing instances during the Vietnam war when the level of missions, as well as the choice of targets, has had political overtones—offsetting a diplomatic search for rapprochement. By June of 1967 the doves in the State Department were painfully conscious of these instances of "the politics of escalation," particularly since the frustration in 1966 of the Polish "Marigold" peace initiative by an elaborate series of bombing "coincidences." Thus those interested in placating Kosygin took steps which they thought would prevent what happened on 18 June from occurring:

> State Department officials went over the North Vietnam target authorizations. . . . They wanted to prevent any awkward coincidences which might irritate Kosygin. They checked to make certain that no dramatic targets such as power plants, harbors, air fields or installations in the Hanoi and Haiphong areas were on the list. *They found none. They also tried to make sure the bombing would be kept at a constant level of activity. They wanted "no humps" in the curve,* as one official put it. *Their research showed there would be none.* (David Kraslow and S. H. Loory, *The Secret Search for Peace in Vietnam*, pp. 85–86.)

The excuse which Kraslow and Loory's account offers for the 166 missions ("exceptionally good weather") fails to explain why the sensitive installation at Kep was bombed, after State Department officials had checked to preclude any such embarrassments.

The pattern of unauthorized attacks against Soviet and Chinese ships in North Vietnamese harbors, after it has been studied in full, can hardly be reduced to a series of "accidents" or "coincidences." But it takes only one or two pilots "accidentally" to attack a ship. The level of missions and choice of daily targets, in contrast, are established (within certain authorizations) at the highest military levels in Saigon and Honolulu. Colonel Broughton has since had to explain to a court-martial why he destroyed flight film from the F-105 gun-cameras. But to my knowledge Admiral Sharp has never had to explain why, on the very day the United States had to apologize to the

Soviet Union for his erroneous "investigation," he renewed the injury by a near-record level of attacks. Washington's repentance, obviously, was not shared in Honolulu.

As for Washington's pledges "to do its utmost to prevent such incidents," their efficacy was demonstrated on 29 June, the date of the very next raid against Haiphong. On that day another Soviet ship, the *Mikhail Frunze,* was attacked in Haiphong harbor: Soviet authorities claimed to possess fragments from at least one pellet bomb which had landed on the ship and damaged it. 29 June has to stand as a record day in the chart of unauthorized ship bombings. Unlike the *Turkestan,* the *Mikhail Frunze* did not stand alone in the closely packed Haiphong harbor. Other ships were also attacked: the British ship *Kingford,* the Chinese ship *Hongqi 157,* and the Italian ship *Bertain.*[4] This time Washington found it advisable to admit the possibility of an "accidental" bombing, even before it had conducted its investigation (*New York Times,* 1 July 1967, p. 1). Its Note of regret on 15 July also shows a changed attitude toward a depressingly familiar scenario:

> Two planes bombed an anti-aircraft battery 600 yards from where the *Frunze* was moored. . . . While the investigation produced no positive indication that these or other aircraft damaged the Soviet vessel, *from the evidence available* the possibility cannot be excluded that some of the ordnance aimed at the anti-aircraft site fell on or near the vessel. (Quoted in *New York Times,* 16 July 1967, p. 10.)

Six weeks before, "lack of evidence" had led the United States to reject the Soviet allegation of an attack. This time it was willing to apologize because the "possibility cannot be excluded." The credibility gap between Washington and Honolulu was beginning to widen.

At the very least, the attacks on the *Turkestan* and the *Frunze* demonstrate a dangerous weakening of civilian and political restraints on the conduct of the war, wherein dangerous improprieties by US officers have been allowed to go unpunished. That Washington's diplomatic assurances of restraint could be so dramatically flouted nine days later, apparently with impunity, suggests also an increase in tension between the President's civilian aides and his commanders in the Pacific. One cannot fully appreciate this tension without reviewing the whole story of the "politics of escalation": the recurring pattern

---

4 One wonders if Admiral Johnson was still voicing his "confidence in the professional skills of our aviators."

of the escalations (whether selective or strategic, particular or overall) which have closed off particularly promising periods in the search for a political settlement. This depressing recurrence is vividly illustrated by the twelve known instances of other attacks against foreign shipping in the Tonkin Gulf. The political contexts of all of them, without exception, do suggest this close relationship to current peace probes which cannot be accidental. To see this we must now consider these contexts, first of the *Turkestan* incident, then of all the rest.

The Context of US-Soviet Relations in May and June 1967

We have now seen at least three separate incidents in the Vietnam air war during June 1967 (the ship attacks and the 18 June "hump" in bombing) that were not only against general policy guidelines but also in spite of specific precautions taken to prevent them at that time. If these incidents cannot be written off as merely coincidental, it becomes important to know more about the relations prevailing at that time between the United States and the Soviet Union—or, more specifically, how those relations might have *appeared* to an observer such as a disgruntled USAF colonel.

To many observers it appeared that the two great nuclear powers were inching slowly but inevitably toward nuclear war. U Thant's view of the war as possibly "the initial phase of World War III" (*New York Times,* 12 May 1967, p. 1) was shared by the influential right-wing *US News and World Report:*

> We are today on the verge of a third world war. . . . A few days ago United Press dispatches from Moscow reported that the Soviet Union now has agreed to grant North Vietnam several hundred million dollars more. . . . The stage is being set for a major war. . . . Is this a time when we should be buttering up Moscow with East-West trade agreements? (15 May 1967, pp. 123–124.)

On 19 May, in opposition to the Joint Chiefs, McNamara prepared a draft memorandum for the President which would in June have terminated all bombing north of 20° N, and replaced it by increased reliance on an electronic barrier (*Pentagon Papers,* pp. 535, 584). Ten days later, *US News* reported accurately that three major proposals were being discussed in Washington to break the deadlock of the Vietnam war. The first was McNamara's project of an electronic barrier to cut off infiltration. "Second is an invasion of North Vietnam with land forces. Third is a blockade of the port of Haiphong" (*US News,* 29 May 1967, p. 39). The two last proposals

would unambiguously have scrapped the political understanding between the United States and the Soviet Union to keep the war on a
a limited level. General Westmoreland was a chief proponent of the
second proposal (which had long been publicly advocated and indeed
promised by General Ky). In August Admiral Sharp was to bring his
support for the third proposal to the Senate Preparedness Subcommittee under Senator John Stennis, and thus ultimately to the US
public.

In this context the deteriorating situation in the Middle East had
ominous overtones as regards the great powers. Both the United
States and the Soviet Union were gathering their warships in the
eastern Mediterranean. On 17 May the commander of the US Sixth
Fleet, Vice-Admiral William Martin, announced that "the continuous build-up of Soviet naval strength" now "is a *significant threat
aimed directly at the Sixth Fleet* . . . a dangerous situation for us and
for them" (*US News,* 29 May 1967, p. 49). After the Egyptians had
blocked the entrance to the Gulf of Aqaba, former Undersecretary
of State George Ball predicted a challenge to the blockade by a
western ship within ten days, and with it "the most serious confrontation between the United States and Russia in five years . . . since
October 1962" (*Washington Post,* 2 June 1967, A18).

If the bombing of the *Turkestan* the next day was in response to
military developments such as these, it would have to be classed as
the act of a madman anxious for nuclear war. There were, however,
other considerations. Although this was not generally known at the
time, the same crises that were driving the two great powers apart
militarily had the opposite political effect of intensifying their secret
lines of diplomatic communication, and the chances of reaching some
kind of mutual understanding or even detente. The total picture of
US-Soviet relations, moreover, was not all dark. Besides the trade
agreements to which *US News* had objected, the text of a nuclear non-
proliferation treaty was nearing completion in Geneva, the US-USSR
Consular Treaty had just been ratified by the Senate, and on 31 May
Aeroflot flights from Moscow to Montreal were announced for June,
with the hope that they would soon extend to New York. More important, the Joint Chiefs of Staff first made it public on 3 May that
they were pressuring McNamara for an anti-ballistic missile system—
US News spoke of an impending public dispute on the issue—and it
was clear that McNamara was still resisting this pressure (as he would
continue to do until his "resignation" in November).

Two interesting Soviet articles, the first hawkish, the second more dove-ish, complained during May of the increase in anti-Soviet statements and actions in and by the United States. On 27 May *Pravda* described the recent defection of Stalin's daughter Svetlana Alliluyeva as part of a general plan to discredit the Soviet Union during the fiftieth anniversary year of the Bolshevik Revolution. It assigned responsibility for this anti-Soviet campaign to a "joint coordinating committee" of the CIA, State Department, and White House; and it charged that this secret high-level campaign discredited public assurances that the United States wanted a normalization of ties. (*New York Times,* 27 May 1967, pp. 1, 7; cf. 23 July, p. 10.)

A more subtle, complex and dove-ish thesis had been presented on 24 May by *Literaturnaya Gazeta,* in an article entitled "Seven Days in May" (*Christian Science Monitor,* 5 June 1969, p. 2). (The anonymous author, "Valentin 008," was identified by the *Christian Science Monitor* as a high-level spokesman for the KGB, the Russian CIA.) The article speculated that when Westmoreland had come to Washington and addressed Congress in late April, he had won approval from Johnson for his escalation plans (which were presumably serious but not necessarily anti-Soviet). Then on 10 and 11 May, the US destroyer *Walker* had "intentionally collided with two Soviet destroyers" (these two mysterious incidents are of course blamed by US officials on the two Soviet ships: see *New York Times,* 12 May 1967, p. 1). "Valentin 008" then noted that the White House press secretary told correspondents that President Johnson was alarmed by the *Walker* incidents, and first released Johnson's remarks to Luci one year before that he did not want to be remembered for World War III (*Washington Post,* 12 May; *New York Times,* 13 May, p. 1). He also drew attention to a pro-Vietnam New York demonstration organized on 13 May by off-duty members of the New York police force and fire departments where right-wing posters carried the ominous message "Russia is the Chief Enemy in Vietnam."

Though the rhetoric might be similar, the KGB article suggests a quite different picture from that depicted by *Pravda:* a situation in which the White House would be more the victim than the author of increased anti-Soviet pressures and hostility. These two articles themselves, like their opposite numbers in *US News* and the *Christian Science Monitor,* suggest an increasing four-way contest between hawks and doves in both Washington and Moscow, a contest with particular implications for the Middle East crisis and the Vietnam war. There is no doubt that at this time there was a major diplomatic effort to reduce tensions in both these areas simultaneously. On 24

May UK Foreign Minister Brown flew to Moscow for a two-day series of meetings with Gromyko; "the Middle East and Vietnam dominated the Anglo-Soviet conversations" (*Christian Science Monitor,* 26 May 1967, p. 2). The same pair of topics were discussed by Johnson the next day in Ottawa (in a surprise flying visit to Canada's Prime Minister Pearson, remembered chiefly for his role in helping to set up UNEF after the 1956 Suez crisis), and again on 3 June in Washington with British Prime Minister Wilson (US Department of State, *Bulletin,* 19 June 1967, p. 909; *Guardian* [Manchester], 2 June 1967, p. 1).

Shortly after the outbreak of the Israeli-Arab war had been followed by Soviet and American appeals for a cease-fire, Washington correspondents began to reveal that the Washington-Moscow "hot line" had been activated to help avoid a larger confrontation between the great powers. According to Murray Marder of the *Washington Post:*

> Secret correspondence between the White House and the Kremlin extended over the period *prior to* and during the outbreak of Israeli-Arab warfare, informed sources said. Through the critical exchange, Washington and Moscow signalled each other that despite their deep differences in the crisis, each superpower was anxious to avoid the risk of being dragged into World War III. These private assurances evidently helped to set the stage for yesterday's turnabout developments in the United Nations on a call for a cease-fire. (*Washington Post,* 7 June 1967, A1.)

The *Christian Science Monitor* spoke more specifically of a personal contact between Johnson and Kosygin:

> President Johnson is known to have been in direct contact with Soviet Premier Kosygin as the Arab-Israeli tension deepened. . . . [He] was so eager to establish the fact that the United States was not partisan in this conflict that his first statement was made 2½ hours from the time he was awakened with the news. . . . [Officials] recalled the numerous occasions that the Soviet Union had used caution as the situation developed. The whole story of this is not yet available for publication. But Soviet diplomats made it known at several danger points that they were acting on the side of restraint. . . . The primary concern of President Johnson . . . is the stability of the big-power relationship while the local brush fire burns itself out. The strong impression here that the Soviet Union has a similar sense of responsibility, and "restraint"—a word used by Premier Kosygin—has helped to keep the American hand steady. (*Christian Science Monitor,* 6 June 1967, p. 1.)

The White House, and ultimately Johnson himself, were belatedly and begrudgingly to admit that the "hot line" had been used (*New York Times,* 9 June 1967, p. 1; 10 June, p. 15; 14 June, p. 18).

As the *Monitor* observed at the time (19 June 1967, p. 2), "News of exactly what was said in Moscow-Washington 'hot-line' exchanges will await the history books." More specifically we do not yet know whether Vietnam, as well as the Middle East, was discussed. To my knowledge no informed correspondent has ever claimed it was, just as no correspondent has ever pointed out that the *Turkestan* strafing, and the Pentagon's incompetent denial of it, occurred in the *very middle* of these secret and sensitive US-Soviet communications. (It is hard to believe that Washington's inept public response to the *Turkestan* incident was not accompanied by some form of secret communications with Moscow; but this is irrelevant.) What matters is not whether the Vietnam air war was really being discussed with Moscow, but only the *appearance* that this was the case. Among a small group of highly placed second-echelon officials who were aware of the hot-line communications even if not of their contents, the fear again grew strong that the controversial bombing of North Vietnam might be reduced or even suspended.

We can learn this also from two separate and neglected news stories which appeared at this time. To understand their significance, we must recall that from 23 December 1966 to 18 April 1967 Johnson had ordered the central areas of Hanoi and Haiphong off-limits to US pilots, in the wake of the Hanoi bombings that had ended the Polish "Marigold" peace initiative (*New York Times,* 12 August 1967, p. 3; 9 May 1967, p. 1).[5] But in mid-April Admiral Sharp flew to Washington and persuaded President Johnson to lift this restriction. On 17 April he held a press conference at the Pentagon, where he stressed the importance of continuing the bombing (*New York Times,* 18 April 1967, p. 2). On 23 April he received the execute order to bomb previously unauthorized targets in and near these two cities, including MIG-capable airfields such as Kep and Hoa Lac, where it was feared Soviet technicians might be based (Admiral Sharp, *Report,* p. 32; *New York Times,* 25 April 1967, p. 1).

On the eve of the *Turkestan* incident, it appeared that the achievements of Admiral Sharp's Washington campaign were all coming unstuck. On 30 May, after the "hot line" had been activated for about a week, the *Guardian*'s Washington correspondent reported

---

5 Official sources speak only of a circle of ten nautical miles around Hanoi; they do not mention a limit around Haiphong.

that "American pilots have once again been ordered not to bomb the North Vietnamese cities of Hanoi and Haiphong. Informed sources, who disclosed this today, did not indicate how long this restriction would last (*Guardian* [Manchester], 31 May 1967, p. 1). (It was later revealed that Hanoi, at least, was placed off-limits from 23 May to 15 July 1967.) And *US News,* which two weeks earlier had spoken of a possible invasion of North Vietnam or blockade of Haiphong, reported in its issue dated 12 June that President Johnson

> is reported by some knowledgeable authorities in Washington to be considering a major shift of strategy. Under consideration: bombing of North Vietnam to be halted by Mr. Johnson to try to win world opinion [for which read "Kremlin opinion," as is made clear by the rest of this sentence] over to his side and force Ho Chi Minh and the Communist regime in Hanoi to de-escalate the war in turn (*US News,* 12 June 1967, p. 29; cf. *Pentagon Papers,* pp. 535, 584).

Rumors of the possibility of a bombing halt were to continue through the next ten weeks, especially in the British press. On 17 July the *Guardian* indicated that "the decision to 'go further' to meet the Russians on the question of bombing has already been taken." At the same time two Frenchmen named Aubrac and Marcovich were en route to Hanoi, bearing the first known American message to the North Vietnamese in six months (Kraslow and Loory, p. 223). As has happened so often in the history of this war, their arrival in Hanoi on 21 July coincided with yet another "hump" in the bombing of the Hanoi-Haiphong areas (FBIS *Daily Report,* July 1967, *passim*).

For whatever reason, the threat of a 1967 bombing halt is not heard of after mid-August. On 9 and 10 August Admiral Sharp, back in Washington for his second political mission in five months, warned the Senate Preparedness Subcommittee that the administration had been considering a bombing cessation "last spring"; any bombing halt, he said, "would be a disaster for the United States" (*New York Times,* 21 September 1967, pp. 1, 3). Faced by the combined opposition of his chief power base in the Senate, Johnson promptly escalated the bombing of North Vietnam (*Pentagon Papers,* p. 540).

The chief issue raised by incidents like the bombing of the *Turkestan* is not whether these attacks *resulted* in terminating a peace threat, but whether this was their *intention.* That these attacks were so intended seems much more likely if we turn now to a large body of evidence not yet considered, the political contexts of all the other known US attacks on foreign shipping in the Tonkin Gulf. It will then be distressingly apparent that every known instance of these "accidents" has fallen into the same pattern of threatening a diplomatic channel opened at that particular time in the search for peace.

The Political Contexts of Similar Attacks on Foreign Ships

To make it easier for the reader to follow the rather cluttered story that follows, I have prepared a simplified schematic chart showing the political contexts for each of the alleged attacks by US planes against foreign shipping (other than North Vietnamese) in the Gulf of Tonkin. I should stress the limitations of a simply schematic formulation and also of the text that follows. Above all, the conclusions that should be drawn from them relate to the overall inductive pattern; any strict or *a priori* deductions from the overall pattern to particular instances would be inappropriate, and I intend to reserve my conclusions about the *Turkestan* incident until the close of this examination. Finally, I feel it necessary to apologize for the chart's superficial neatness: it is not intended as a total explanation of its subject. As I am sympathetic to the "patternless" approach to history associated with Lewis Namier, I can only wish it exhibited one or two prominent loose ends.

With these apologies—history cannot always be as untidy as we would wish it to be—the following generalizations must still be made:

a) Although port facilities (other than Haiphong) were raided repeatedly and frequently throughout this two-year period, attacks against foreign ships are not scattered randomly, or in proportion to fluctuation in overall bombing levels (as we would expect from "accidental" bombings).

b) The attacks tend to be concentrated in periods of particular political sensitivity—precisely when it is diplomatically most urgent that such incidents be avoided. (In both June 1967 and January 1968, when most of the attacks occurred, the port of Haiphong was placed off-limits to US pilots, clearly to avoid what Rusk later called "particularly difficult incidents.")

c) Only those alleged attacks against Chinese vessels have in the end been denied by US officials; in every instance of an alleged attack against Soviet or Polish shipping the attack, or at least the "possibility" of it, has in the end been conceded.

d) If any credence is to be given to the victims' accounts of such attacks (and these have withstood investigation better than US denials), then on repeated occasions these attacks clearly could not have been accidental.

97

ALLEGED US ATTACKS AGAINST VESSELS, OTHER THAN NORTH VIETNAMESE, IN THE TONKIN GULF

ALLEGED INCIDENT	POLITICAL CONTEXT	US RESPONSE
19 April 1966: Polish M/V *Beniowski* in "harbor near Haiphong": "bombs and rocket missiles exploding near the ship."	April 1966: Polish ICC representative, Janusz Lewandowski, arrives in Vietnam to initiate "Marigold" peace initiative; calls on DRV Foreign Minister 20 April.	No known response at time. In June 1967 officials reveal that US acknowledged damage could have been caused accidentally.
28 May 1966: Chinese fishing vessels sunk; 21 fishermen killed. (12 May: US planes attack Chinese border; down first Chinese plane.)	May 1966: Rumanian official visits Hanoi via Peking (11 May) after Harriman meets Rumanian premier 4 May. Official reports to Harriman in Bucharest 27 May.	
(9 July, 4 August, 1966: USSR Notes charging Soviet vessels in Haiphong "imperilled.")	June 1966: first phase of "Marigold" in Saigon. 21 June: Canadian diplomat Ronning tells US of his findings in Hanoi (Hanoi-Haiphong raids authorized 23 June).	9 July: Note accused of "inaccuracies and false allegations." US embassy refuses to accept 4 August Note.
29 August 1966: 1 Chinese vessel sunk, another damaged. Bombed and strafed "for as long as 3 hours." 9 killed, 7 wounded. (5 September: US planes bomb China.)	US and Chinese ambassadors to resume Warsaw talks 7 September "amid reports of a new American effort to discuss the Vietnam situation with Peking."	29 August: Navy A-4s sank 2 North Vietnamese patrol boats. 5 September: awaiting "more complete information" from Saigon. 6 September: "no basis in fact to support the Chinese Communist charge."
30 November–1 December 1966: 6 Chinese fishing vessels sunk in Tonkin Gulf. 27 killed, 17 wounded. (2 December: Hanoi bombed.)	Late 1966: Rumanian Premier Maurer on secret mission to Peking. 6 December 1966: DRV and US representatives supposed to meet in Warsaw.	5 December: investigating charges. 13 December: State Dept. denies attacks both on ships ("we have found no evidence") and on downtown Hanoi (later confirmed by H. Salisbury).
20 February 1967: Chinese fishing-boats strafed.	28 January 1967: North Vietnamese statement on talks.	
25 April 1967: UK ship *Dartford* in Haiphong rocketed.	April 1967: Canadian and American proposals for DMZ pullback (State Dept. officials tried but failed to cancel Haiphong raid).	27 April: investigating charges. 5 May: "no deliberate US attack." 12 May: ship's officers call strafing "an accident."

ALLEGED INCIDENT	POLITICAL CONTEXT	US RESPONSE
2 June 1967: USSR M/V *Turkestan* in Campha bombed and strafed by two F-105s "from different directions." 1 killed, 6 wounded.	Late May–early June 1967: direct White House-Kremlin "hot line" exchanges over possibility of common approach to Middle East and Vietnam. 23 May: Hanoi and Haiphong again placed off-limits.	2 June: asks CINCPAC to supply flight plans of planes in area. DOD, 3 June: "no US aircraft bombed or strafed the ship." 18 June: 20-mm gunfire "may have struck the *Turkestan.*" 20 June Note: US will do its utmost to prevent such incidents.
29 June 1967: *Mikhail Frunze* (USSR), *Hongqi 157* (China), *Kingford* (UK), *Bertain* (Italy) pellet-bombed by CBUs in Haiphong harbor.	23, 25 June: Johnson sees Kosygin at Glassboro. 26 June: Johnson sees Rumanian Premier Maurer at White House; Maurer then leaves on secret Vietnam mission to China with message from Johnson.	30 June: commanders asked to examine flight plans and post-flight photography. 15 July Note: "possibility cannot be excluded" that ordnance fell on *Frunze.*
(11 September 1967: US officials report 1 Polish and 1 Italian vessel sprayed by North Vietnamese shrapnel in Haiphong; DRV recalls attack on *Turkestan* in protesting raid.)	6–12 September: de Gaulle in Warsaw. 12 September: joint communiqué condemns war and calls for "cessation of foreign intervention."	
25 November 1967: Chinese ship *Hongqi 154* in Hongai dive-bombed, damaged; 8 wounded.	November 1967: Rumanian officials return from Hanoi, see Harriman in Bucharest 27 November.	2 December: State Dept. declines comment.
3 January 1968: Chinese ship *Hongqi 158* in Hongai bombed by 4 US planes. 5 bombs damage ship; wound 4. 5 January 1968: USSR ship *Pereslavl-Zalesskiy* in Haiphong trapped in circle of delayed-action bombs from 2 to 100 meters off. 20, 27 January 1968: Chinese ships *Hongqi 152* and *153* attacked in Hongai and Campha harbors.	1 January 1968: Hanoi publishes Foreign Minister Trinh's statement 29 December that talks "will" (rather than "could") follow cessation of bombing North Vietnam. In January Rumanian official returns to Hanoi with US message. 16 January: Mai Van Bo, DRV representative in Paris, specifies talks would begin after "a suitable time."	No known response. 5 January: investigating charges. 5 January Note: "any damage . . . was inadvertent and is regretted." Haiphong again placed off-limits to avoid "difficult incidents." (Rusk) 1 February: investigating Chinese charges.

e) All of the attacks without exception can be related to concomitant developments in the diplomatic search for a negotiated settlement.

f) This relationship is sophisticated and selective: the attacks are related to diplomatic developments not only in time but also by being directed against ships of a particular nation.

g) On many occasions this relationship would only have been apparent at the time to a highly sophisticated observer, or one with access to highly classified information.

These last two features are particularly important in attempting to understand the political significance of the *Turkestan* attack. The first recorded attack against a foreign Communist vessel visiting North Vietnam was on 19 April 1966, when US bombs and rockets allegedly fell around the Polish M/V *Beniowski* in a harbor near Haiphong. Sometime in the same month of April the ambitious young Polish diplomat, Janusz Lewandowski, arrived in Hanoi to initiate the important and highly secret Polish peace initiative (known as "Marigold" in the US State Department's secret files) which ultimately was to be nullified by a series of crucially timed bombings against Hanoi.[6] US-Polish cooperation and trust, essential to the success of "Marigold," clearly were not helped by the attack. Yet the Poles waited one week before protesting formally in a Note to US Ambassador Gronouski, and yet another day before they made this protest public (*New York Times*, 29 April 1966, p. 3; FBIS *Daily Report*, 28 April 1966, FF1; 29 April, FF1). (This unexplained delay suggests that State Department files will someday reveal more about the secret diplomatic context of the incident.) It is interesting that on 1 April 1966 CINCPAC had been authorized to plan and prepare for targets in the Haiphong area, but that these targets remained on the restricted list, despite increasing political pressure in Washington, until mid-June (CINCPAC, *Report on the War in Vietnam as of June 30, 1968*, pp. 24–25). The day after the *Beniowski* attack, before any news of it had been released, US officials were to make it clear that Hanoi and Haiphong were still out of bounds (*New York Times*, 21 April 1966, p. 2).

After the *Beniowski* incident, there was no reported attack on foreign merchant vessels until 29 August 1966. On that day, according to a delayed Peking announcement one week later, two Chinese ships were bombed and strafed continually "for as long as three

6 For the "Marigold" story see, *inter alia, Ramparts,* March 1968, pp. 56–58; Kraslow and Loory, *The Secret Search for Peace in Vietnam,* pp. 3–88; Chester Cooper, *The Lost Crusade* (New York: Dodd, Mead, 1970), pp. 320–68; *Pentagon Papers,* pp. 523–24.

hours": both ships were damaged and one of them sank (*New York Times,* 6 September 1966, p. 1). The diplomatic consequence of this attack was shortly to prove both clear and indisputable. On 7 September US Ambassador Gronouski and Chinese Ambassador Wang Kuo-chuan were scheduled to hold their first meeting in six months, "amid reports of a new American effort to discuss the Vietnam situation with Peking" (*New York Times,* 7 September 1966, p. 1). This was a particularly important meeting, inasmuch as over the preceding summer the first dramatic events of the Chinese Cultural Revolution had amazed and baffled western observers, causing increasing speculation that a more militant and anti-Soviet stance in Peking might be linked with a greater desire to avoid a direct confrontation over Vietnam with the United States (Franz Schurmann, "What Is Happening in China?" *New York Review of Books,* 20 October, 1966, pp. 18–25). Hopes for the 7 September meeting had been particularly raised by surprising reports that Chinese Foreign Minister Chen Yi had told visiting Japanese MPs that China was "not necessarily dismissing" the possibility of Vietnam talks with the United States (*New York Times,* 8 September 1966, p. 1). Apparently Chen Yi, also, drew attention to the importance of the Warsaw ambassadorial talks.[7]

In this hopeful context, Washington officials were demonstrably disappointed by Ambassador Wang's intransigence at the 7 September meeting, where instead of negotiating he took the unprecedented step of releasing publicly a long résumé of US provocations against China and Vietnam (the 130 previous Warsaw meetings had been conducted with the highest degree of confidentiality). Two incidents in particular were singled out as evidence of American bad faith: the 29 August attack against Chinese cargo vessels and an attack the preceding 28 May against Chinese fishing vessels in the international waters of the Tonkin Gulf, when twenty-one fishermen were allegedly killed (*New York Times,* 8 September 1966, p. 3).

This earlier incident, too, had had diplomatic implications, if for the moment we give credit to the Chinese story. In early May Harriman (the US "roving" ambassador whose task was to pursue peace-

---

7 Though the reports of Chen Yi's actual words differ, by all accounts he was surprisingly open to the usefulness of talks: "China supports the idea of Sino-US talks on the settlement of the Vietnam dispute. The idea of peaceful settlement is Chinese foreign policy" (Tokyo Radio, 6 September 1966); "Communist China does not completely rule out the possibility of negotiating with Washington for a peaceful solution of the Vietnam war" (Tokyo Radio, 6 September 1966); "It is wrong to think that China has no intention of having talks with the United States, and the two countries will continue negotiations at Warsaw at the ambassadorial level. A settlement of questions through talks is China's basic policy." (*Mainichi Shimbun,* Tokyo, 7 September 1966; FBIS *Daily Report,* 7 September 1966, BBB5–6).

feelers) was rumored to have seen Rumanian Premier Maurer in Geneva, possibly in hope of arranging an exchange of prisoners-of-war in Vietnam.[8] At the same time an important Rumanian delegation, led by First Deputy Premier Emil Bodnaras, left (via Geneva) for Hanoi and Peking. From 5 to 9 May, while Bodnaras was in Hanoi, US planes attacked new targets in the Hanoi area, closer to the capital than ever before. On 12 May, one day after Bodnaras had arrived in Peking to see Chou En-lai, US planes were reported to have shot down their first Chinese MIG during a rocket attack against the Chinese border. On 27 May Bodnaras reported for three hours on his trip to the US ambassador in Bucharest, and asked him further questions about the United States's attitude toward conditions for a political settlement (*New York Times*, 25 June 1966, p. 6). Peking could hardly fail to interpret the attack against fishing vessels the next day as a brutal but eloquent answer.

As our chart will show, President Johnson continued to work with the Rumanians as possible emissaries to the pro-Peking faction in Hanoi, just as the Poles, much closer allies of the USSR, carried messages to the pro-Soviet faction. In late 1966 Premier Maurer himself went on a secret mission to Hanoi and Peking, at about the time of the notorious December 1966 raids against Hanoi which ended the Polish peace initiative "Marigold." Again the Chinese reported a lethal attack against their fishing-boats (the first since 28 May); and in the unprecedented raids of 13–14 December against downtown Hanoi, an American rocket damaged three adjacent embassies—the Chinese, the Polish, and the Rumanian (*New York Times*, 6 December 1966, p. 7; 15 December, p. 3; 18 December, p. 3; Kraslow and Loory, p. 69; Harrison E. Salisbury, *Behind the Lines—Hanoi*, New York: Harper & Row, 1967, p. 69).

Despite these discomforting honors from US pilots, the Rumanians continued to show interest in playing the role of intermediaries. The stakes for this newly independent country—economic as well as political—were high. Since the death of old-line Stalinist Georghiu-Dej in 1965, Rumania had sought an international role not unlike that of France under de Gaulle, of profiting from trade and political relations with all three major powers so as to maximize its own au-

8 It is known that Harriman and Maurer were in Geneva together, as well as the Bodnaras delegation of Rumanian officials on the way to Hanoi (*New York Times*, 4 May 1966, p. 3). Although it is not certain that Harriman met Maurer personally, both men conferred with the president of the International Committee of the Red Cross. In December, at about the time of Maurer's visit to Hanoi and Peking, the US was full of rumors about the possibility of a prisoner-of-war exchange through the ICRC. Harriman was said to have discussed this matter with the ICRC again in Algiers (*New York Times*, 12 December 1966, p. 1).

tonomy. On 26 June 1967, one day after he had seen Kosygin at Glassboro, President Johnson received Premier Maurer at the White House—the first time that any Communist head of government had received or accepted such an invitation from him. Rumanian officials later confirmed that Johnson offered US backing for Rumania's candidate for presidency of the next regular UN General Assembly (*Guardian* [Manchester], 18 July 1967). On 2 July, Maurer left with a delegation of twenty officials for a fortnight's secret mission to Peking, where he reportedly conveyed "an offer from President Johnson to China to live and let live" (*Guardian* [Manchester], 18 July 1967; see also Belgrade Radio, 3 July, in FBIS *Daily Report,* 5 July 1967, JJ1; *New York Times,* 7 July 1967, p. 6; 11 July, p. 1). Peking, in considering such an offer, would have had to appraise its sincerity against the 29 June bombing of its ship the *Hongqi 157.*

The undauntable Mr. Maurer made yet another secret journey to Hanoi in November 1967, amid reports that raids against new bombing targets had endangered commercial airliners at Hanoi's Gialam International Airport (*New York Times,* 7 November 1967, p. 1; 8 November, p. 9). On one of these raids at least four US missiles exploded over downtown Hanoi, killing an Indian member of the International Control Commission (*New York Times,* 18 November 1967, p. 9; 19 November, p. 3). Whether or not US officials knew at first of this mission is unclear, but on 20 November *Times* correspondent Peter Grose reported from Washington that Ambassador Harriman would visit Bucharest on 27 November to hear from Rumanian officials who "have made frequent visits to Hanoi in the last two years" (*New York Times,* 21 November 1967, p. 11). Harriman did meet Premier Maurer as planned; but meanwhile, on 25 November, the *Hongqi 154* had reportedly been bombed. Diplomatic files may someday reveal whether or not this bombing inhibited the fruitfulness of the Maurer-Harriman meeting.

In January 1968 it at least seemed more likely than ever before that the long diplomatic search for peace talks, to follow a US cessation of the bombing of North Vietnam, was about to produce results. On New Year's Day the North Vietnamese published a new diplomatic position, formulated by Foreign Minister Trinh on 29 December 1967, which stated that a cessation of bombing "will" (rather than "could") be followed by "conversations with the United States on relevant problems." As was noted at the time:

> This would seem to be exactly the "authoritative message from Hanoi" for which Ambassador Goldberg appealed in the UN last

September 21: "No such third party—including those governments which are among Hanoi's closest friends—has conveyed to us any authoritative message from Hanoi that there would in fact be negotiations if the bombing were stopped. We have sought such a message directly from Hanoi without success" (*New York Times*, 22 September 1967, p. 16). It would also seem designed to meet the president's promise (in his San Antonio speech of 29 September and interview of 19 December) that "We will stop bombing immediately provided you will have prompt and productive discussions" (*New York Times*, 20 December 1967, p. 16). Thus the president no longer linked a stop in the bombing to a prior assurance that North Vietnamese infiltration into South Vietnam had already ceased (*Ramparts*, March 1968, p. 56).

Kraslow and Loory report that, in response to the new Trinh statement, the US State Department empowered "a high-ranking Rumanian official" to return to Hanoi with a secret inquiry, possibly linked to further US concessions about what would be acceptable levels of infiltration (Kraslow and Loory, p. 229). This visit seems to have had the usual potent effect on foreign shipping: four separate instances of unauthorized attacks by US planes (a record) are reported for the month of January. Three of these were against Chinese vessels of the *Hongqi* class. The fourth attack was against a Soviet vessel in Haiphong harbor, and the Soviet account of the attack suggests a studied evasion of strict commands from Washington against a repeat of the *Turkestan* incident. According to Hanoi Radio, at 3:40 on the afternoon of 4 January, fifteen planes flew in from the northeast, of which four "concentrated their attacks on the Soviet ship *Pereslavl-Zalesskiy*. They came from three directions, forming a triangle, the center of which was the ship. Each of them dropped about ten delayed-action demolition bombs from two to 100 meters *around* the ship" (FBIS *Daily Report,* 9 January 1968, JJJ2). (As in the case of the Chinese ship attacked the previous day in Honggai the weather was good, visibility was reported perfect, and the attack had been preceded by overflights of US reconnaissance aircraft.) The *Pereslavl-Zalesskiy* was thus "seriously damaged" without any one pilot having *directly* attacked it, just as, in the preceding June, the *Frunze* had been damaged by pellet-bombs from Cluster-Bomb Units (CBUs) exploding in the immediate vicinity. Immediately after this incident, Hanoi and Haiphong were again placed off-limits to US pilots for at least three weeks, to avoid what Secretary Rusk later called "particularly difficult incidents" (On "Meet the Press," 4

February 1968; Dept. of State *Bulletin,* 26 February 1968, p. 268). This order protected Russian ships, but not the smaller Chinese vessels, for it did not extend to the nearby small ports of Honggai and Campha, where in late January two more Chinese vessels were reportedly attacked.

Conclusions

Though the "accidental coincidence" hypothesis might explain one or another of the incidents that we have reviewed, it can hardly erase the recurring pattern that emerges from all of them. Like the patterns of the air war itself, particularly against the cities of Haiphong and Hanoi, the timing of these attacks suggest that in general they were politically inspired; and deliberately timed to diminish the chances of peace talks that could mean an end to the bombing of North Vietnam. In other words, they fit into the general pattern explored in *The Politics of Escalation:* even as late as January 1968 the response to a political concession by the other side seems to have been an unprecedented wave of American aggressive acts. And by 1968, it should be remembered, there were virtually no options for escalation left that did not directly threaten a war between great powers.

It is particularly important to recall the bombings of the Hanoi-Haiphong areas in April, June, and December 1966, the undeniable effect of which was to frustrate the Polish peace initiative "Marigold" in that year. From one point of view it is not surprising that the timing of these raids should have been politically inspired. After all, as White House and Pentagon spokesmen never tire of pointing out, the reasons for *not* bombing Hanoi and Haiphong were also political: there were no military reasons for preserving those two enclaves in the general rain of destruction over North Vietnam. Thus it is not extraordinary that the Johnson administration, in allowing a peace-feeler to go forward, should at the same time escalate the bombing to make sure the other side would not negotiate from strength. As James Reston observed at the time: "everything in the Johnson strategy seems to be done in twos—something for the hawks and something for the doves" (*New York Times,* 9 February 1966, p. 38; see also Arthur Krock, *New York Times,* 19 April 1966, p. 40). In particular the notorious Hanoi raids of December 1966 which ended "Marigold" (and which the Pentagon Papers study claimed "were launched inadvertently") were authorized by the President in Texas on 12 November 1966.[9] This was just one day after he had heard Harriman report to the LBJ Ranch on "Marigold" after a whirlwind tour of world capitals with Chester Cooper.[10] Johnson thus ensured that, if the North Vietnamese did negotiate, it would be in a context of humiliating US air strength.

The chronology of the ship attacks in 1966 fits neatly into the larger story of this double dove-hawk strategy. Though the attacks might be illegal under international law, there is no evidence to suggest that their perpetrators were directly violating the wishes and instructions of their American superiors. (The incidents involving Polish and Soviet shipping caused no damage or casualties, while the more serious attacks on Chinese ships were hardly inconsistent with other US-Chinese hostilities in the same period.) In 1966, then, there is no evidence of an "illegal conspiracy."

After May 1967, however, the relationship of the ship attacks to overall US peace policy, while still strikingly apparent, becomes more complicated and sinister. Slowly in 1967 Johnson came to see that the war would not be over and won in time for the 1968 elections; he directed more and more of his energies to seeing that there would at least be some form of negotiations (*Pentagon Papers,* pp. 529, 539–41, 567–68). His growing disenchantment provoked the visits of Sharp and Westmoreland to Washington in 1967, the latter imbued with all the political overtones of MacArthur's return sixteen years before. After June 1967 there are increasing rumors of a public political challenge to Johnson's policies by his generals, possibly by the Joint Chiefs of Staff. These rumors were not to disappear until March 1968, when Johnson stepped out of the political arena by announcing he would not run for reelection.

In this period we see that the relation of ship attacks to raids on the Hanoi-Haiphong area changes. Whereas in 1966 and early 1967 such attacks occur when raids on Hanoi and Haiphong have just been secretly *authorized,* by 1968 they are occurring when such raids have just been secretly *prohibited.* One such prohibition was issued on 23 May 1967: it was followed by the attacks on the *Turkestan* and on four other vessels. Another was issued in January 1968; yet this

---

9 *Pentagon Papers,* p. 524; cf. Kraslow and Loory, p. 5 ("The President and his top civilian lieutenants had forgotten"). The date of 12 November, revealed by Admiral Sharp (*Report on the War in Vietnam,* Washington, GPO, 1968, p. 25), proves that the President made this important decision in virtual isolation. The "Tuesday lunch" meeting of 15 November in Washington, to which Kraslow and Loory attribute the decision (p. 32), must (like other such meetings) have merely recorded a decision already made.

10 *New York Times,* 12 November 1966, p. 8; Kraslow and Loory, p. 32; Chester Cooper, *The Lost Crusade,* pp. 320–21.

month, near the climax of the long search for peace talks, saw more separate attacks on foreign ships (four in all) than any other. It is in this context that the charge can be laid of an illegal conspiracy, acting secretly in collusion to subvert high-level secret policies of the administration. It would appear that those whom Johnson had used in his diplomatic bombing maneuvers were now playing the game against their Commander-in-Chief.

About at least one such incident, the bombing of the *Turkestan,* enough is now known to warrant the charge. It is now certain that the strafing by two planes did occur despite orders to avoid such engagements, that a third officer acting in collusion suppressed and destroyed relevant evidence, that all three were in the end cavalierly exonerated by a USAF court-martial and review board. It is almost as certain that a consciously misleading denial was prepared at CINCPAC headquarters and issued over the signature of Admiral Sharp. The cautious evasions of this document suggest that it was intended to deceive, not the Russians who were fully aware of the incident, or the outside public who were wholly ignorant of it, but other members of the US administration.

The political context, on the eve of a new war threatening direct US-Soviet confrontation, makes it almost inconceivable that Johnson could have wished such an incident. The reports of an imminent cessation of bombing, which were published just at the time the *Turkestan* was attacked, accurately reflected the President's urgent concern to reach at least a minimal understanding with the USSR. All of these considerations make it difficult to accept any of the possible non-conspiratorial explanations of the incident: a) that it was just a little accident, b) that it was the overexuberant act of two carefree hotshot pilots, and c) that it was duly ordered from above in accordance with official responsibilities.

The fourth possibility, that there was an illegal conspiracy (presumably to avoid an agreement that would limit the air war), is not easy to believe either. This charge must now be laid; and the onus of proof now lies with those who would deny it. Some duly constituted authority of the United States, possibly a subcommittee of the Senate Foreign Relations Committee, should arrange for a review of the facts outside the military bureaucracy. It might begin with testimony from the officers involved in the court-martial, from the author of the spurious denial, and from Admiral Sharp who signed it. It would, I hope, extend to those involved in similar incidents as well.

The real ceiling on the American commitment, the [Pentagon] analysts suggest several times, was imposed primarily by President Johnson's refusal to be pushed by the military leaders into asking Congress to mobilize reserve forces—both former servicemen on inactive status and organized units of these servicemen. Mobilization, the analysts assert, became the "political sound barrier" that President Johnson would not break.

The Pentagon Papers

Chapter Five
Pueblo: 1968

The *Pueblo* incident, like the Tonkin Gulf episode it so resembles, is one most Americans
would just as soon forget. Even those who would
justify US policies in Asia are silent about the
Pueblo; while many who would condemn the
same policies find the *Pueblo* incident too technical and complex for their moral fervor. But
the issues posed by the incident are ominous and
enduring, with respect both to Korea and to the
entire conduct of US foreign policy.

More and more, among informed students
of Asian affairs, one hears speculations that the
military stand-off in Korea will not remain stable
much longer. The military restraints imposed by
the 1954 agreements have grown increasingly
anachronistic with the failure to reach a political

settlement; and the *Pueblo* incident has led to their being flagrantly violated on both sides. Those who read only the American press may find it difficult to appreciate the gravity of this consequence, since what we have been told has not led us to consider seriously the alternative possibility of Korean reunification through political processes. But if it is true that the present stand-off cannot remain stable, the prospect of detente and eventual political reunification may have to be revived if the *Pueblo* incident is not, like the Tonkin Gulf incidents, to be followed by a new American war. It is almost certain that this prospect cannot be contemplated until some of the false evidence, "proving" the North Koreans guilty of deliberate piracy, has been exposed for what it is.

The *Pueblo* crisis needs to be understood, and dealt with, even in the unlikely event that the Korean crisis subsides. There are too many indications that the many alleged "errors" and "coincidences" on the American side, without which the incident would not have occurred, were in fact not errors and coincidences but part of an enduring pattern of artificially induced provocations and/or "crises," the recurrence of which has contributed to the increasing militarization of US foreign policy (and the breakdown of congressional restraints) since the all-too-comparable U-2 incident of 1960. The U-2 and RB-47 shot down by the USSR in 1960, the *Maddox* incident in the Tonkin Gulf in 1964, all had much in common with the *Pueblo* in 1968. To begin with, all were on highly sensitive intelligence missions, so dangerous that they had to be approved by the secret Special Group (later known as the Senior Interdepartmental Group, or 303 Committee) on the deputy secretary level.[1]

The original explanation for the timing of the U-2 disaster was the weather, as explained by former Special Group member Robert Murphy:

> American newspapers and speech-makers demanded why had our government ordered a surveillance flight at such an inappropriate time, when the Russian, British, French and American heads of state were about to negotiate? . . . I inquired of my former colleagues in Washington and was told that weather was one important consideration. There were urgent reasons why the flight should be made, and it was calculated that weather conditions were likely to be unfavorable *for some weeks* because fog and heavy clouds make high altitude flights unsuitable for photography. Careful consideration was given

---

1 Harry Howe Ransom, *The Intelligence Establishment* (Cambridge, Mass.: Harvard University Press, 1970), p. 249; Trevor Armbrister, *A Matter of Accountability: The True Story of the Pueblo Affair* (New York: Coward-McCann, 1970), p. 192.

to the scheduled Summit Conference, but nothing was expected from that event anyway—that is, there would have been no benefit from the talks even if they had taken place.[2]

Apart from the candid admission in the last sentence, Murphy's hypothesis of "fog and heavy clouds" conflicts with Gary Powers' new revelations, that the two U-2 flights scheduled over Russia in April 1960 were the first of any such flights in at least six months (possibly much longer), and that his own flight was "the first time we had attempted to fly all the way across the Soviet Union."[3] Powers himself comes up with the canny suggestion that his U-2 overflight was no coincidence but a conscious US condition for proceeding with the Summit Conference:

> I knew there had been no overflights for months and then suddenly two in close succession. . . . Could Eisenhower have *wanted* Khrushchev to know of the flights? We knew that the Russians had radar-tracked most if not all of the overflights, so the chances were that these last two U-2 flights would not have gone undetected. Might Eisenhower or his advisers have felt it to be to our advantage, psychologically, to have Khrushchev to know, to have this very much on his mind. . . . Eisenhower smug in the knowledge that we could overfly Russia at will, and Khrushchev not able to do a thing about it; Khrushchev inwardly raging but unable to protest, because to do so would be to admit that his country did not have missiles capable of reaching the planes (p. 229).[4]

In like manner the *Pueblo* was not on a routine patrol (as we were first told) but on a mission of unprecedented risk in Korean waters, at a time when secret diplomacy was beginning to show public re-

2 Robert Murphy, *Diplomat Among Warriors: Secret Decisions That Changed the World* (New York: Pyramid, 1965), p. 491, emphasis added.

3 Francis Gary Powers, *Operation Overflight* (New York: Holt, Rinehart and Winston, 1970), p. 71: "Most of 1958, all of 1959, and thus far in 1960, there had been a drastic reduction in the number of overflights. Months would pass without one. . . . Then, suddenly, after a long pause, two flights were scheduled for the same month, April 1960" (pp. 69–70); "During the six months following the October 31, 1959 embassy meeting, there were only two overflights of the USSR. . . . April 9, 1960 [and] May 1, 1960" (p. 358); "from early 1958 until April, 1960, we made almost none" (p. 374).

4 Further than this Powers does not speculate. He does, however, inform us that at the last minute his own plane was replaced by another known to be "a 'dog,' never having flown exactly right. Something was always going wrong" (p. 76). He thus innocently corroborates the unprovable rumor told Paul Jacobs nearly four years ago (by "an aircraft engineer who had been in a position to know a great deal about the U-2 program") that " 'The U-2 Powers was flying was a dud. It was supposed to go down.' " (Paul Jacobs, "Did the Real Gary Powers Really Fall Down?" *Ramparts*, June 1967, p. 6.) This is only one of the many intriguing analogies between the U-2 incident and that of the *Pueblo*, which was also assuredly a "dog" (particularly with respect to its vital direction-finding equipment) and concerning which the rumor circulates today that it too was meant to be captured.

sults: the North Vietnamese statement of 29 December 1967, which envisaged the opening of public negotiations to end the Vietnam war.

To understand why the United States sent the USS *Pueblo* on its unprotected and ill-fated spy mission off North Korea in January 1968, it is necessary to go back to mid-October 1966. Both sides agree that the current radical aggravation of the Korean crisis began about that time, though each accuses the other of having begun it. Later Evans and Novak speculated that one reason for the increased activity on the North Korean side was the Vietnam war: "to stop South Korea from sending another division of highly-trained . . . ROK troops to Vietnam" (where they were sorely needed because of the rigid US troop ceiling of 525,000 men).[5]

In any case, between October 1966 and February 1967 seven Americans patroling the DMZ had been killed, against a total of three for the preceding fourteen years.[6] On 14 March 1967, a joint US-Korean statement in Washington envisaged (in apparent violation of the Korean armistice agreements) US aid for "modernization of Korean armed forces"; a North Korean newspaper charges that this new commitment was first made by President Johnson in Seoul on 31 October 1966.[7] By the end of 1967 there were 445 incidents of various types affecting the DMZ, compared to a total of 37 in all of 1966.[8] In November 1967 the US Command in South Korea submitted its first report to the United Nations since 1953, and Ambassador Goldberg complained to the UN Security Council about "recent sharp increases in the scope and intensity of the North Korean military attacks."[9]

The east coast of North Korea in particular was affected by the increase in tension. On 19 January 1967 a North Korean shore battery shelled and sank a South Korean Navy patrol boat, the first such sinking since 1953. The ship admittedly had crossed north of the DMZ line, with a fleet of South Korean "fishing vessels," well inside the twelve-mile limit claimed by North Korea, but just outside the three-mile limit recognized by South Korea and the United States.[10]

---

5 *Washington Post,* 26 January 1968, A21.

6 *New York Times,* 3 November 1966, p. 15; 26 February 1967, p. 11.

7 Department of State, *Bulletin,* 3 April 1967, pp. 552–53; *People's Korea* (Tokyo), 8 May 1968, p. 6.

8 US Congress, House, Committee on Armed Services, *Inquiry into the U.S.S. Pueblo and EC-121 Plane Incidents, Hearings,* 91st Cong., 1st Sess. (Washington: GPO, 1969), p. 684 (hereinafter cited as *Hearings*).

9 Department of State, *Bulletin,* 20 November, p. 692.

10 *New York Times,* 20 January 1967, p. 3.

The South Koreans announced "certain retaliatory measures"; thereafter the number of incidents involving "fishing vessels" off the North Korean east coast also dramatically increased. Fifty of these ROK fishing boats had been seized by North Korea by the end of 1967, though the boats and crews were usually released.[11]

One reaction of the United States was to seek more information about North Korean intentions, by using its tiny ELINT (electronics intelligence) ships, the *Banner* and the *Pueblo*. Unlike the destroyer *Maddox* used in the all-too-similar Tonkin Gulf mission of August 1964, these ELINT ships were unarmed until January 1968, when, in response to the Israeli attack on their larger sister-ship the *Liberty* in July 1967, two token .50-caliber machine guns were mounted on the *Pueblo*'s deck. The guns spoiled the ships' cover as peaceful vessels engaged in oceanography, so they were by orders kept under tarpaulins.

In January 1967, shortly after the sinking of the ROK Navy vessel, Admiral Sharp (CINCPAC) obtained approval for the first ELINT mission by *Banner* off North Korea in February. CINCPAC estimated the risk of this patrol to be "minimal"; but this was CINCPAC's estimate for *all* ELINT patrols: a higher risk category would increase the possibility of civilian interference in Washington.[12] The admiral in charge of *Banner* (Admiral Frank L. Johnson, Commander of Naval Forces, Japan) concurred; his staff treated the *Banner* mission as routine and did not request an Air Force alert. General McKee, Fifth Air Force Commander in Japan, sent out an order notwithstanding that both US and South Korean (ROK) planes in Korea should be placed on alert, just in case.

The order to alert ROK planes in Korea was countermanded by General Bonesteel, the US and UN commander in Korea. General Bonesteel could hardly do otherwise; only a few days before he had had to persuade the South Koreans not to use their planes, already launched, in retaliation for the sinking of the ROK patrol boat. *Banner*'s mission may have gathered useful information, but it also had the result of demonstrating to the North Koreans (if they were interested) that Admiral Sharp, at least, had no intention of being intimidated by Kim Il Sung. The unarmed *Banner* was sent to spend a day off Wonsan harbor, one area recognized as being especially sensitive. General Bonesteel pointed this out in protesting to the Navy: "Had the Navy forgotten how just a few months ago North Korean fighters had 'flushed' on U.S. reconnaissance planes near Wonsan?"[13] This inter-service flap over *Banner* in January 1967 was a factor in the planning for *Pueblo* one year later. It may well explain why, in 1968, the normal precaution of an airstrip alert was not requested.[14] And the lack of available aircraft was probably a major reason why the *Pueblo*'s mission resulted not only in an incident (as might have been foreseen) but in capture as well.

The background to the *Pueblo* patrol was different from *Banner*'s only in that it was far more perilous. A new speech by Kim Il Sung on 16 December 1967 called for preparations in North Korea for "the liberation of South Korea and the unification of the fatherland at the earliest possible date."[15] This speech, the third of its kind, was taken seriously by the United States: like the Department of State's Intelligence Bureau in Washington, so also Ambassador Porter and General Bonesteel in Korea considered that "the next eighteen to twenty-four months could be critical . . . characterized by Kim's willingness to commit rash acts and to run risks of war, even though unsupported by Russia."[16] The situation on the DMZ had deteriorated to the point of "artillery exchanges and at least one small tank battle."[17] General Bonesteel's Eighth Army Command in Korea had by January "already designated the hall where daily news briefings, similar to those in Saigon, will be held if war should break out again."[18]

Once again Admiral Sharp on the advice of Admiral Johnson (COMNAVFORJAPAN) and Admiral Hyland (CINCPAC-FLEET) recommended, on 23 December, an ELINT patrol off North Korea.[19] Though this would be the third such patrol, it would be the first for the recently commissioned and inexperienced *Pueblo*. More important, as was explained later by General Carter of the National Security Agency (which shared responsibility for these patrols with the Navy): "This was . . . the *first* voyage in which we were having a vessel linger for *a long period of time* [eighteen days, as opposed to four and a half for *Banner*] near North Korean waters. It

13 Armbrister, *A Matter of Accountability: The True Story of the Pueblo Affair*, p. 123. Before *Banner*'s "minimal risk" mission, an Air Force general told its skipper, "If there is a war, *Banner* will be the first to know, the first to go, and may be the cause of it" (p. 122).

14 *Ibid.*, pp. 196–97.

15 *People's Korea*, 20 December 1967, p. 2.

16 Townsend Hoopes, *The Limits of Intervention* (New York: David McKay, 1969), p. 135; cf. Andrew Tully, *The Super Spies* (New York: William Morrow, 1969), pp. 137–38.

17 *Washington Post*, 2 February 1969, B6.

18 *New York Times*, 24 January 1968, p. 14.

19 The first proposal for a January 1968 patrol off North Korea, the only one proposed in a six-month schedule, seems to have been in COMNAVFORJAPAN's cable of 28 November 1967 (*Report*, p. 1639).

was therefore *a special mission as we saw it.*"[20] Like everyone else up and down the line, Admiral Sharp, who studied the proposal for "fifteen to twenty minutes,"[21] estimated the risk once again to be "minimal."

The Special House Subcommittee investigating the *Pueblo* incident, headed by hawkish former Marine bomber pilot Otis Pike, concluded (pp. 1622–23) that "no level of authority . . . was sensitive to the abundant evidence" of a more dangerous Korean situation. Their assumption that the absurd risk categorization was an "error," rather than a deliberate reckless showing of the flag, is central to Armbrister's intelligent, well-documented, valuable, but often misleading book. But the committee's and Armbrister's distortions of the evidence available, which we shall examine one by one, are themselves grounds for contemplating the alternative, that Admirals Sharp and Moorer (the chief of naval operations) were happy to risk a showdown, just as they were four years earlier in the Tonkin Gulf incidents.

One has to remember that in late 1967 the relations between the generals and their civilian overseers were also deteriorating, even after McNamara's "resignation" was announced on 29 November. Admiral Sharp lobbied vigorously in Washington for an end to political restraints on the bombing of North Vietnam, and in particular for the closing of Haiphong, despite the risk of increasing Soviet intervention or otherwise widening the war.[22] (There were increasing press speculations in this period that North Koreans piloted the MIGs which occasionally opposed US raids into North Vietnam.) In late 1967 and early 1968 Sharp campaigned just as vigorously against the secret diplomatic efforts, then reaching fruition, to halt the bombing of North Vietnam and open negotiations: US casualties in South Vietnam, he warned, would probably increase.[23] More and more, the eccentric clusters of US bombing raids under Sharp, by what Chester Cooper calls a "tragedy of errors," appeared to be grouped in direct proportion to the intensity of diplomatic initiatives at that time.[24]

20 Testimony in Secret Executive Session, cited in *Report,* p. 1654, emphasis added; cf. *Hearings,* p. 715: "But, Admiral, you had never had a mission of this kind before the *Pueblo,* and you haven't had one since." Cf. also *Hearings,* p. 744.

21 *Hearings,* p. 798; *Report,* p. 1651.

22 *New York Times,* 10 August 1967, p. 1; 21 September 1967, pp. 1–2; 14 October 1967, p. 2.

23 Hoopes, p. 131.

24 Chester Cooper, *The Lost Crusade* (New York: Dodd Mead, 1970), e.g. pp. 337, 339, 379; David Kraslow and Stuart H. Loory, *The Secret Search for Peace in Vietnam* (New York: Random House, 1968), pp. 3–6, 43–74, 210, 224.

Most alarming were the eight reported bombing and strafing attacks on Soviet and Chinese vessels between June 1967 and 27 January 1968—virtually all of them occurring at times when Hanoi and/ or Haiphong had secretly, for political reasons, been placed briefly *off-limits* to US planes. On 6 January 1968, two weeks before the *Pueblo* was seized, the *New York Times* noted editorially (p. 28) the "cause for concern" about these events, which might seem to suggest a "politics of escalation."

These developments were no more extraordinary than the *Pueblo*'s unprotected mission into the sensitive waters off Wonsan. The South Korean "fishing boat" incidents in this area were increasing: twelve such boats were seized by North Korea in the first eleven days of January (compared to fifty for the whole of 1967).[25] In December North Korea began warning publicly that it would tolerate no more spy missions off its waters, directing its warnings principally to the United States: "As long as the US imperialistic aggressors conduct reconnaissance by sending spy boats, our naval ships will continue to take determined countermeasures."[26] The CIA included two of these warnings in its *FBIS Daily Report* of foreign broadcasts (cf. 8 January 1968, GGG1), a basic information document for intelligence agencies and State Department officials, and even for friendly governments and university depository libraries such as at Berkeley.

Its decision to report these warnings may indicate an informed concern *before* the *Pueblo* incident, an "intelligence battle" within the government echoed after the incident by a second *Times* editorial, "The Pueblo Warnings," on 28 January. But the House Subcommittee found that the warnings in these FBIS reports of 8 and 11 January were not known to the HQ of either CINCPACFLEET or COM-NAVFORJAPAN (the Subcommittee said nothing about the HQ of CINCPAC, that is, Admiral Sharp).[27] Nor were they communicated to Captain Bucher aboard the *Pueblo,* which left Sasebo, Japan, for its ill-fated mission on 11 January. We are asked to believe that no one responsible in the intelligence community read the FBIS reports.

Captain Bucher, finally, was never told of North Korea's formal protest about US "armed spy boats" at Panmunjom on 21 January,

25 *Hearings,* p. 683 (information supplied by DOD). This information claims that no ROK vessels were sunk in the episodes, but Hoopes (p. 134) reports that one was sunk by collision. Deliberate collision (which might sink the thin-shelled *Pueblo*) was feared up and down the line by the mission's planners, from Bucher to Sharp, and the risk was foreseen in the authorizing cables (*Hearings,* p. 767).

26 North Korean broadcast in English of 11 January 1968, quoted in a *New York Times* editorial, "The Pueblo Warnings," 28 January 1968, p. 28.

27 *Report,* p. 1620.

two days before the incident.[28] If the then Congressman Melvin Laird's sources can be believed, the North Korean representative also "warned us about the surveillance-type ships in the area" at meetings on 19 and 20 January.[29] It is certain that on 24 January he protested that more than a hundred South Korean boats had intruded north on each of the three preceding days, to points only some sixty miles from the course of the *Pueblo*.[30]

These were not the only, perhaps not even the most serious, North Korean warnings, which had apparently begun in December. Both the Subcommittee and Armbrister attach much importance to a so-called "warning message" of 29 December from NSA civilians to the Joint Chiefs in Washington, whose "action" recommendation of increased ship protective measures was unaccountably changed, on its receipt by Air Force General Steakley, into a message for "information" only.[31] Though one would not guess it from the sanitized text released by the Pike subcommittee and Armbrister, the NSA message was based partly on "warnings . . . from the North Koreans," warnings apparently received not from open broadcasts but from "sensitive . . . special intelligence."[32] These may or may not have been the "intercepted North Korean messages," warning of " 'diversionary tactics' against American forces in the neighborhood," which McNamara is said to have reported to the first White House *Pueblo* meeting on 23 January.[33] But there were undoubtedly warnings. No less an authority than President Nixon stated that (in contrast to the case of the ELINT EC-121 plane shot down in 1969) "the North Koreans warned and threatened the *Pueblo* for a period of several weeks before they seized it."[34]

28 *New York Times,* 28 January 1968, p. 28; Hoopes, p. 134. Not till much later did he hear of the unprecedented attempt the same day by a North Korean guerrilla team to assassinate South Korean President Chung Hee Park.

29 US Congress, House, Committee on Appropriations, *Department of Defense Appropriations for 1969, Hearings,* 90th Cong., 2nd Sess., p. 36 (cited hereafter as *Appropriations Hearings*).

30 *New York Times,* 26 January 1968, p. 7.

31 Armbrister, p. 194; *Report,* p. 1655. The Pike subcommittee (p. 1656) found the subsequent disappearance of this message to suggest "at best . . . an unfortunate coincidence of omission; at worst . . . the highest order of incompetence." There is of course a third possibility: that the burial was deliberate.

32 *Report,* p. 1654; Armbrister, pp. 193–94 (censored text); *Hearings,* p. 819; cf. Rear Admiral Daniel V. Gallery, Ret., *The Pueblo Incident* (Garden City, N.Y.: Doubleday, 1970), p. 12; *Hearings,* p. 715.

33 Andrew Tully, *The Super Spies,* p. 126.

34 *New York Times,* 19 April 1969, p. 14; Department of State, *Bulletin* (5 May 1969), p. 381. One member of the Pike committee called Nixon's statement "unfortunate," "a slip of the tongue" (*Hearings,* p. 906). It is true that, as General Wheeler commented (p. 894), this was *Pueblo*'s first mission; but the warnings may well have been directed to monitoring operations in this area though not to the specific ship.

What the *Pueblo* actually did off the shore of North Korea from 15 to 23 January in the wake of these warnings is still unknown and still being actively misrepresented. That is the chief conclusion one draws from the four books on the *Pueblo* published just before the 1970 elections, all of which agree in many minute details with each other, and all of which are in certain essential points incompatible with the few scraps of hard intelligence buried in the Pike material and elsewhere.[35] I do not mean to dismiss the authors as simple liars, nor to suggest that their books have no value. On the contrary, the books, Armbrister's and Schumacher's in particular, give a much clearer picture of the whole incident than was hitherto available, and a much more ominous one to boot.

To begin with, it will henceforth be difficult to credit seriously the Pike committee's solemn assurances that "at no time during its mission did the USS *Pueblo* ever penetrate North Korean territorial waters" (*Report,* p. 1661)—if by these waters we understand the twelve-mile limit claimed *de jure* by North Korea, and recognized *de facto* in the *Pueblo*'s declassified "sailing order" of 5 January.[36] We learn from Armbrister in particular that the ship's loran position-finders were suspected of inaccuracy (p. 21), and yielded positions off from those established by dead reckoning by as much as five or even seven nautical miles (pp. 35, 45). When working only fourteen miles from the coast this gave rise to uncertainty and concern (pp. 34–35) since the ship was forbidden to verify its position by radar (and thus break electronic silence) until after it knew it had been detected by the North Koreans. (This known detection did not occur until 21 January, after all but two of the seventeen alleged "intrusions" which were afterwards claimed by North Korea.) Armbrister indicates that erroneous loran fixes were entered (as required by Navy regulations) in Ed Murphy's quartermaster's log (p. 35), including at least one "inside the 13-mile line" (p. 45).

This is Armbrister's rationalization for the North Korean claims of six (later seventeen) territorial intrusions by the *Pueblo*: "The 'evidence' . . . was preposterous—the erroneous loran fixes which Mack and the other inexperienced navigators had written in the ship's

---

35 Commander Lloyd M. Bucher (with Mark Rascovich), *Bucher: My Story* (New York: Doubleday, 1970); F. Carl Schumacher, Jr., and George C. Wilson, *Bridge of No Return: The Ordeal of the USS Pueblo* (New York: Harcourt, Brace, Jovanovich, 1970); Armbrister; Gallery. The Bucher, Armbrister, and Schumacher books often have recourse to identical wording, because all three follow closely the unpublished testimony at the Navy's Court of Inquiry.

36 Text of Sailing Order in *Hearings,* pp. 768–69; Gallery, p. 153; Bucher, p. 421: "The closest point of approach . . . will be thirteen nautical miles."

position log. . . . Couldn't the North Koreans understand that the
lines his [Murphy's] men had drawn through these fixes meant that
they were mistakes?" (p. 260) But this rationalization of the "preposterous" evidence in the position log—photographs of which were
released by the North Koreans and shown over NBC television in
April 1968—confirms that this evidence was not forged by the North
Koreans; it thus effectively negates Murphy's own earlier story that
he was "coerced into marking in [the] points of intrusion."[37] And the
photographs of recorded fixes inside the twelve-mile limit included
fixes reached both by loran *and* dead reckoning, in contexts which
suggest no discrepancy between them. Despite what we are led to
expect by Armbrister, there are no lines drawn through them.[38] Even
if one granted that all these fixes were erroneous, the North Koreans
could hardly then be blamed for believing that their waters had been
violated, or for insisting on an apology.

Doubts about the ship's actual course become much graver when
we turn from Armbrister's account to Bucher's. Bucher testifies that
the "LORAN was fairly good . . . so there was never any question
about our position" (p. 157), and his book is the only one rash enough
to plot the *Pueblo*'s mission on a chart. (The chart is incompatible with
the evidence in the *Hearings* as well as in the position log, but this
could be attributed to artistic simplification.) Bucher tries an opposite
approach from Armbrister to rationalize his quartermaster's admission at a North Korean press conference on 12 September 1968 of
seventeen intrusions: these were, he suggests, not accidental errors
but deliberately fantastic, to outwit the slow-witted "KORCOMS"
and alert the American people. ("KORCOM" is official Pentagonese
for "Korean Communist," and the term itself, as well as Bucher's use
of it, reflects some of the racism explicit in Admiral Smith's "Mon-
golian savage,"[39] or Admiral Gallery's "rabble of gooks."[40])

> The KORCOMS had decided to break the news to the world of addi-
> tional "intrusions" which they discovered we had committed. To prove
> that these intrusions were ordered by the US government, they made
> use of an Instruction which we had aboard the ship. The daffy logic
> used in making their point using this Instruction, proved to me that this
> time they were cutting their own throat, and I gladly complied. . . .

37 *Christian Science Monitor,* 1 July 1969, p. 10.

38 *Naked Act of Aggression by U.S. Imperialism Against the Korean People* (Pyongyang:
Foreign Languages Publishing House, 1968), III, p. 27.

39 Armbrister, p. 265.

40 Gallery, p. ix.; cf. p. xi: "By 'gook' I mean precisely an uncivilized Asiatic Communist.
I see no reason for anyone who doesn't fit this definition to object to the way I use it."

> We were now up to seventeen intrusions, and although most of them
> would have required the *Pueblo* to go supersonic, the KORCOMs
> somehow failed to see any contradiction. Ed Murphy did a marvelous
> job of explaining the new "intrusions." . . . I had no way of knowing
> whether any of the correspondents present would do the calculations
> needed to give the lie to our confessions, but I knew that our own
> people at home would not fail to do so.[41]

Captain Bucher has already suffered much for the sins of others,
and one hesitates to add to his difficulties. But what he says here is
quite simply untrue, both in the letter and in the spirit. The seventeen
intrusions reported from the press conference, far from being impossible, are on the surface (except for one apparent typo) quite plausible.[42] None are very deep, all are consistent with the general times
indicated by the Armbrister account, and all but one are in specific
zones of special interest indicated by the redoubled course plots on
the Bucher chart. Why can the Captain not admit and discuss this
candidly? Is it that he was forced first by the North Koreans to admit
things that were true, and has been forced since (after the grotesque
threat of a US Navy court martial) to produce a denial that is false?

Bucher's effort to ridicule his testimony of those days is systematic; he has reconstructed from memory a "final confession" in which
he allegedly admitted spying for Hawaii's "kingpin of all provoca-
teurs . . . Fleet General Barney Google" (p. 427). But his confession
on that unhappy 12 September was in no wise so happy-go-lucky; it
was sober, detailed, and in most respects demonstrably true. Ed
Murphy on the same day referred the eleven new "intrusions" (over
the original six) to precisely the loran apparatus which Armbrister
identifies (pp. 21, 35) as being "susceptible to atmospheric dis-
turbances."

Personally I have no knowledge whether or not the *Pueblo*
crossed the twelve-mile limit, and it may well be (if Armbrister is
right about the loran's unreliability) that the Pentagon does not know
either. Restrictive limits to territorial waters (whether of three or of
twelve miles) should not be taken too literally; they have been established above all by great maritime powers such as Britain, and have

---

41 Bucher, p. 344; cf. Ed Murphy, *Christian Science Monitor*, 1 July 1969, p. 10: "the
Pueblo would have had to been [*sic*] steaming at speeds several times faster than that of
which she was capable."

42 One indication of their plausibility is that they were apparently never reported by the
US press (apart from the left-wing *Guardian*) so that "our own people at home" were once
again denied the chance to calculate for themselves. The press conference is, however, reported in the *People's Korea* (3 October 1968), cf. p. 2.

by no means been universally acceded to.[43] As the US State Department's intelligence bureau noted in 1965, "The itinerary of any naval vessels close along a foreign coast or through strategic waters may be tantamount to creating tension and precipitating crises, even among otherwise friendly states. . . . The most peaceful coastal patrol may loom as a war scare."[44]

These limits become even less meaningful where espionage (or, if you prefer, intelligence-gathering) is concerned. As a research associate at Harvard Law School has pointed out, "It is hardly unexpected for small coastal countries to question the appropriateness of granting absolute immunity to electronic intelligence vessels or to seek other means for redressing their comparative technological disadvantage. . . . To conclude the *Pueblo* posed no threat begs the question. Its threat was acquisition of data that could make the coastal state defense establishment vulnerable."[45]

The hostility aroused by ELINT vessels became undeniable after July 1967, when Israel used both planes and ships to kill thirty-four Americans on board the USS *Liberty*. This incident occurred more than a mile outside Egypt's territorial waters, and a good deal farther from Israel's. It was still fresh in everyone's mind when Admiral Sharp (as CINCPAC) cabled on 23 December: "Risk to *Pueblo* is estimated to be minimal since operations will be conducted in international waters."[46]

The persistent dissembling after the fact, however, suggests that the Navy does know the truth about the *Pueblo*'s movements and has taken considerable pains to conceal them. For example it maintains that the *Pueblo* kept radio silence until the two relatively dull SITREPS (situational reports) which it broadcast on the morning of its capture.[47] The Navy Court of Inquiry summarized the secret testimony of Bucher and Stephen Harris (in charge of *Pueblo*'s ELINT technicians) as saying that "the ship's mission was unproductive up to the point of seizure."[48] But at a background briefing for US newsmen a high State Department official revealed that Harris' NSA detail

43 For a useful review of this subject, see Joseph Goulden, *Truth Is the First Casualty*, pp. 224–26.

44 US Department of State, Bureau of Intelligence and Research, *Geographic Bulletin #3: Sovereignty of the Sea*, April 1965, p. 3; quoted in Goulden, p. 16.

45 William E. Butler, quoted in *New Republic*, 24 May 1969, p. 8.

46 *Report*, p. 1651.

47 None of the books discussed, in supporting this claim, answers the State Department's correction of it on 13 February 1968, stating that the *Pueblo* first broke silence on 20 January, three days before the incident (*New York Times*, 14 February 1968, p. 9).

48 Goulden, p. 15.

aboard the *Pueblo* had transmitted additional "purely technical messages" which "did not come through command [i.e. military] channels at all."[49] These messages, he conceded, added to the "uncertainty" about the *Pueblo*'s route. Andrew Tully reports that

> In Washington, both military and civilian intelligence sources snickered up their sleeves at . . . the *Pueblo* Court of Inquiry . . . summary . . . declaring that the vessel's spy mission was "unproductive." In fact, the *Pueblo* relayed all sorts of vital intelligence to Washington, including . . . information on North Korean military equipment. . . . Eavesdropping on conversations between fighter pilots, the ship's electronic listeners learned . . . that they were having problems with a certain type rocket launcher. From another message, intelligence in Washington got its first news of the delivery of a new type of Russian tank to the North Korean Army.[50]

What the *Pueblo* really did on 23 January is as obscure as ever: the outsider can speak with confidence only of the ship's partially declassified orders and cable traffic. From this small residual core of information we are told that the ship first broke radio silence the night before, and after sixteen hours of unsuccessful efforts established radio teletype communication with Japan at either 9:30 or 10:45 A.M. Korean time. (This radio circuit was kept open continuously until the ship was boarded less than four hours later.)[51] At around noon Korean time the *Pueblo,* then dead in water at a reported position (39–25.2N, 127–55.0E) some fifteen miles from the nearest island, was approached from the south by a North Korean SO-1 subchaser. After asking for and learning the *Pueblo*'s nationality, the SO-1 at 12:27 hoisted flag signals, "Heave to or I will open fire on you."[52]

According to Armbrister, "Bucher was dumbfounded" (p. 50). But according to the Navy both at the time and later, the order to "heave to" under threat of fire was "a routine incident"—"harass-

---

49 *Ibid.,* p. 116. Only two such INTEL/TECH Reports are indicated in the Navy's *Chronology;* both are called "routine," and neither can have been very long.

50 Tully, pp. 124, 129. The new books, like the Court of Inquiry, suggest that Marine Sergeants Chicca and Hammond, the two Korean-speaking interpreters under Harris, were unable to translate intercepted messages competently (Armbrister, p. 31; Bucher, pp. 181, 196; Schumacher, p. 86). But even this is open to doubt; the *Pueblo* was somehow able to cable "They plan to open fire on us now" at 1:26 P.M., four minutes before the firing occurred, and the man who spread the warning through the ship was Sergeant Chicca (Gallery, p. 162; cf. Armbrister, pp. 57–58; Schumacher, p. 90). Whatever the facts, somewhere on ship or shore Americans were monitoring North Korean messages, including those which led up to the seizure and capture of the *Pueblo.*

51 *Hearings,* p. 669 (Gallery, p. 157); *Report,* p. 1658.

52 *Hearings,* p. 842; *Report,* p. 1666.

ment... no worse than expected nor as bad as previously experienced by *Banner*."[53] Admiral Sharp himself (who had predicted the risk to the *Pueblo* as minimal) later assured the Pike committee that ELINT vessels "had had that type of harassment before, and that was nothing unusual."[54]

Bucher himself determined on that day that the situation was harassment and "not that critical." His reaction to "harassment" had been discussed earlier in briefings and was regulated closely by his operational and sailing orders. Under a recent special order from Admiral Moorer, now the Chief of Naval Operations, no US ships were to permit themselves to be intimidated.[55] An XP to his operational orders 301–68, under the heading "Hostile, harassing or embarrassing tactics," specified that "Retirement under any circumstances should be slow and gradual, and at variance of any course prescribed by the non-friendly unit."[56]

Lieutenant Schumacher, the *Pueblo*'s Operations Officer, tells us that two references in the *Pueblo*'s Sailing Order of 5 January (Refs C and D) applied in case of harassment.[57] The first of these (Ref C, CINCPACFLEET Instructions 003120.24A of 28 February 1966) was the Instruction cited with "daffy logic" by Lieutenant Murphy when he confessed to the *Pueblo*'s seventeen intrusions, at the famous North Korean press conference of 12 September 1968. In particular Murphy quoted paragraph b.2 (a) as stating that (in contradistinction to a twelve-mile limit set for patrols off China and the Soviet Union), "surface patrols to the three-mile limit off North Korea are authorized."[58]

The response of the State and Defense Departments in Washington the next day was to confirm Murphy's language; they argued however that CINCPACFLTINST 003120.24A of February 1966 had been "superseded" by the Sailing Order of 5 January 1968,[59] which set a thirteen-mile limit. This announcement by Robert McCloskey of the State Department, like so many he has made about

53 *Hearings*, pp. 667, 670 (Gallery, p. 161).

54 *Hearings*, p. 831; cf. p. 833. General Wheeler (who approved the minimal risk classification) later explained that "We had the same thing happen to *Banner* from a Soviet destroyer ... about a year before ... and there was no fire opened" (*Hearings*, p. 914).

55 Bucher, p. 182.

56 *Hearings*, pp. 760–62; Armbrister, p. 54.

57 Schumacher, pp. 67–69. Text of Ichthyic One Sailing Order also printed in Bucher, p. 420; Gallery, p. 153; *Hearings*, pp. 768–69.

58 *People's Korea*, 3 October 1968, p. 2; cf. *Guardian* (New York), 28 September 1968, p. 12.

59 *Washington Post*, 14 September 1968, A6; cf. 13 September 1968, A1; *New York Times*, 13 September 1966, p. 20.

the US in Asia, was false. Paragraph 6 (g) of the Sailing Order states explicitly that the provisions of 003120.24A "apply regarding rules of engagement."[60] According to Schumacher, "This meant that the dictums in 003120.24A, about brazening it out if harassed, applied. . . . The same instructions said the skipper of an American ship being harassed should brazen it out, *even if this meant steaming toward the harasser's land.* The lightly armed *Pueblo,* under these instructions, was supposed to act brave if harassed but not provocative."[61]

It is clear that Admiral Moorer's views on standing up to harassment had not changed much between his instructions of 1966 (when he was CINCPACFLEET) and his special order of 1967 (when he was Chief of Naval Operations). McCloskey was probably wrong in September 1968 when he attributed the 1966 orders to Admiral Sharp (CINCPAC) rather than Moorer (CINCPACFLEET).[62] But the distinction is immaterial. The coincidence between Sharp's and Moorer's extraordinary views on retaliation had already been demonstrated by their conduct during the Tonkin Gulf incidents, when Sharp was CINCPAC and Moorer CINCPACFLEET. And the orders and behavior of the *Maddox* in August 1964 are all too suspiciously similar to those of the *Pueblo* in January 1958.

Did the *Pueblo,* after being harassed, steam toward the harasser's land, as the *Maddox* is said by some to have done on 2 August 1964? Almost certainly its first movement at 1:15 P.M. was northeast in the opposite direction, but what happened later is less clear. Bucher's first official message (PINNACLE I) sent at 12:52 P.M. Korean time (twenty-five minutes after the "heave to" order) announced that his intentions then were "to remain in area if considered feasible, otherwise to withdraw slowly to northeast."[63] Almost immediately, however, the situation changed for the worse. At about 1:00 P.M., if not earlier (before the "heave to" order at 12:25, according to Bucher, pp. 179–80), three torpedo boats approached rapidly from the southeast. After two MIGs and a second subchaser had joined the action, the *Pueblo* by all accounts did depart the area, about 1:15 P.M., and at first it withdrew slowly to the northeast at course 080, directly away from shore.

Armbrister and Bucher add that this course was in defiance of

---

60 *Hearings,* p. 769; Gallery, p. 155. The text in Bucher (p. 422, "declassified authority Deputy Secretary of Defense [Paul Nitze] 12 September 1968") is garbled so as to conceal this application.

61 Schumacher, pp. 69, 67, emphasis added.

62 *Washington Post,* 13 September 1968, A1.

63 Text of PINNACLE I in *Hearings,* p. 842; cf. Armbrister, p. 51; Schumacher, p. 86.

North Korean orders and maneuvers, and hence led (after a brief respite) to the first Korean gunfire at 1:30 P.M. Bucher states categorically that the torpedo boats tried to prevent his withdrawal, even though the subchaser, in contrast, actually hauled down her flag signal to heave to: "Two of them stuck close to our stern, the other two porpoised around our bows, zigzagging as close as ten yards with the obvious purpose of blocking our withdrawal."[64]

Schumacher, however, raises the possibility that the North Korean vessels had precisely the opposite purpose, to escort the *Pueblo* out to sea:

> The torpedo boats . . . stayed with us, surrounding us in a diamond formation. The two lead boats crisscrossed back and forth about twenty yards in front of our bow. It was still the tense game of chicken, but still according to the rules. The torpedo boats could be just showing off, rubbing it in that they were forcing us to move farther out.[65]

Goldberg's speech to the UN Security Council on 26 January, while claiming like Bucher that the *Pueblo* was prevented from withdrawing, interestingly raised the alternative of an escort out to sea as a legitimate possibility envisaged under international law: "The North Korean vessel . . . under international law, if there had been an intrusion—which there was not—should have escorted the vessel from the area in which it was. However . . . the *Pueblo* attempted peacefully to withdraw from this encirclement but was forcefully prevented from doing so and brought to a dead stop."[66]

---

64 Bucher, p. 186. Armbrister (p. 56) says that the first subchaser, though it lowered its flags, soon closed "rapidly on *Pueblo*'s port quarter, an obvious attempt to force Bucher back toward land."

65 Schumacher, p. 90.

66 Department of State, *Bulletin,* 12 February 1968, p. 195. Like the Pentagon press release of three days earlier, Goldberg's statement is incompatible in many details with the story now told. For example, he stated that the *Pueblo,* after being ordered to heave to, "maintained its course and kept its distance from the shore"; we are now told that the ship remained dead in water as before.

Goldberg's reference to international law derives from Article 23 of the 1958 Convention on the Territorial Sea, which deals with sovereign warships and states that "The coastal State may require the warship to leave the territorial area." This also suggests that Goldberg, a lawyer, may not have seen the cables. In PINNACLE I Bucher had taken pains to point out that the "*Pueblo* hoised the U.S. ensign, then ran up [flag] code Hotel Juliett Delta, translated 'Hydrographer'" (*Hearings,* p. 842). He thus made it unambiguous that he had identified himself not as a sovereign Navy warship, but as a "government ship operated for non-commercial purposes." This would invite treatment by North Korea under Articles 16 and 22, under which the inviolable sovereignty of vessels is not recognized, and the coastal state is expressly granted the right to "prevent passage which is not innocent." (Text of Convention in Department of State, *Bulletin,* 30 June 1958, pp. 1111ss). The precision of Bucher's cable suggests that the Navy was aware of these legal niceties. If so, it was asking for trouble.

Armbrister's detailed account of this crucial period before the first gunfire supports the "obstruction" version of Bucher and Goldberg, which was also arrived at by the naval court of inquiry. Unfortunately his account suppresses certain key items of information, which, when restored, tend instead to corroborate the "escort" possibility raised by Schumacher.

> Eight or ten soldiers in full battle dress were stepping now from the deck of the subchaser to the deck of the lead P-4. And the P-4 was backing down toward *Pueblo*. [Murphy] shouted for Bucher. It was 1:17. . . . Bucher stared at the troops in the boarding party, stunned by their sheer gall. Those guys were serious. *Well, he'd be damned if he'd let them get away with a stunt like that.* He would withdraw. But slowly—in a dignified manner befitting an American ship. The special instruction attached to his operations order was very specific about this . . . the sentence beginning "Retirement under any circumstances . . . [should be slow and gradual, *and at variance of any course prescribed by the nonfriendly unit,* cf. *supra*]. . . . Bucher was not a man to violate orders. . . . "Right to zero-eight-zero," Bucher told the helmsman. . . . "All ahead to one-third." . . . . *Pueblo* swung around in a wide circle and aimed for the open sea. . . . Schumacher finished drafting the second JOPREP PINNACLE:
>
>> ". . . SO1 has sent international code translated 'Follow in wake; I have a pilot aboard.' . . . Two MIGs sighted on starboard bow circling; [P-4] 604 is backing toward bow with fenders rigged with an armed landing party [on bow. Attempting to board] *Pueblo* all ahead one third [right full rudder and departing area *under escort.*] Intentions to depart the area."[67]

Whatever the course undertaken by the *Pueblo,* the suppressed words "under escort" indicate that its seaward course was initially in compliance with, not in defiance of, the intent of the North Koreans (there were no other American ships nearby) and hence a course in violation of Moorer's special instructions.

---

67 Armbrister, pp. 53–55, emphasis added; compare the at times almost identical wording in Bucher, pp. 184–85, and Schumacher, p. 89. These all follow closely the wording of Bucher's testimony at the naval court of inquiry (*Washington Post,* 2 February 1969). The more complete text of PINNACLE II is in *Hearings,* p. 843; the crucial words "under escort" are corroborated by Admiral Moorer, p. 691, Admiral Sharp, p. 830, and General Wheeler, p. 914. But even the fuller text may have been censored to conceal *Pueblo's* direction. It seems inconceivable that, even in times of stress, an officer of a ship dead in water would cable the uninformative words "right full rudder" in place of his compass course.

Murphy implies that he persuaded the captain to "come to course 080" *after* the first firing (at 1:30 P.M.), but then says that they "were generally on the 080 heading *through* the early firing" (*Christian Science Monitor,* 17 June 1969, p. 5).

Bucher (pp. 185–86) and Armbrister (p. 56) agree that the first subchaser appeared for a while to accept the *Pueblo*'s departure, fell behind the *Pueblo* and actually hauled down its flag signal to "heave to." The final crisis and the first shooting occurred some thirteen minutes later, after the subchaser belatedly approached the *Pueblo* with its "heave to" order again flying. Why matters should have so deteriorated is unclear. It may be that the North Koreans themselves abandoned the idea of a seaward escort, as Schumacher implies. But Armbrister's account, when its omissions have been restored, suggests that possibly the difficulties arose from Bucher's reluctance to disobey order 003120.24A ("Retirement under any circumstances . . . should be . . . at variance of any course prescribed by the unfriendly unit").

Such a possibility is corroborated by the coordinates given in the ship's cable chatter between 1:28 and 1:31 P.M., which, although somewhat garbled and possibly confused, seem to indicate it was already on a course of 220 into shore toward Wonsan harbor.[68] Bucher himself talks of evasive movement to the starboard, to present a smaller target to the subchaser; and he says that "while I was considering that any more right rudder on my part would inevitably bring our heading back toward North Korea, she [the subchaser] suddenly opened fire."[69]

If Bucher did follow 003120.24A to the letter, it is of course easy today to question his hurried judgment, although even a 220 course toward land was not *ipso facto* illegal outside of the twelve-mile limit. The 1966 instructions for defiance may have made some sense for a destroyer that could defend itself against smaller craft, but not for the unarmed and extremely vulnerable AGERs. The orders however were not his idea but Honolulu's, where the admirals, like others interviewed by Armbrister, never seem to have adjusted to the idea of these little spitkits—"the nearest thing you could get to

68 The position at 1:28 P.M. was 39–25.5N, 127–54.9E; at 1:30 P.M. it was 39–25N, 127–54.3E. The times for these coordinates can be established by comparing Armbrister (p. 55) with the abridged (and censored) "chronology of all radio transmissions" in *Hearings* (pp. 670–71), *Report* (pp. 1659–60) or Gallery (p. 162). A third fix shortly thereafter is incompatible with the first two and apparently garbled slightly: the positions 38–24.1(N), 1+7–54E, followed by 39–34N 127–54E, should apparently read 39–24N, 127–54E, a fix which accords with the southwestern track and speed established by the first two fixes. Even if we do not emend the last coordinates (which were repeated three times), but let them stand, they are still wholly incompatible with the 080 course suggested by Goldberg, as well as with the preceding sets of coordinates.

69 Bucher, p. 186; Armbrister, p. 58: "*Pueblo* was already maintaining a course of 110 degrees. . . . Too much of a turn. . . . and he would be heading toward the North Korean coast."

a fishing boat"[70]—as commissioned ships of the US Navy. It seems only too likely that the order of 28 February 1966, drafted shortly after the first AGER was commissioned in the Pacific, represented in large part a simple failure of CINCPAC to adjust to the new risks which the defenseless AGER patrols would face. It is likely furthermore than the Navy, even after the airstrip alert controversy over *Banner*'s 1967 mission, never properly assessed the limitations on US resources of air support.[71]

Much about the *Pueblo* concept, design, and equipment represented an unhappy compromise, satisfying nobody, between civilian and military conceptions of the Navy's intelligence role in the Far East. The *Pueblo*'s two .50-caliber machine guns were but one symptom of this compromise—enough armament to be provocative and compromise the ship's civilian cover, but not nearly enough to offer defense in any significant armed engagement. More important was the compromise—imposed by budgetary limitations—of reconverting old slow ships from the mothball fleet, where the original civilian concept had called for swift, easily extricated vessels. I. F. Stone has described how the F-111 was rendered impracticable by successive modifications, which crammed more and more high-priced electronic gear into a frame that could not carry it.[72] The same problem arose with *Pueblo*, which in the end had millions of dollars of Ling-Temco-Vought's most sophisticated equipment stuffed into a mothballed World War II coastal freighter that was barely seaworthy. Ultramodern in her inner gadgetry, ponderous, clumsy and at times unmanageable in her overall design, *Pueblo*'s paradoxes of wealth and squalor were only too symbolic of the policy and government that produced her.

70 Admiral David L. McDonald, former CNO, as quoted in Armbrister, p. 90.

71 In retrospect one can also fault the assumption that the North Koreans, in the best of circumstances, would be as restrained in their reactions to ELINT patrols as the Soviets or even the Chinese. To begin with, the United States had fought a war against North Korea, a war which had never been properly ended, and in which perhaps two million civilians had died. According to Armbrister the fault here was NSA's rather than the Navy's, which had wanted to restrict *Banner*'s patrols to the coast of the Soviet Union: "The Russians, it reasoned, would never attack the ship on the high seas. A *quid pro quo* existed here [because of the Soviet unarmed ELINT trawlers]. . . . But . . . officials at the National Security Agency . . . became a little greedy. They wanted to 'task' *Banner* against North Korea and China. The Navy said this would be dangerous. . . . The *quid pro quo* would no longer apply" (pp. 119–20). This, however, cannot be the whole story. Admiral Sharp himself told the Pike committee that the intelligence needs of both the Navy and NSA required that the *Pueblo* "operate close to the North Korean shores," that for this patrol the Navy requirements were in fact primary, and that the planned delay in the sensitive Wonsan harbor area was in pursuit of Navy requirements alone. (*Hearings*, pp. 797; cf. p. 707.)

72 I. F. Stone, "In the Bowels of Behemoth," *New York Review of Books*, 11 March 1971, p. 34.

But more was wrong here than simple bureaucratic stupidity, inertia and compromise. For one thing, the contrast between *Pueblo*'s obsolete hull and costly innards reflected accurately the comparative strengths of America's shipbuilding and aerospace-electronics lobbies. Thus I. F. Stone may have been too sanguine in suggesting that the answer lies in better civilian control over greedy generals and admirals. There *was* civilian review of the AGER program as it developed; it was exercised by McNamara's deputy Cyrus Vance. There is no sign that Vance challenged the conversion of *Pueblo* into a floating warehouse for LTV equipment. Like every Deputy Secretary of Defense in over a decade, Vance could not be wholly disinterested in the matter of defense contracts in aerospace and electronics. The Wall Street law firm from which Vance (along with Johnson's confidante, Ed Weisl) came, Simpson, Thacher and Bartlett, was intimately linked to the investment firm of Lehman Brothers, which had a direct stake in Ling-Temco-Vought.

In like manner, more may have been wrong with the planning of *Pueblo*'s maiden mission than a simple bureaucratic failure to imagine the special risks involved. Too often (especially in the preceding six months) CINCPAC headquarters, and Admiral Sharp in particular, had reacted to periods of impasse or uncertainty in the war by pressing recklessly to the outer limits of established US policy —in large part out of frustration at the restraints of civilian control. Sharp in the next few days would show that his outlook had not changed. Though it seems unthinkable that anyone in the US Navy could have wanted the *Pueblo* captured, the prospect of a showdown with North Korea was not so unattractive. Bucher, and many others in the US Navy on that day, looked to the Fifth US Air Force to send jet fighters in response to *Pueblo*'s calls for help. In this case the *Pueblo* mission might well have led to a major international conflict whether or not the ship itself was lost.

Above all, if Hawaii had wanted to keep out of trouble on this delicate mission, it certainly should not have chosen an untried ship and an untried commander with only submarine experience.[73] Bucher's possibly overliteral interpretation of 003120.24A was just what would have been expected from this gung-ho career man and near-John Bircher, of whom one former crewman observed, "Bucher has more guts than the law allows."

Whatever the true facts, it is now agreed that, by 1:45 P.M. at

---

73 *Banner*'s first patrol of Korean waters one year earlier was also assigned to a new and inexperienced commander.

the latest, the first gunfire was over; and the *Pueblo,* after stopping briefly, was "being escorted" (as the *Pueblo*'s informal radio chatter reported at that time) southwest on a course of 220 into Wonsan.[74] At 2:00 P.M. Bucher stopped his ship in order to allow more time for destruction and possible rescue, but after a renewed salvo (which killed Fireman Duane Hodges), he again ordered his ship ahead one-third, at a speed of five knots.[75] Sometime after 2:32 P.M. (at 2:50 P.M., according to Bucher) the *Pueblo* was finally boarded.[76]

This consensus of events after the first firing is irreconcilable with the story presented by US Ambassador Goldberg to the UN Security Council three days after the incident. Goldberg argued that between the first encounter at noon and the *Pueblo's* reported boarding at 1:50 P.M., "The location of the *Pueblo* was constantly far away from Korean shores, always away from the 12-mile limit. . . . The *Pueblo,* in seeking to escape the encirclement, did not move in the direction which would have transgressed the 12-mile limit."[77] He also displayed a map which showed the *Pueblo* moving constantly seaward in a straight line on course 080 (the original course chosen by Bucher when he first departed the subchaser), to a point five miles ENE of the noon encounter.

Goldberg's tidy demonstration is now discredited on two points. The *Pueblo* did not keep to a straight course of 080; and it was boarded, not at 1:50 P.M., but some forty to sixty minutes later.[78] Goldberg's apparent errors could be easily forgiven and forgotten if it were not for the apparently incontrovertible evidence with which he documented his story. Like McNamara before the Fulbright committee's Tonkin Gulf hearing a month later, Goldberg's chronology was corroborated by intercepted radio messages from the North Koreans as well as by messages from the US ship, with the North Korean traffic confirming our own.

At that time the Pentagon had indeed received a cable which has been variously summarized as follows:

> We are now being boarded by NK personnel at 23/0445Z [1:45 P.M.]
> . . . . The ship reported that the boarding took place at 127 degrees,

74 *Report,* p. 1660, cf. Armbrister, pp. 67, 75; Bucher, p. 197; Schumacher, p. 97.

75 Bucher (p. 202), has corrected the obvious self-contradiction of his earlier testimony to the Court of Inquiry (quoted in Schumacher, pp. 96–98), in which he reported making "a large sweeping circle" toward Wonsan after the *second* gunfire (when he was already on course 220) as well as after the first.

76 *Report,* p. 1661; Bucher, p. 193; Armbrister, p. 84; Schumacher, p. 101.

77 Department of State, *Bulletin,* 12 February 1968, p. 196.

78 *Report,* p. 1661; Armbrister, p. 84; Schumacher, p. 101; Bucher, p. 193.

54.3 minutes east longitude; 39 degrees, 25 minutes north latitude [a point one mile southwest of the noon fix of 127–55E, 39–25.2N]. The time was 11:45 P.M. EST [1:45 P.M. Korean time].

Later research, however, established that this 1:45 cable had originated not from the *Pueblo* but from the US Navy in Japan, being no more than a relay of earlier mistaken "chatter" about a boarding at 1:26 P.M. from the men below the decks on the *Pueblo*.[79]
Such confusions are inevitable and relatively innocent.

What catches our eye is the corroboration of a mistaken relay between Japan and Washington by an alleged enemy intercept five minutes later.

At 1:50 P.M. Korean time, within a few minutes of the reported boarding of the *Pueblo,* North Korean vessels reported their position at 29–26 NL 128–02 EL [five miles or so ENE of the noon and 1:28 P.M. fixes] .... The North Korean vessel at 1350—1:50 P.M.—... reported boarding the *Pueblo*.[80]

In other words, this alleged intercept not only echoed Japan's mistaken report of a boarding one hour before the event, its coordinates also echoed the mistaken US impression that the *Pueblo* and its escort were still moving ENE on its original course at 080, rather than southwest (for at least 40 and perhaps 80 minutes) on course 220. These are two remarkable coincidences. It is easy to believe that Japan could have been mistaken about the boarding, or even the *Pueblo*'s communications officer in the SOD hut below decks. It seems incredible that exactly the same error could have been made simultaneously by the North Korean PT boat.

It is of course possible that the error did not lie in the original message, but arose innocently in the course of interception, translation, and transmission to Washington. This benign explanation of the coincidences would not strain our beliefs unduly, were it not for the unfortunate parallel with the Tonkin Gulf incidents, when "a North Vietnamese 'intercept' reported information which echoed the cables sent by the *Maddox* and the *Turner Joy* but which later turned out to have no convincing basis in fact."[81] Another possibility, less benign but hardly outrageous in these days of deepening credibility gaps, is

79 *Report*, p. 1664, cf. p. 1660; Department of State, *Bulletin,* 12 February 1968, p. 189; cf. Armbrister, p. 55.

80 Department of State, *Bulletin,* 12 February 1968, pp. 195–96.

81 Peter Dale Scott, "Tonkin Bay: Was There a Conspiracy?" *New York Review of Books,* 29 January 1970, p. 34.

that the "intercepts" were invented or altered *ex post facto* to facilitate the US representation before the Security Council. This was certainly not the case with the Tonkin Gulf intercepts, which played a key role in triggering the US response in 1964, and then remained a closely kept secret for almost four years. According to Armbrister (pp. 255–57), the North Korean intercepts would have remained secret also, if Goldberg had not persuaded the President they were necessary to his case, over the protests of the Pentagon that the intercepts were "too secret to reveal."

To judge by its subsequent behavior, the revelation which the Pentagon feared most may have been the insubstantiality of its intercepts, which soon had to be altered more and more freely as additional hard information came in. By 14 February a full 52-page log of the cable traffic (including the informal "chatter") had been compiled, showing that the *Pueblo* had not been boarded at 1:45 P.M. as originally reported. On that day Robert McNamara, in one of his last acts as Defense Secretary, gave a much more detailed report on the "intercepts" to the House Appropriations Committee.[82] From this list the alleged "intercept" of 1:50 P.M. (which "reported boarding the *Pueblo*") has simply been dropped. In its place is a new intercept of 1:59 P.M., in which "the North Koreans reported conditions not right for boarding." But this attempt at reconciliation only makes the record worse. If the 1:59 "intercept" was available earlier, why was the 1:50 "intercept" used by Goldberg to create a false narrative? And if it was not available earlier, from what belated but convenient source did it arise?

The record is further muddied by a full table of allegedly intercepted coordinates of enemy ships which was supplied to the Pike committee.[83] All but one of these positions lie outside North Korea's twelve-mile limit; if plotted on a chart, however, they produce a widely erratic and improbable course which is irreconcilable with the *Pueblo*'s official messages and informal cable chatter, as well as with the new eyewitness accounts, and with the tidy fictionalized report presented by Goldberg. In particular both the coordinates and the content of Goldberg's 1:50 "intercept" have been altered. The position (formerly 39–26N, 128–02E) is now 39–29N, 128–08E, some six nautical miles farther out to sea; and the *Pueblo* is no longer reported as being boarded but as "following SC-35 [the subchaser] with MTB's [the patrol boats] escorting."

82 US Congress, House, Committee on Appropriations, *Department of Defense Appropriations for 1969, Hearings*, 94th Cong., 2nd Sess., pp. 4–5.
83 *Report*, p. 1662.

A *third* version of the 1:50 "intercept" (one which might seem to restore some credibility to Goldberg's version) is supplied by Armbrister: "According to present instructions we will close down the radio, tie up the personnel, tow it, and enter port at Wonsan. We are on our way to boarding. We are coming in. . . ."[84] But this message was a different intercept, which had been placed by McNamara at 1:06;[85] and it indeed echoes, once again, a message from *Pueblo* at 1:15 (PINNACLE II: "Patrol boat backing towards bow with fenders rigged . . . attempting to board. *Pueblo* all ahead one third right full rudder and departing area under escort").

Clearly an intercept record so nebulous and continuously altered should not be treated with respect. It would be serious enough if this persistent alteration of the intercepted record represented a deliberate effort to mislead the UN Security Council and world and domestic public opinion. But deliberate falsification of the intercept record before 26 January would constitute not only a lie but probably a crime: a deliberate and conspiratorial attempt to mislead the US government while it was seriously considering possible acts of war. Particularly if authorities in Washington had to work with the PINNACLE II text just quoted (with the meaningless course indication of "right full rudder"), the 1:06 intercept would supply the false impression that the *Pueblo* was being escorted *under orders into Wonsan* rather than (as Schumacher reports) out to sea in the manner authorized by international law.

Ambassador Goldberg, a lawyer by profession as well as an OSS veteran, made precisely this point to the Security Council:

> The North Korean vessel . . . under international law, if there had been an intrusion—which there was not—should have escorted the vessel from the area. . . . Further compounding this offense against international law, and the gravity of this warlike act, is the fact that the North Koreans clearly *intended to* capture the *Pueblo,* knowing that it was in international waters, and *force it to sail into the port of Wonsan.* This aim is made clear by messages exchanged among the North Korean vessels themselves which we monitored including the following: "By talking this way it will be enough to understand according to present instructions we will close down the radio, tie up the personnel, tow it, and enter port at Wonsan. At present we are on our way to boarding. We are coming in." This is an exact voice broadcast

84 Armbrister, p. 255.

85 *Appropriations Hearings,* p. 4; cf. *Washington Post,* 2 February 1969, B2; Schumacher, p. 89. Admiral Moorer, on 4 March 1969, told the Pike committee that he had "no knowledge" of the 1:06 intercept (*Hearings,* p. 692).

from the ship which acknowledges the instruction that it was following.

Now, Mr. President, *in light of this, this was no mere incident,* no case of mistaken identity, no case of mistaken location. It was nothing less than a *deliberate premeditated armed attack* on a United States naval vessel on the high seas.[86]

As in the case of the Tonkin Gulf "intercepts," the "proof" of a premeditated armed attack was corroborated by our own traffic, in this case PINNACLE II's ambiguous reference to an "escort." But the 1:06 "intercept" becomes as implausible as that of 1:50, when we learn from Armbrister, Bucher, and Schumacher that the escort at 1:15 P.M. was not in toward Wonsan but in the opposite direction, "forcing us," in Schumacher's words, "to move farther out."[87]

The issue of the *Pueblo*'s precise location on 23 January 1968 is in my view less important than the issue (raised also by the Tonkin Gulf incidents) of whether or not there was a deliberate conspiracy to induce a more warlike US response, in part by the feeding in of false "intercepts." The last eleven years have amply illustrated the disastrous impact of spies and spy missions on international relations, particularly during peaceful diplomatic initiatives in US presidential election years. In 1956 this was not so: the antics of the frogman Commander Crabb were not serious enough to cause the cancellation of Bulganin and Khrushchev's first Soviet state visit to the west. But the U-2 flights of April 1960, the first in some eighteen months, caused the collapse of the projected summit meeting between Khrushchev and Eisenhower. The Tonkin Gulf incidents of August 1964 were not only a prelude to the Americanized Vietnam war; they are also said by some to have contributed to the downfall two months later of Khrushchev and his line of "peaceful coexistence."

Many of the questions that have been posed about the Tonkin Gulf incidents[88] should also be put to Admirals Sharp and Moorer about the *Pueblo*. Is it merely a coincidence that both of these patrols (the first in some six months) occurred at times of major diplomatic initiatives to bring about negotiations to end the Vietnam war? Were both of these patrols said to constitute minimal risks? Did both of them have secret orders to close to land in the case of anticipated "harassment"? Is it merely a coincidence that our local allies (in this case, the South Koreans) had been contemporaneously involved in

86 Department of State, *Bulletin,* 12 February 1968, pp. 195–96, emphasis added.
87 Schumacher, p. 90; Bucher, p. 186; Armbrister, pp. 54–56.
88 *New York Review of Books,* 29 January 1970, p. 36; cf. Goulden, pp. 246–47.

an increasing number of warlike incidents in the waters chosen for our ELINT patrol?

Why, in both cases, did we not only ignore enemy warnings against such patrols, but direct our ships to linger in the precise areas known to be most sensitive? Why, in both cases, did unexpected warning messages from within the Defense establishment not reach their addressees, and thus remain hidden from civilian eyes, until too late? Why, in both cases, was air cover or support withheld? (In 1964 this was in violation of an explicit presidential order of 3 August; in 1968 it was against previous practice for particularly sensitive missions.) [89] All in all, the overkill in these twin scenarios for catastrophe appears to surpass by far the stratagems of Claudius in the last act of *Hamlet*.[90]

Turning now to the conduct of Admiral Sharp, is it really a coincidence that on 23 January 1968, as on 2 August 1964, he was in the course of leaving Vietnam by airplane, and thus unreachable from Washington, while an aircraft carrier (the *Constellation* in 1964, the *Enterprise* in 1968) was ordered into the area by local commanders? His movements in 1968 are particularly qustionable. Sharp left a meeting with Westmoreland in Danang at 4:00 P.M. Korean time (2:00 A.M. EST), four hours after the first PINNACLE message and almost three hours after the second (the so-called trigger message).[91] His CINCPAC HQ in Honolulu had received a third urgent (CRITIC) message at 1:55 P.M. Korean time ("*Pueblo* now surrounded and NK boats plan to open fire") and had discussed this with the Pentagon by telephone fifteen minutes later.[92] Admiral Bringle, the Seventh Fleet commander a few miles from Danang in the Tonkin Gulf, first heard of the *Pueblo*'s "trigger message" a few minutes after 1:00 P.M. Korean time.[93] Is it really credible that Admiral Sharp was not notified of the *Pueblo* crisis until he arrived as planned aboard Admiral Bringle's flagship at 5:00 P.M. Korean time? Why was he not notified before his flight?

The conduct back in Washington of Walt Whitman Rostow, the president's representative on the secret 303 Committee which approved the 1964 and 1968 patrols, is just as inexplicable. Rostow has

89 General Gavin was reported to have been "appalled" at the lack of air cover for *Pueblo* (*New York Times*, 27 January 1968, p. 3).

90 One task in a properly constituted body would be to pursue the indications that the chronologies of both incidents (as now presented) have been tampered with, perhaps so as to indicate a longer time span than is in fact the case.

91 *Hearings*, p. 796.

92 *Report*, p. 1664; *Hearings*, p. 886.

93 Armbrister, p. 210.

137

been described by Hoopes as "the closest thing we had near the top of the US government to a genuine, all-wool, anti-Communist ideologue and true believer."[94] "An early and unremitting advocate of bombing North Vietnam," Rostow was shortly after the *Pueblo* incident the only civilian adviser (with Generals Wheeler and Taylor) to support Sharp's proposal for mining Haiphong harbor (thus possibly provoking a confrontation with the Russians).[95] Yet on the night of the *Pueblo* incident in Washington, Rostow was as uncharacteristically slow in his response as Sharp on the other side of the globe. Both PINNACLE II of 1:15 P.M. Korean time or 11:15 P.M. EST ("attempting to board . . . departing area under escort") and the Japan CRITIC of twenty-one minutes later ("*Pueblo* now surrounded and NK patrol boats plan to open fire") had reached Washington by 11:46 P.M. EST.[96] Yet, alerted by the White House Situation Room about this time, Rostow did not decide that this was a "serious crisis" until nearly an hour later (12:45 A.M.), by which time the *Pueblo* had reported its definitive capture. Why not?

Rostow then drove to the White House, but, reportedly on the advice of Rusk and McNamara, did not wake the President until 2:00 A.M.[97] By this time it was too late to send air cover and the *Enterprise* was steaming north toward North Korea, leaving (as Chalmers Roberts promptly reported) the President with "no option open on whether or not to respond with a show of force."[98]

Chalmers Roberts' informant was apparently resentful about this loss of options through the delay: "If the President . . . had been informed in time, air cover might have been sent to drive off the torpedo boats." Rostow should perhaps not be blamed for this specific inaction; even though he had personally approved the *Pueblo* mission three weeks before (as a member of the 303 Committee),[99] he might have mistakenly assumed that such steps had been planned for or taken. But this extraordinary delay in reacting (he did not even phone McNamara until 12:23 A.M. or later) corroborates the impression in

94 Hoopes, p. 20.

95 *Ibid.,* pp. 21, 177.

96 *Report,* pp. 1664, 1667.

97 Armbrister, pp. 215, 231.

98 *Ibid.;* Chalmers Roberts in *Washington Post,* 25 January 1968, A14. McNamara said he was first telephoned about the crisis at 12:23 A.M. (*Appropriations Hearings,* p. 34). He claimed that this report was based on the first PINNACLE message ("Heave to, or I will open fire"), but according to the Pike committee *Report* (pp. 1664, 1667) PINNACLE I did not reach the Pentagon until 1:24 A.M., while the Japan CRITIC ("NK patrol boats plan to open fire") had arrived at 11:40 P.M. Gen. Wheeler told the Appropriations Committee (p. 33) that he was alerted at 12:03 A.M.

99 Armbrister, p. 192.

Armbrister (p. 215) that the reported imminent attack upon *Pueblo* did not at first strike him as a "serious crisis." Why not? Surely the reports of an escort, attempted boarding, surrounding of the *Pueblo,* and plans to open fire must have constituted more in his opinion than the contemplated "minimal risk."

A certain mystery also obscures what was going on in the mind of Admiral Sharp. According to Armbrister (p. 232), he suggested "sending a lone US destroyer with air cover into [N.B.] Wonsan harbor." Sharp himself testified that he asked the Joint Chiefs to "reconsider" their cancellation of CINCPACFLEET's order (from Admiral Hyland in Honolulu) to send a destroyer with air cover off Wonsan just *outside* the twelve-mile limit: "We thought . . . that at least we ought to have a ship up there that would reassert our right to do that patrol."[100] But Sharp's own testimony makes it clear that he saw the destroyer only as part of a larger scenario:

> We wanted to station the destroyer off Wonsan and have it ready to accept the *Pueblo* crew if they would act and demand that they be returned, ship and crew, and that if this didn't succeed, then we would have to take other steps. . . . Once the *Pueblo* entered Wonsan harbor, any major U.S. countermoves would then be of a retaliatory nature. I therefore viewed the situation from this point on as one involving major U.S. forces in a confrontation *that could result in a second Korean war.*[101]

In this context, Sharp's first reported orders at 10:54 P.M. Korean time on the night of the incident are particularly interesting: "Do not understand what useful purpose will be served by repositioning [deleted]. . . . Suspend movement of aircraft [deleted] until further notice."[102] Sharp, in other words, called off the newly ordered air cover on 23 January but apparently did not call back the destroyer. It is of course true that the *Pueblo* reportedly had docked by 8:30 P.M. in Wonsan, while the *Enterprise* with her special supporting task group of destroyers did not reach her station at 32–30N (400 nautical miles to the south) until 9:00 P.M.[103] Sharp's call might suggest that he saw no useful purpose to a destroyer patrol *until* an air-

100 *Hearings*, pp. 835, 857–59.

101 *Ibid.,* pp. 834, 797, emphasis added. The order to position a destroyer with air cover off Wonsan came from CINCPACFLEET (Admiral Hyland) in Honolulu, at 7:21 P.M. Korean time, 23 January (*Hearings*, p. 847).

102 *Ibid.,* p. 851. Sharp's first reported message (time group apparently garbled) asked Honolulu to tell him the authority for Hyland's order positioning a destroyer (*Hearings*, p. 849).

103 *Report*, p. 1658; *Hearings*, p. 852.

craft carrier and task group had been fully assembled to back it up. (This task group 70.6 soon included six carriers, three cruisers, and eighteen destroyers—"the largest task force the United States had assembled since the Cuban missile crisis of 1962."[104] But in that case Sharp should have cancelled the destroyer patrol along with the air cover. The cable suggests that he may have let the destroyer proceed into the troubled area, while cancelling the air cover ordered for it— exactly what led to the alleged second Tonkin incident in 1964.

If so, Sharp's recommendation of the next day ("that at least we . . . reassert our right to do that patrol") was part of a series of actions (the cancellation of air cover, the unauthorized sending in of an aircraft carrier) which closely paralleled the context of Honolulu's cable of 4 August 1964 (to "demonstrate United States resolve to assert our legitimate rights in these waters"). In other words, it might appear that Admiral Sharp's envisaged solution for the *Pueblo* incident was a second incident (a confrontation, in his words, "that could result in a second Korean war"), the preparations for which paralleled almost exactly Honolulu's incredible orders leading to the second Tonkin Gulf incident, and all that followed it.

The parallels with Honolulu's actions in 1964 would be almost complete if in 1968 Sharp had again recommended retaliatory air strikes. The record is confused as to whether Sharp "recommended" air strikes, or merely "made up a lot of plans for strikes" for the Joint Chiefs.[105] We do however learn from other sources that the Joint Chiefs proposed bombing the *Pueblo* in Wonsan harbor.[106]

Fortunately, the Johnson administration, already at the limits of its resources in Vietnam, had no appetite for an exact rerun of the Tonkin Gulf scenario. This time the bombing proposals from Sharp were never authorized; and an order from Washington at 10:25 A.M. EST 24 January prevented the destroyer, or any other ships, from

---

104 Armbrister, p. 257.

105 When pressed by Congressman Pike, Sharp backed away from the word "recommend": "Mr. SLATINSHEK. Did you at any time after the fact . . . recommend some retaliatory corrective action? Admiral SHARP. *Oh yes,* we have a whole series of strikes that we had by that time made up and sent in to JCS. . . . Mr. PIKE. I am going to be very fussy about this language here, because the word Mr. Slatinshek uses is 'recommendation' (*sic*) . . . . Did you recommend these attacks? . . . . Admiral SHARP. Well, I don't remember whether I did or not, to tell you the truth . . . . in the scale of attack that we are talking about, first you had to get your attack built up, *you had to get your ground forces built up,* your ammunition built up, which we never did completely, I believe. . . . I am not willing to say I did recommend. I could tell you that we made up a lot of plans for strikes, and I don't remember—" (*Hearings,* pp. 858–59, emphasis added). His cables to the JCS were supplied to the Pike committee (pp. 854–55), but for the most part not published.

106 Tully, p. 126; cf. George Christian, *The President Steps Down* (New York: Macmillan, 1970), p. 139.

sailing closer than eighty nautical miles to North Korea when north of the 38th parallel.[107] These two actions later prompted Assistant Defense Secretary Warnke, a member of the White House ad hoc *Pueblo* "Planning Committee," to observe, "This was one helluva lot different than the Tonkin Gulf deliberations. Tonkin Gulf, as I understand it, the idea was that if you showed firmness, the Reds would back off. Now everyone figured this sort of approach didn't work with Asian Communists."[108]

But in two respects, one of which has had lasting consequences, the Tonkin Gulf lesson was not learned as well as Warnke suggests. First, at least one dangerous military response seems *not* to have been blocked by the Planning Committee: Walt Rostow's proposal to entrap a Soviet trawler. "Rostow opined, on the basis of no visible evidence, that Russia had very probably instructed North Korea to seize the *Pueblo.*"[109]

> At that moment the aircraft carrier *Enterprise* lay off the South Korean coast. A Soviet intelligence ship, the *Gidrolog,* was shadowing her diligently. This gave Rostow an inspiration. Why not lure *Gidrolog* into South Korean waters and then encourage the ROK's to seize her? "Walt was all excited about it, hopping around," Steadman recalls. "He kept referring to the 'symmetry' of this response." . . . Now the Secretary of State looked directly at Rostow. "The only symmetry," he said, "is its equal outrageousness."[110]

Hoopes, Armbrister, and George Christian all suggest that, "although no formal votes were taken, the Planning Committee's members [including Christian] had . . . effectively ruled out" Rostow's proposal.[111] So indeed the members of the Planning Committee may have imagined. But a UPI story buried in the *Washington Post* reported, from South Korean military sources, that the *Enterprise,* "last reported off North Korea, had changed course and entered the South Korean port of Pohang."[112] If so, the *Enterprise,* either deliberately or by coincidence, did exactly what Rostow had proposed; and we can hardly congratulate the Planning Committee for the Soviet self-

---

107 *Hearings,* p. 886; *Report,* p. 1668.
108 Armbrister, pp. 251–52.
109 Hoopes, p. 136.
110 Armbrister, p. 253.
111 *Ibid.;* cf. Hoopes, p. 136; Christian, p. 139.
112 *Washington Post,* 27 January 1968, A11. The report originally appeared in the South Korean newspaper *Hankook Ilbo,* 26 January 1968.

restraint in not accepting this bait.[113] One would like to hear an explanation for this reported meneuver by the *Enterprise,* and to hear Mr. Rostow's assurance that he did not discuss his "effectively ruled out" proposal with the US Navy.

Despite Rostow's busy cerebrations, the long-range effect of the *Pueblo* incident was to increase US-Soviet collaboration in the Korean area: one year later, when the North Koreans shot down a US EC–121 ELINT plane, Soviet vessels took part in the futile rescue operations and later transferred the salvage debris to a US ship.[114] This is not surprising. By 1969, thanks to the *Pueblo,* the US and USSR were now for the first time facing each other "eyeball to eyeball" in Korea, as in so many other parts of the world. This result, though it probably corresponds to the objectives of one Washington faction, is more in the interests of empire-builders there and in Moscow than in the long-range interests of peace.

The most significant and long-lasting US response to the *Pueblo* incident was its stock response to all previous Asian crises since 1950: to increase vastly its deployment of men and matériel to the area. One hundred fifty late-model US planes were promptly flown to South Korea to augment the eighteen F-4s and obsolete F-86s already there under "United Nations" (i.e., US) command.[115] This act amounted to the first wholesale scrapping by the United States of the prohibition on introducing new foreign matériel in the 1953 Korean armistice agreements;[116] and it can hardly have been surprising that North Korea, which in marked contrast to South Korea had been free of foreign troops since 1958, soon introduced SAM missiles and other new matériel. In other words, the most important long-range result of the *Pueblo* incident has been an internationalization of the Korean crisis and a radical step-up in the military commitment by the two superpowers on both sides, with a further weakening of the armistice agreements and above all of the chances for a political solution to the problem of Korean reunification. Here then is another analogy with the Tonkin Gulf incidents, which were fol-

113 It is however possible that US Ambassador Thompson's gentle threat in Moscow on 25 January ("that governments friendly to the United States might seize one of the Russians' eavesdropping vessels," Tully, p. 126) may have had the fortunate side effect of alerting the Soviets to Rostow's stratagem.

114 *Hearings,* pp. 906, 921.

115 Hoopes, p. 136; *New York Times,* 28 January 1968, p. 1.

116 Korean Armistice Agreement, Art. II, 12: "The Commanders . . . shall . . . (d) Cease the introduction into Korea of reinforcing combat aircraft, armored vehicles, weapons, and ammunition; provided, however, that combat aircraft [etc.] may be replaced on the basis of piece-for-piece of the same effectiveness and the same type." Text in US State Department, *American Foreign Policy, 1950–1955: Basic Documents,* I, pp. 727–29.

lowed by massive movements of US aircraft and the virtual scrapping of the similar matériel restrictions in the 1954 Geneva agreements. (In 1964 some of the forbidden new aircraft had been flown secretly into Vietnam in advance of the Tonkin Gulf incidents.)

Many in the United States may question this analysis of the *Pueblo* affair, believing that there never were any good chances for a political solution. But a scholarly essay by Benjamin Page in the *Nation* three years ago suggests that the reunification proposals by the Democratic Peoples' Republic of Korea (North Korea), far from being unacceptable, are similar to the conditions of the 1954 Geneva agreements on Vietnam which the United States has moved belatedly toward recognizing:

> The DPRK would most like to see elections, by secret ballot and supervised by mixed teams of North and South Koreans, to create a single government for the country. If this be unacceptable to the government of the South, the DPRK would be prepared to negotiate a confederation, each government remaining as it now is, with mixed commissions to work out economic problems and the like, and with unification the ultimate goal. Should this also be unacceptable, the DPRK is prepared to set political questions aside for the present and work out economic, postal, cultural and personal visit exchanges. The Rhee government stood steadfastly against any such contacts from the outset of its rule in 1948; the government of Pak Chung Hee continues this policy, forbidding even postal service across the border.[117]

The dilemma is precisely that of Vietnam: in Korea the United States calls for a settlement prior to its withdrawal; the DPRK wants this timetable reversed.

Mr. Page quotes a revealing UPI despatch from Tokyo on 23 November 1960, which indicates only too clearly a chief source of opposition to *any* political rapprochement in Korea:

> North Korea is waging an intensive campaign to establish direct contacts between North and South Korea . . . with proposals for cultural, commercial, postal and other exchanges between North and South. . . . High United Nations Command [i.e., United States] sources said that the UNC would exert its influence to prevent the South Korean Government from falling into, or being forced into these "traps."

And he adds: "It is not irrelevant to ask how closely the military *coup*

117 Benjamin Page, "Signals from North Korea," *Nation,* 19 May 1969, p. 622.

d'etat that brought General Chung Hee Park, formerly a major in the Japanese army, to the Presidency in April 1961 was related to such 'influence.' "[118]

Here then are two further analogies to the Vietnam story. In 1961 the US State Department White Paper on Vietnam called "the nation-wide [Vietnam] elections scheduled in the accords for 1956 . . . a well-laid trap."[119] And the military coup that brought General Nguyen Khanh, formerly a Groupe Mobile commander in the French army, to the Vietnam premiership in January 1964 (allegedly with the aid and encouragement of his American adviser, Colonel Jasper Wilson) followed closely on US fears that a political rapprochement might be in the making.[120]

A side-effect of the 1968 US build-up in South Korea seems to have been a considerable augmentation to the captivity and sufferings of the *Pueblo* crew. Soon after their capture it became apparent that the North Korean conditions for their return were essentially two: an apology for the "intrusions" and withdrawal of the 150 illegally intro-duced new planes and other matériel.[121] Ultimately the United States did apologize (while simultaneously declaring the apology was mean-ingless and invalid), but there are no reports that it gave ground on the new deployments. It would appear once again that some elements in Washington cared more about increasing the US build-up than about the welfare of the *Pueblo* crew; and this is one more indication that the *Pueblo* incident, apart from the ignominy of having a US vessel captured, was for some people not an unhappy "accident" to be regretted.

In addition to deploying 150 new planes to Korea, President Johnson also announced the call-up of 14,787 reservists. This was the largest call-up of reserves since the Berlin crisis of 1960–61 (ex-ceeding that of the 1962 Cuba missile crisis); and White House Press Secretary Christian hinted that it might just be the beginning.[122] Soon, without any formal announcement, there were reports that US Na-tional Guardsmen and reserves were fighting, and dying, in Vietnam. Also in Vietnam a newly augmented Asian B-52 fleet (apparently in-creased through Johnson's *Pueblo* order by 50 percent, from 50 to

118 *Ibid.*

119 US Department of State, Publication 7308, 8 December 1961, *A Threat to the Peace*, quoted in I. F. Stone, *In a Time of Torment* (New York: Vintage, 1968), p. 217; Marvin Gettleman, *Vietnam* (New York: Fawcett, 1965), p. 322.

120 Franz Schurmann *et al.*, *The Politics of Escalation* (New York: Fawcett, 1966), pp. 26–34.

121 *New York Times*, 14 February 1968, p. 9.

122 Armbrister, p. 254; *New York Times*, 26 January 1968, pp. 1, 6.

75 planes)[123] promptly inaugurated the new Vietnam military tactic of saturation tactical bombing around Khesanh.[124] Today the reservists have gone home; but the B-52 saturation bombing has become the backbone of the so-called Nixon policy of Vietnamization, a policy whose origins date back to early 1968.[125]

In other words the long-range results of the *Pueblo,* in the form of escalated levels of deployment, still haunt us today in Vietnam as in Korea. This is the final analogy with the Tonkin Gulf incidents. They too were accompanied by secret deployments which paved the way for a new phase of the war; and the Fulbright committee heard a disturbing rumor (which the Pentagon in a carefully worded response failed to deny) that some of these deployments actually began *before* the alleged second Tonkin Gulf incident which was supposed to have triggered them.[126] Just as in the long run the Tonkin Gulf deployments of new aircraft and of reserves were probably more significant than the actual retaliatory strikes of 5 August, so the *Pueblo* deployments may someday prove to have been more significant for escalation than the Joint Chiefs' bombing proposal which was turned down.

In the case of the *Pueblo,* it appears that the call-up of reserves, at least, had been urgently requested by CINCPAC before the *Pueblo* crisis, and (as in 1964 before Tonkin) were the source of increasing friction between the generals and the civilians in Washington (*Pentagon Papers,* pp. 516, 528, 531, 537, 595–96). The call-up of US reserves for Asia, which had been requested repeatedly by the Joint Chiefs since the spring of 1965,[127] had become a major internal political issue by late 1967. In the acrimonious debate over troop levels in Vietnam which is said to have contributed to McNamara's political demise, it was generally agreed that the next major troop increase could only come from a mobilization of reserves. In addition the government was then at the limits of its budgetary resources: civilians

---

123 *New York Times,* 9 February 1968, p. 2. Technically this report refers to B-52s in Asia under the Strategic Air Command, but I can find no other reports of B-52 movements in this period.

124 Peter Dale Scott, "Cambodia: Why the Generals Won," *New York Review of Books,* 18 June 1970, pp. 31–32; citing Hoopes, p. 213.

125 *Ibid.* The withdrawal of USAF squadrons in Southeast Asia remained frozen throughout phases V and VI of the so-called Vietnamization program, from April 1970 to 1 May, while troop levels in this period were cut from 425,000 to a scheduled 284,000.

126 The question whether any units had been alerted prior to the incidents was answered by the Pentagon with neither a yes nor a no, but as follows: "We have not identified any air unit which had been alerted for movement . . . prior to the Tonkin Gulf incidents" (*Tonkin Gulf Hearing,* p. 23). As I. F. Stone pointed out, this "is an obvious evasion. The JCS doesn't even say they *cannot* identify such units" (*New York Review of Books,* 13 February 1969, p. 6).

127 *New York Times,* 26 January 1968, p. 6.

argued that this call-up should be accompanied by a shift to wartime economic controls to avoid a disastrous weakening of the dollar.[128] Fearing the political consequences of these two steps, Johnson through late 1967 supported the freeze on authorized troop levels for Vietnam. The *Pueblo* incident provided Sharp and Westmoreland with the means to shatter the civilian inhibitions (or what the Pentagon Papers study called the "political sound barrier") about calling up reserves, even if this first call-up fell far short of the 90,000 immediate "mobilization package" of National Guard and reservists which was then put forward by the Joint Chiefs in mid-February.[129]

Sharp's appearances before Congress and the US press through 1967 indicate that he was deeply interested in ending the political inhibitions limiting the US air and ground wars in Vietnam. It is even possible that, in their absurd proposals to bomb Wonsan harbor, the Joint Chiefs knew very well that this time they would be overruled, and in fact were far more interested in obtaining the "compromise" result of calling in more modern planes and the reserves to fly them. Sharp's testimony to the Pike committee in particular refers to the inadequate forces available to him "because of the Vietnam war," so that it was impossible to contemplate saving the *Pueblo* in the six hours between its capture and docking in Wonsan.[130] His testimony about US vulnerability in the area strengthens the suspicion that he knew very well there was more than a "minimal risk" in sending the *Pueblo* to the sensitive area outside Wonsan harbor; and that the risk was in fact as great as when, in 1964, Honolulu altered a Washington directive and sent the *Maddox* repeatedly into the sensitive area around Hon Me island.

To call such actions "criminal" may well be empty rhetoric. So far as command-and-control procedures are concerned, Sharp (like Wheeler and Westmoreland) seems to have stayed scrupulously within the levels of discretion afforded him by higher authority.[131] But

---

128 London *Times*, 28 November 1966, p. 7; Cooper, p. 391. The *Washington Post* (26 January 1968, A20) noted editorially that the "*Pueblo* affair has given the Administration a comparable justification for tapping the military reserves on a scale which would have been difficult to justify solely in terms of the highly controversial conflict in Vietnam."

129 Hoopes, p. 148; *Pentagon Papers*, p. 516. The Joint Chiefs' package would have called up immediately "two National Guard divisions and some Army reserve units (totaling 50,000 men) plus the Fourth Marine division and its companion air wing (totaling another 40,000 men)." Christian, in announcing the *Pueblo* call-up of reserves, had "hinted that this might be just the beginning, that Army and Marine reservists might be summoned, as well" (Armbrister, p. 254).

130 *Hearings*, p. 828; cf. p. 835.

131 This was less clear in 1964, when (according to McNamara) Sharp told him that all concerned "were satisfied" the 4 August attack was a real one. If Sharp did say this, he lied. But Sharp's public record of falsehoods is not so amply documented as McNamara's.

what are we to make of the two "intercepts" of 1:06 and 1:50 P.M.—
the "intercepts" which echoed US secret cables of that period and
created a tidy picture of intentional North Korean piracy which later
turned out to be false? Here the analogy with the Tonkin Gulf incidents raises the possibility that the "intercepts" may once again have
been not merely false, but altered or manufactured to deceive civilian
authorities in Washington.[132] If so, someone should investigate the
possibility that "fictitious or fraudulent statements or representations"
were "knowingly and willfully" made in contravention of 18 USC
§1001. No doubt it could be argued, justly, that there is ample precedent for intelligence agencies feeding to their governments falsified
information of the type which some of its leaders wanted to receive.[133]
But, at least under the US Constitution where residual power is reserved to the people, such precedent does not constitute authority.

The charge of conspiratorial war-making is not a moot or historical question. It is true Admiral Sharp has since retired to become
consultant to firms such as General Dynamics whose planes he once
consumed, at an admitted rate of 500 a year in 1967, over North
Vietnam. (Old admirals do not die, they become corporation con-
sultants.) But Admiral Moorer since has been promoted by Nixon
to succeed General Wheeler as Chairman of the Joint Chiefs of Staff.

More generally, the U-2, Tonkin Gulf, and *Pueblo* incidents, all
of them ultimately authorized by the same secret "Special Group" or
303 Committee in Washington, have amply demonstrated the extent
to which the international relations of this country can be affected,
if not manipulated, by those with responsibility for intelligence missions.[134] The Tonkin Gulf and *Pueblo* incidents in particular (in
contrast to the flagrant attack on the *Liberty*) suggest that the key to
producing highly controversial escalation from ELINT patrols may lie
in the "highly classified" but "unimpeachable" "intercepts" whose
texts and whose sources no civilian is ever allowed to see.

Even if the Tonkin scenario is now too threadbare to see service
a third time, the Cambodian crisis of election-year 1970 suggests that
the political influence of our military intelligence agencies is as pervasive and as devious as ever.

132 If the intention had been to deceive public rather than official opinion, it is unlikely
that those responsible for the reporting of the intercepts would have objected so strongly
(cf. *supra*) to their being published.

133 An obvious example would be the alleged "missile gap" of 1960, when not a single
Soviet ICBM was in fact deployed. Cf. Sidney Lens, *The Military-Industrial Complex*
(Philadelphia: Pilgrim Press, 1970), p. 53.

134 Armbrister reports tersely that "The 303 Committee has been dissolved" (p. 379). If
true this probably means that there is today even less civilian review of ELINT patrols
than before.

Cambodia is the Nixon doctrine in its purest form.

President Nixon, 12 November 1971

Chapter Six
Cambodia: 1970

The issue of the Pentagon Papers must not be substituted for the issue of the Vietnam war. Although they throw light on the process by which the US war effort was escalated, and particularly on the role of systematic deception, they do not cover the whole of that process. The Pentagon Papers, written from the viewpoint of the bureaucracy, suffer from at least three serious limitations of vision. They are insufficiently cognizant of the *covert* decisions and operations in Asia of US intelligence agencies (the para-structures of our government). They say far too little about the domestic political and economic pressures influencing presidents and their advisers. And they tend to focus our attention on the past.

As a result the role of bureaucratic rationalization in the National Security Council, which hitherto has been systematically under-reported, may now be given too much emphasis; assuredly the war was not uniquely the product of secret decisions in the White House or Pentagon. Moreover, the Nixon administration has quietly encouraged an image, strengthened by the Pentagon Papers, of the Indochina war as one which proceeds from the original momentum given it by Democratic executives who are now departed from office and no longer accountable.

To dispel both of these false images, particularly the latter one, I would like to supplement my earlier analysis, published in June 1970 in *The New York Review of Books,* of the secret "crisis" decision to send regular US ground troops into Cambodia. That analysis, which detailed the strategic requirements of the air war impelling the Joint Chiefs and the National Security Council, was limited in the same way as the Pentagon Papers. At the same time, there are clues in the Pentagon Papers—e.g., that covert US air operations against North Vietnam immediately *preceded* the Tonkin Gulf incidents[1]—which justify greater emphasis on the role of the covert US air and ground operations in Cambodia, preceding Nixon's decision to invade that country.

One can now see the strategic requirements of the air war in a broader context, political and economic rather than military, both in Cambodia and in America itself. At first glance these other considerations might seem to overshadow the role of intelligence agencies to which I drew passing attention. On the contrary this larger perspective reinforces and even explains the role of covert operations and bureaucratic intrigues, rather than overshadows them. It also raises grave questions about the role of President Nixon and his political backers.

An undoubted crisis had been slowly aggravating for some years in Cambodia, under the more and more nominal leadership of Sihanouk. In retrospect one can see that Sihanouk's efforts to maintain a neutralist posture were increasingly hopeless and anachronistic, for economic as well as strategic reasons. Lon Nol's coup[2] of March 1970,

---

1 Report to Assistant Secretary of State Bundy, 7 November 1964, in *New York Times,* 13 June 1971, p. 37, col. 6; *The Pentagon Papers* (New York: Bantam, 1971), p. 306.

2 The phrase "Lon Nol's coup," though frequently encountered, is admittedly an over-simplification: many others participated in the overthrow of Sihanouk, which was finally approved by an unanimous vote of the Cambodian legislature. The technical point that such a vote had no constitutional validity is less important than the weakness of the Sangkum in the face of a prior *de facto* takeover by Lon Nol and his allies. At least two successive coups in Laos were similarly "ratified" by votes of the Laotian legislature in 1960.

which paved the way for the American and South Vietnamese invasion, was only the ultimate and most visible stage in a rightward shift of power that had begun some three years before. This was because of

> pressures which were in part the result of steadily deteriorating economic conditions. Over the past several years the Cambodian economy has become subject to increasing strains. Cambodia has been extraordinarily dependent on manufactured imports, both for day-to-day consumption and . . . for industrial development. The exports exchanged for these goods have been rubber and rice. But the surplus of these commodities has never been enough to meet the country's foreign exchange needs. Until 1963 these needs had been met largely by U.S. economic and military assistance. When in 1963 Sihanouk terminated the aid agreements with the United States in his efforts to remain free of political pressure from Washington, the flow of dollars stopped, and since 1964 there has been a growing balance of payments deficit.[3]

By the fall of 1967 Sihanouk was forced to seek a rapprochement with the American-dominated World Bank, International Monetary Fund, and Asian Development Bank (all of which linked the prospects of aid to the abandonment by Sihanouk of his faltering experiments in "Buddhist socialism" and nationalized foreign trade. In this context Sihanouk shifted to the right, received Chester Bowles in January 1968, and began increasingly to crack down on *Khmer rouges* and NLF troops. In August 1969 Sihanouk formed a new government headed by Lon Nol and Sirik Matak, the men who would soon overthrow him. Meanwhile, in June 1969, Sihanouk resumed diplomatic relations with Washington; the US embassy, in 1959 caught red-handed in the act of plotting against him, was allowed to reopen. "Economic necessity, not fear of the Vietnamese Communists, seems to have been the prime reason."[4]

In Washington new political and economic pressures lent weight to the strategic arguments of the Joint Chiefs of Staff for widening the war into Cambodia. Defense Secretary Laird, a "hawk" by anyone's standards in 1968, found himself increasingly by-passed and over-ruled by military demands for escalation in 1969 and 1970—in the same way that McNamara, a "hawk" in 1964, found himself increas-

---

3 William Rosoff, "Dissension in the Kingdom," in Jonathan Grant, Laurence Moss, and Jonathan Unger (eds.), *Cambodia: The Widening War in Indochina* (New York: Washington Square Press, 1971), p. 89.
4 Rosoff, p. 90.

ingly by-passed and over-ruled in 1965 and 1966. The reason lay in the White House. In both cases a President who had been recently elected on a program of peace proved to be highly receptive to military proposals that promised to end the war quickly, more receptive than a Defense Secretary who saw these proposals as an overcommitment of limited resources which increasingly weakened the US military posture in the world as a whole. Nixon and Kissinger began to deal with the Joint Chiefs over the head of Laird the way that four years earlier Johnson and McGeorge Bundy had dealt with them over the head of McNamara.

By the time of Nixon's election in 1968, moreover, the interests of large American oil companies had been drawn to the possibility of offshore oil discoveries in the neighborhood of Cambodia. Leases in the adjacent offshore waters of Thailand had been awarded in September 1967 to six oil companies (five of them American); this lent urgency to unresolved offshore border disputes between Thailand and Cambodia that were somehow quickly settled after the Lon Nol regime took over in 1970.[5] Meanwhile, in the wake of US Navy-sponsored hydrographic and geomagnetic surveys dating back to 1957, the months of November and December 1968 saw a "highly successful" seismic refraction oil exploration survey around the South Vietnamese island of Poulo Panjang, which lies directly south of Cambodia.[6] This survey was only the last and most promising of a preliminary series, conducted under the auspices of the United Nations Economic Commission for Asia and the Far East (EC-AFE). State Department denials notwithstanding, official documents reveal that the great bulk of the technical assistance for these surveys came from the US Naval Oceanographic Office (NAVOCEANO). According to NAVOCEANO's Annual Report for 1968,

> The Navy's coastal survey ships [which included no less than seven chartered from commercial petroleum survey services] were completely employed in charting operations off the east and west coasts of South Vietnam.

Furthermore,

> The following magnetic studies were carried out during [fiscal year] 1968: A complete low-level aeromagnetic survey of South Vietnam

5 Malcolm Caldwell, "Oil and the War," *Liberation* (Spring 1971), p. 59.

6 United Nations, Economic Commission for Asia and the Far East, Committee for Co-Ordination of Joint Prospecting for Mineral Resources in Asian Offshore Areas, Report of the Sixth Session, 21–27 May 1969 (E/CN.11/L.239), pp. 9, 66–70.

[including all of the land surface and at least part of the offshore waters, "for military and/or scientific purposes"]; a detailed survey of the Formosa Strait off the coast of Taiwan (in fulfillment of a U.S. offer to provide aeromagnetic surveys of the Asian continental shelf area as a contribution to the United Nations Economic Commission for Asia and the Far East.[7]

This language explains the chicanery of the State Department's written assurances to Senator Fulbright that the US government "has not provided South Vietnam any technical assistance relating to offshore oil exploration."[8] Strictly speaking, the assistance was not provided to South Vietnam, but either as "support of the fleet" (in the case of the charting) or "as a contribution to ECAFE" (in the case of the aeromagnetic surveys).

The Poulo Panjang seismic survey was in an area close to Cambodia and affected by the unresolved border dispute between the two countries over offshore islands. It was also very close to an Esso concession northeast of Malaysia in which, according to reported rumors, oil has already been discovered.[9] This may help to explain why ECAFE proceeded, before June 1967, to make "a broad regional study of the northeastern portion of the Sunda shelf of Southeastern Asia, including the Gulf of Thailand and the adjoining offshore areas of Cambodia and the Republic of South Vietnam,"[10] even though Cambodia at this time was not a member of ECAFE and may not even have been consulted. In 1969 the same ECAFE committee formulated proposals for further seismic refraction surveys in selected Cambodian offshore waters, as "suggestions" to be forwarded "to the Cambodian authorities for consideration."[11] Meanwhile, the special aeromagnetic survey planes of the US Navy proposed to carry out aeromagnetic profiles across the Sunda shelf "at opportune times while in transit between major projects in this region," ostensibly as part of the US Navy's Project MAGNET (originally a project "to provide world-wide charts of magnetic declination for safety in navi-

7 US Naval Oceanographic Office, *Annual Report, 1968,* pp. 1, 16; cf. pp. 7, 73, UN Doc. E/CN.11/L.216, p. 5. The seven charter survey vessels were leased from Alpine Geophysical Associates, Marine Acoustical Services, and Texas Instruments, Inc.

8 Letter of 10 February 1971 from David M. Abshire, Assistant Secretary of State for Congressional Relations; quoted in *San Francisco Chronicle,* 11 June 1971, p. 17.

9 *Wall Street Journal,* 22 Sept. 1970, p. 34.

10 United Nations, Economic Commission for Asia and the Far East. Committee for Co-Ordination of Joint Prospecting. Report of the Third Session (24 June–4 July 1967) (E/CN.11/L.186), p. 32.

11 UN Doc. E/CN.11/L.239, p. 9.

gation at sea").[12] These surveys of Cambodia's offshore areas, apparently never asked for by Sihanouk's government, should be investigated closely by Congress. For by the end of 1970, when it appeared to many that the Lon Nol regime could not possibly survive without increased US support, "Union Oil of California . . . had a concession for all on-shore Cambodian oil and much of the off-shore, former French, concession as well."[13]

All these diverse economic and political factors, both in Cambodia and in America, will suggest to liberal minds a picture of historical complexity, and to Marxist minds a picture of historical inevitability; and either of these pictures might seem to rule out the hypothesis that conspiracy played any major role in prompting the US invasion of Cambodia. However, if we now look at covert US military and intelligence operations for the same period, the complex picture becomes a much simpler one in which the long-range operation of economic factors turns out to have been helped along considerably by bureaucratic means.

In particular the Cambodian balance-of-payments crisis, which forced Sihanouk to install his domestic enemies in power and reopen relations with a hostile United States bureaucracy, represented a historical process that had been considerably accelerated by US covert operations. From as early as 1964, but with particular intensity in April–May 1969, US planes from South Vietnam systematically defoliated as much as one-third of the French-owned rubber plantations in Cambodia, the chief source of Cambodia's export revenue. Although the Department of Defense denied at first that the plantations had been deliberately sprayed, a visiting team of American biologists found this denial incredible:

> The fact that rubber plantations (which are readily distinguishable from the air) were so heavily hit (one-third of all this major Cambodian crop) suggests an attempt at punitive action on the part of the United States. That U.S. pilots are, we are told, under standing

---

12 UN Docs. E/CN.11/L.239, p. 93; E/CN.11/186, p. 36; cf. E/CN.11/L.216, pp. 7–8. One suspects that "safety in navigation at sea" was as important in this survey as in the same planes' aeromagnetic survey of the entire land area of South Vietnam.

13 Malcolm Caldwell, *Liberation* (Spring 1971), p. 59. However, a recent French report announces that the new Cambodian government will allow no foreign oil companies to drill independently in its offshore waters. All will have to work through a government board in which French oil interests are still prominent (AFP, 2 July 1971). This would suggest that covert US-French competition for Cambodia is not yet resolved.

orders in South Vietnam to avoid the spraying of rubber adds further support to the hypothesis that this particular action was deliberate.[14]

The biologists concluded that the spraying, carried out just before the beginning of the growing season, had caused up to 80 percent damage in some areas, and represented an economic loss in 1969 of approximately $11 million in rubber, plus an additional $1.2 million in other crops. These losses totaled more than half of Cambodia's exports in 1968 ($22.9 million), of which rubber represented 64 percent ($14.6 million).[15] An ensuing economic crisis (including a budgetary deficit of $20 million) induced Sihanouk to talk publicly in July and August 1969 of accepting direct US aid, and even of resigning.[16]

After being questioned by a House Foreign Affairs subcommittee, Thomas R. Pickering of the State Department finally sent written confirmation "that the greatest part of the damage was caused by a deliberate and direct overflight of the rubber plantations."[17] He claimed, however, that "there were no US missions targeted for the Cambodian areas involved, nor were the investigators able to determine that any US aircraft were directly involved in spraying these areas." As in the case of covert US operations against Cambodia in 1959 and 1967, the public was allowed to draw the conclusion that some other government, presumably South Vietnam, was responsible. But one cannot accept this excuse for a defoliation program dating back eight years, to the days when the rudimentary South Vietnamese air force was in fact largely flown by US pilots. Another explanation might be that Air America planes and pilots were involved, since Air America officials have admitted to extensive defoliation programs against insurgent areas in Thailand, and US officials have frequently fallen back on the excuse that Air America's planes, based in Taiwan, Thailand and South Vietnam, are not "U.S. aircraft."[18]

US responsibility for this extensive and repeated use of its de-

---

14 *Report on Herbicidal Damage by the United States in Southeastern Cambodia,* by A. H. Westing (Windham College), E. W. Pfeiffer (University of Montana), J. Lavorel, and L. Matarasso, reprinted in Thomas Whiteside, *Defoliation* (New York: Ballantine, 1970), p. 131.

15 United Nations Statistical Office, *World Trade Annual,* 1968 Supplement (New York: Walker and Co., 1969), V, 410.

16 Rosoff, in Grant (ed.), *Cambodia,* p. 90.

17 US Cong., House, Committee on Foreign Affairs, *Chemical-Biological Warfare . . . , Hearings* (91st Cong., 1st Sess.), p. 198; cf. Whiteside, p. 130.

18 In this respect it seems relevant that Mr. Pickering is a former naval and State Department intelligence official who had been named prior to this testimony as a CIA agent.

foliants for international aggression cannot be denied. It is particularly instructive to learn from a pre-invasion article in the authoritative *Far Eastern Economic Review* that "last spring (April–May 1969) . . . Henry Kissinger and Nixon ordered bombing strikes against communist bases in Cambodia."[19] In other words, secret strikes for the two months of the covert defoliation program were ordered by the adviser who, as Chairman of the National Security Council's Special Action Group, presided over the secret decision to invade Cambodia one year later.

President Nixon's covert operations against Cambodia in the first year of his presidency are part of a series dating back to the era when he was Vice-President. In 1958 and 1959 the CIA financed, equipped, and advised the brief military uprising of the Khmer Serei, whose part-Vietnamese political leader, Son Ngoc Thanh, had been premier of Cambodia under the Japanese. To show CIA complicity in the uprising, Sihanouk is said to have given as evidence the fact that a political officer from the US embassy, Victor Masao Matsui, was found in the Khmer Serei rebel headquarters. As far as I am aware, it was eleven years before this fact was even alluded to in the "responsible" US press:

> South Vietnamese undercover agents who had directed the uprising subsequently explained that Matsui's presence on the scene was only accidental. They disclosed, however, that the CIA had financed the operation.[20]

Matsui's presence appears less accidental when we learn that he was with the US Army for twelve years until just before joining the US embassy in Cambodia as a "political officer"; and that in 1966 he was expelled for a second time from Pakistan for renewed charges of subversion.

Throughout the 1960s the CIA in Saigon continued to use its contacts with Son Ngoc Thanh and the Khmer Serei in at least three ways: for intelligence-gathering (in both Cambodia and South Vietnam), for special missions inside Cambodia, and for the recruitment and training of paramilitary forces from the large ethnic Khmer minority of the delta provinces of South Vietnam.[21] Many if not most of

19 Harold Munthe-Kaas, *Far Eastern Economic Review,* 25 December 1969, p. 668.

20 Stanley Karnow, *Washington Post,* 28 March 1970, p. A10. For a typical press censorship of Sihanouk's charge, cf. *Time,* 16 March 1959, p. 34. William Worthy, "The CIA Plot Against Cambodia" (*Le Sangkum,* Phnom Penh, September 1965, p. 17), speaks of a covert flight to Siem Reap by an Air Vietnam plane on 7 February 1959. It is known that many of Air Vietnam's pilots are in fact Americans flying with Civil Air Transport.

21 *New York Times,* 28 January 1970, p. 1. *San Francisco Chronicle,* 29 May 1970, p. 14.

the latter were taken in from the armed bandit Khmer Kampuchea Krom (KKK), of whom an unflattering portrait can be found in Robin Moore's book *The Green Berets.* Trained by US Special Forces, by the Khmer Serei, and later by Thai officers in Thailand, these troops became part of the CIDG or so-called Mike Force of ethnic minorities, who were controlled (along with US Green Berets and the 34-A Ops teams working against North Vietnam) by the Saigon-based "Studies and Operations Group" (SOG, or MACSOG). SOG in turn reported in theory to Generals Westmoreland and Abrams (COMUSMACV); but it is said to have reported in practice to the CIA, which originally set it up.

The US public was given a hint of the deep splits within both the US military and the intelligence communities in the wake of the two Green Beret murder scandals of 1969; some of the resulting leaks concerned Cambodia. Both of the murdered agents, it developed, had operated in Cambodia; at least one of them (Inchin Hai Lam) had been a member of the Khmer Serei. Shortly before Sihanouk's overthrow, a *New York Times* report revealed that the United States had used the Khmer Serei, an organization "dedicated to the overthrow of the legitimate government of Cambodia on covert missions into that country in 1967, according to testimony at the trial of a Green Beret captain convicted in 1968 of killing one of the members of the sect."[22] 1967 was the year in which Sihanouk renewed his charges that the CIA was still plotting against him, as it had in 1959; and the year in which Khmer Serei harassment, especially along the Thai border, markedly increased.[23] The charges have since been corroborated: "A Green Beret officer says he took part in a secret mission in 1967 designed to aid in the overthrow of Cambodia's Prince Norodom Sihanouk. . . . Capt. John McCarthy . . . said the clandestine operation in Cambodia was directed from South Vietnam by the Central Intelligence Agency. . . . The mission was known as 'Operation Cherry' . . . and involved McCarthy, working under cover, and members of the Khmer Serai."[24]

According to the same *New York Times* story, "sources said that the several hundred former [Khmer Serei] members in Cambodia had pledged allegiance" to the Sihanouk government. This did happen in 1967, when Lon Nol was briefly prime minister, but the indications are that the Khmer Serei retained their identity, their militant opposi-

22 *New York Times,* 28 January 1970, p. 1. The testimony was offered by Maj. Patrick J. McKernan, "chief of the Army counterintelligence operations branch" in Saigon.
23 *New York Times,* 19 February 1967, p. 25; *Le Monde,* 6 May 1967, pp. 1, 3.
24 *San Francisco Chronicle,* 23 May 1971.

tion to pro-left elements in Sihanouk's coalition, and their links with US intelligence circles. Of these last, DIA at least continued to maintain a "safe house" in Phnom Penh, even when diplomatic relations with Cambodia were broken off and US personnel officially withdrawn.[25]

Wilfred Burchett has charged that the more violent events surrounding the overthrow of Sihanouk—the planned raids against the North Vietnamese and PRG embassies on 11 March and the ensuing massacres of ethnic Vietnamese civilians in the Cambodian countryside—were all spearheaded by CIA-trained Khmer Serei cadres.[26] In the weeks and months since the coup of 18 March 1970, it has become abundantly clear that the most reliable cadres in the Cambodian Army are those recruited and trained by the Khmer Serei and Green Berets in South Vietnam.[27] Although the majority of these have entered Cambodia since the coup, their central role lends credence to the Burchett hypothesis. So do the unprecedented and unexplained "demonstrations on March 8th and 9th . . . in the eastern province of Svay Rieng, where villagers (*sic*), with the help of Cambodian troops, seized weapons from Vietnamese guerrillas."[28] These must have been well-trained villagers to accomplish, without US air support, what the best Cambodian troops have been unable to do since. Their prodigious achievement was followed on 15 March, three days *before* the coup, by the first publicly announced and conducted joint operation between Cambodia and South Vietnamese troops.[29] Given the usual suspicion and hostility between the two peoples and their armies, it seems likely that special Khmer Serei cadres from South Vietnam were involved.

The special relationship between Lon Nol's army and the Khmer Serei-KKK units at its center implicates the US intelligence community, not only in the coup itself, but also in the ensuing "strategy of provocation," in which a series of hopeless attacks on larger and superior enemy forces brought about a debacle followed by official US intervention. This involvement of US intelligence personnel, above all the paramilitary personnel under SOG and the CIA, does not imply that Cambodian history in 1970 followed a master blueprint emanating from CIA headquarters. The intelligence parastructures of other nations were also involved, in addition to those of the United States, Thailand, and South Vietnam. Sihanouk

25 Andrew Tully, *The Super Spies* (New York: William Morrow, 1969), p. 201.

26 *Guardian* (New York), 25 April 1970, p. 1.

27 *New York Times*, 5 May 1970, p. 16; *San Francisco Chronicle*, 29 May 1970, p. 14.

28 Robert Shaplen, *The New Yorker*, 9 May 1970, p. 136.

29 *Bangkok World*, 18 March 1970, p. 1.

himself has since claimed that much of the plotting took place in Japan, between Prince Sirik Matak (a coup leader who was then ambassador to Tokyo), Song Sak (a Khmer Serei leader and alleged CIA agent who fled Phnom Penh in 1964 with $10 million), and CIA personnel.[30] An analysis of the coup in *Le Monde Diplomatique* refers to the contacts of a third coup leader with "Japanese secret societies manipulated by the CIA";[31] and Son Ngoc Thanh himself owes much of his influence to his three years in Japan during World War II.

A country that was more directly involved, as *Newsweek* reported, was General Suharto's Indonesia:

> A team of Cambodian officers secretly visited Indonesia last November [1969], and again in January, to study in depth how the Indonesian Army managed to overthrow President Sukarno [in 1965]. This, some Indonesians say, gave Djakarta advance knowledge of Cambodian General Lon Nol's coup against Prince Norodom Sihanouk last March. It also helps explain Indonesia's prompt offer to send arms to Lon Nol.[32]

Psychological warfare "experts" from Indonesia arrived in Phnom Penh within days of the coup. According to Wilfred Burchett, they "advised" in the xenophobic anti-Communist campaign against ethnic Vietnamese that is one of the most striking similarities between the Indonesian and Cambodian coups.[33]

These additional external factors suggest a prevailing trend toward right-wing repressive capitalism for which the United States and its agencies are not solely responsible. At the same time, all the known facts about foreign involvement reemphasize the central coordinating role of US intelligence, and in particular of the paramilitary faction in the CIA, that faction known to the public through the operations of Civil Air Transport/Air America. CAT supplied "complete logistical and tactical air support" for the abortive Indonesian military uprising of 1958;[34] and Tony Poe, their legendary ground

---

30 Press conference of Prince Sihanouk, as reported in Wilfred Burchett, *The Second Indochina War* (New York: International Publishers, 1970), pp. 55–56.

31 Daniel Roy, "Le Coup de Phnompenh," *Le Monde Diplomatique,* April 1970, pp. 12–13; translated in Martin Gettleman *et al.* (ed.), *Conflict in Indochina* (New York: Random House, 1970), p. 350.

32 *Newsweek,* 25 May 1970, p. 25.

33 Burchett, p. 65; cf. Jonathan Grant, "The Regime of Lon Nol," in Jonathan Grant *et al., Cambodia,* p. 121.

34 Lansdale Memo of July 1961, in *Pentagon Papers,* p. 137; cf. David Wise and Thomas B. Ross, *The Invisible Government* (New York: Bantam, 1965), pp. 145–56.

operative who spearheaded guerrilla operations against Tibet and (in Laos) South China from 1958 to 1970, has been identified as working also with the Khmer Serei insurgents in southwestern Cambodia.[35] Air America and its personnel, finally, do contract work in Southeast Asia for the large oil companies,[36] many of whom maintain their own "intelligence" networks recruited largely from veterans of the CIA.

In contrast to nineteenth-century flag imperialism, the twentieth-century equivalent is multinational, like the large corporations whose sphere of influence is enlarged, and whose syndicates, since the fall of Sihanouk, have proceeded to divide up the whole of the southern South China sea for oil exploration. The participation of Indonesia in the planning of the Lon Nol coup is in this respect particularly instructive, for it is a striking fact that the successful military coup against Sukarno in 1965, like the unsuccessful military uprising of 1958, both have not only been linked to the CIA, but followed publicly announced moves by Sukarno to nationalize the rich Indonesian oil industry. The power of US and Japanese oil interests with the new Suharto regime is likewise a matter of public record.[37]

The Lon Nol coup of 1970, like the right-wing coups of January 1964 in Saigon and April 1964 in Laos, would have been counterproductive if they had not been swiftly followed by a stepped-up US involvement. In 1964 the CIA intervened before the military, with the initiation of clandestine 34-A operations against North Vietnam in February 1964, and the initiation of T-28 bombing raids, with Thai and Air America pilots, in Laos in April and May.[38] In both cases these provocations, while inadequate by themselves to improve the US military position, aggravated conflict in such a way as to bring about the first open commitment of US military forces. In this respect the "coinciding" of the first covert T-28 and 34-A Marine attacks against North Vietnam, in such a way as to help provoke the Tonkin Gulf incidents, indicates that this CIA faction wanted escalation, even while some members of the Lansdale or "left-CIA" faction were beginning to contemplate disinvolvement.

35 *San Francisco Chronicle,* 4 September 1970, p. 24.

36 *New York Times,* 5 April 1970, pp. 1, 22.

37 *Wall Street Journal,* 18 April 1967, p. 30 quoted in Michael Tanzer, *The Political Economy of International Oil and the Underdeveloped Countries* (Boston: Beacon Press, 1969), pp. 363–64.

38 34-A and Special Force–Air America operations in Vietnam were controlled by the CIA's "Studies and Operations Group" (SOG), as were the Mike Force ethnic mercenaries later infiltrated into Cambodia. Lt. Col. Conein, who acted as General Khanh's case officer and maintained contact with the 1963 and 1964 coups, is said to have also handled covert operations inside North Vietnam.

The Pentagon Papers that have been published indicate that the CIA hawks had the support of Director McCone,[39] but that they kept other key administration personnel in the dark as to their plans. McNamara in particular claims to have been ignorant of 34-A operations accompanying the ELINT mission of the USS *Maddox,* even while he released the order for the 5 August bombing of North Vietnam. Later in 1964 a State Department official could only report that the T-28 bombings of 1 and 2 August "probably" took place, as the North Vietnamese had claimed, and McNamara denied.[40]

In like manner the overt US intervention in Cambodia in 1970, although vital if months of covert US operations were not to collapse, seems only to have been accomplished after intrigue, secrecy, and deception within the massive US bureaucracy. The only significant change in role from 1964 seems to have been that of the CIA director. In 1964 John A. McCone, an in-and-outer, held $1 million worth of stock in Standard Oil of California, one of the two largest US oil firms in Indonesia and Southeast Asia, whose subsidiary Caltex accounted for 70 percent of Sumatran oil production. That he should be revealed as one of Washington's most ardent hawks in 1964 and 1965 does not weaken the case of those who offer an economic explanation for US military policy. Richard Helms, director in 1970, in contrast is a career intelligence officer, with no particular commitment to, or economic stake in, the Far East.

Like other disputed escalations in the Indochina war, the 1970 invasion of Cambodia was preceded by an "intelligence battle" in Washington. A policy debate was disguised as a factual one, over the relevance of the deteriorating scene in Cambodia to US prospects in Vietnam. In this debate the issues that emerged were the truth or falsity of two propositions, finally subscribed to by President Nixon in his invasion announcement of 30 April: (1) in the so-called Cambodian sanctuaries lay "the key control center" COSVN, "the headquarters for the entire communist military operation in South Vietnam"; (2) the enemy was "concentrating his main forces in these sanctuaries where they are building up to launch massive attacks on our forces [in South Vietnam]."[41]

The military imagination, as revealed to *Newsweek,* seems to have envisioned COSVN ("the Central Office for South Vietnam") as a setting for the denouement of a James Bond spy thriller: "Near the

39 *Pentagon Papers,* pp. 386, 440.

40 *Ibid.,* p. 261.

41 President Nixon, speech of 30 April 1970, reprinted in Gettleman, *Conflict in Indochina* (Random House), pp. 382, 384.

town of Memot [Mimot] . . . COSVN's reinforced concrete bunkers are believed to spread 15 to 20 feet beneath the jungle's surface and to house some 5,000 men, many of them specialists in communications and ordnance. . . ."[42] But other "intelligence analysts" in Saigon said flatly that COSVN "is not a static location," but "a mobile group of individuals . . . who seldom sleep more than one night in the same bed."[43] The latter analysts predicted confidently and correctly that COSVN would not be found.

There was similar skepticism within the bureaucracy about alleged captured documents from "Allied intelligence sources" revealing plans for "a series of attacks in South Vietnam the first week in May," "as violent as those of the 1968 Tet offensive," even though these plans were taken seriously by the National Security Council apparatus.[44] Two staff members of the Fulbright committee, who received a quite different impression from briefings in Washington before 29 April and in Vietnam on 2 and 3 May, alluded to these documents acidulously in their report: "There seem to be captured documents to prove almost any point or to support, retrospectively, almost any conclusion."[45]

Both of Nixon's two propositions were finally discredited by the failure of US forces to find either COSVN or massed troop formations in the Cambodian sanctuaries. But long before 30 April the propositions had been authoritatively and repeatedly refuted in the US press. Robert Shaplen, an informed journalist with "left-CIA" contacts since at least the early 1950s, cited "reliable reports" that the so-called COSVN had been moved out of the sanctuaries area "at the time of the [18 March] coup against Sihanouk"; he was corroborating "authoritative reports" in the *New York Times* a month earlier, with a detailed map, showing that COSVN had been moved from near Mimot in Cambodia into virtually inaccessible areas in South Vietnam itself, "in Tayninh between Katum and Somracht" and "in Binhlong between Cheampdau and Khtarek."[46]

Early reports pinpointed General Wheeler and Admiral Moorer as the key hawks in the administration, with plans for a thirty thousand

42 *Newsweek*, 11 May 1970, p. 25.
43 *San Francisco Chronicle*, 4 May 1970, p. 13.
44 *Ibid.*, 2 May 1970, p. 7; *Wall Street Journal*, 28 April 1970, p. 1.
45 US Cong., Senate, Committee on Foreign Relations, *Cambodia: May 1970*, Staff Report (Washington: US GPO, 1970), p. 5; cf. p. 6.
46 Robert Shaplen, "Letter from Indochina," *The New Yorker*, 9 May 1970, p. 139; *New York Times*, 4 April 1970, p. 3; cf. *Washington Post*, 5 April 1970, A6.

man amphibious US" invasion,[47] and corroborated Jack Anderson's *ex post facto* report that the Joint Chiefs endorsed the false picture of COSVN:

> The President is furious with the Joint Chiefs for misleading him about the possibility of destroying the Communist headquarters. They visualized the enemy command center, apparently, as a jungle version of their own elaborate, Pentagon-style headquarters. But other intelligence specialists had warned the headquarters, like a floating crap game, could be folded up quickly and re-established later in some other jungle hideout.[48]

Although this story appears to be itself one more missile in the intelligence battle, it has the ring of truth. In early 1971 there were rumors that the President then relied far less on DIA and more on CIA than he did before Cambodia.

In another leak Jack Anderson traced the false information about COSVN to alleged enemy radio messages intercepted by US Army Intelligence in Vietnam:

> General Creighton Abrams . . . thought he knew where COSVN was located, because the Army had intercepted radio messages from the North Vietnamese command center. Crack troops quickly zeroed in on the location but found no sign of the headquarters. By continuing to monitor enemy radio transmissions, the Army frantically chased but never caught up with COSVN. Army Intelligence finally concluded that the North Vietnamese had set up their mobile radio transmitters a safe distance from the secret headquarters, with runners to carry the messages back and forth.[49]

This new information does not "explain" the error of Army Intelligence and the Joint Chiefs. On the contrary, it increases the probability of an "intelligence conspiracy" to bring about the 30 April invasion of Cambodia by deliberate misrepresentation. What was at issue was not a particular set of geographic coordinates, but the Army's claim of a fixed concrete installation housing five thousand men. Did the intercepted messages corroborate the existence of such

---

47 Oakland *Tribune*, 2 May 1970, p. 1.

48 *San Francisco Chronicle*, 14 May 1970, p. 43. Cf. "End Run by Joint Chiefs? Laird Pushes JCS Reorganization," *Christian Science Monitor*, 14 May 1970: "Many civilians in the Defense Department believe that the Joint Chiefs pulled an end run in their efforts to get the attacks against the border areas approved."

49 *San Francisco Chronicle*, 30 March 1971, p. 33.

an installation or not? Was the reported volume of communications compatible with the failure of twenty-five thousand US and Vietnamese troops to find a headquarters anywhere in the Fishhook area, not just at one location? Above all, did the content of the intercepts corroborate the "captured documents" that spoke of a new Tet offensive in early May, or did they refute them? If the former, the intercepts were probably false; if the latter, they were probably concealed from the White House decision-makers.

Much is unclear about these intercepts, but one conclusion is clear. If Senator Fulbright's committee is serious about unearthing the origins and course of US intervention in Indochina, it will have to examine the recurring importance of alleged "intercepts" in provoking escalation in response both to the Tonkin Gulf incidents in 1964, and in Cambodia in 1970. In particular it must examine the recurring pattern of 1964 and 1970, in which covert aggression by Air America and paramilitary forces under SOG and the CIA, which help to provoke a crisis, are followed by intelligence "intercepts" which falsely indicate enemy offensive actions, and/or provide grounds for open US military retaliation.

The possibility of an intelligence conspiracy, by no means proved but demanding to be investigated, suggests the context of a US President who for some reason is reluctant to escalate. The complex role played by Nixon in the election year 1970 is suggestively like that played by Johnson in the election year 1964. Both men had early in their administration committed themselves to a long-range policy of hanging on in Indochina, even while cultivating a popular public image as seekers of peace. Both men had thus given initial encouragement to CINCPAC and Pentagon fantasies of "victory" in Indochina. As days of electoral reckoning neared, however, both men were increasingly reluctant to approve escalation proposals favored by the Joint Chiefs of Staff. Both Nixon and Johnson reverted to a posture of reluctance and indecision, with overtones of increasing tension between them and their Joint Chiefs, *after* as well as before their swift, spectacular, and highly dubious escalations.

Nixon and Johnson were no doves; what they above all wished to avoid was not escalation, but personal responsibility for the decision to escalate. Such indecision invited parapolitics, in the form of covert operations and manipulated intelligence which effectively took the decision out of the President's hands. What was subsequently resented, by Nixon in particular, was not so much that false intelligence was presented, as the embarrassment that this falsity was so swiftly and easily penetrated by the public.

Such speculations—they are only that—do not address the question whether either President may have encouraged such an intelligence conspiracy against their own administrative procedures. This question, too, is worth exploring, for both leaders owed much of their political success to the oil and aerospace interests that have been lobbying for a strong stand in Indochina.

Nixon's personal role in the Cambodian "crisis" is particularly open to question. On 28 April, the day of the Fishhook decision and two days before his own congressional leaders would hear of it, Nixon told "several private citizens" from eleven "veterans and patriotic organizations" that the action he was soon to order "was imperative if we were to escape the probability of total and humiliating defeat in Vietnam."[50] One needs to ask why Nixon, the professed "strict constructionist" of the Constitution, did not consult with his own Congress over an impending invasion, but instead shared his secret with a small group of retired military officers and their friends. The answer may well be that some of these officers were linked to the American Security Council, a powerful lobby with strong links to Nixon himself, to the US intelligence community, and to the Los Angeles oil and aerospace interests who contributed so much to elect Nixon in 1968.

It is, I think, no digression to look at these links more closely. Among the members of the ASC's National Strategy Committee are Admiral Felix B. Stump, Air America's board chairman and former CINCPAC, and Henry O'Melveny Duque, Nixon's former law partner who sits on the board of California's Union Bank with two directors each from Union Oil of California (the beneficiaries of the Cambodia coup) and TRW (Thompson-Ramo-Woolridge, a leading defense aerospace contractor). Also working with the ASC are vice-presidents from Atlantic-Richfield, Standard Oil of California, and General Dynamics, and Admiral Robert W. Berry, Pacific Coast director for the rarely mentioned but powerful National Security Industrial Association. These interlocks between the ASC, Nixon, intelligence personnel and Pacific-oriented oil companies could be expanded to fill pages.[51]

---

50 *San Francisco Examiner,* 21 May 1970, p. 1.

51 In the ASC library is to be found a bound set of HUAC hearings from 1938 to 1941 "which the flyleaf says is the property of Senator Richard M. Nixon" (*New York Times,* 17 August 1970, p. 21).

An additional word should be said here about the NSIA, which describes itself as a "non-lobbying organization of more than 400 [defense contractors] conceived by James Forrestal in 1944":

> NSIA has won a reputation with both Industry and Government for fair dealing by expressing only those points of view which can provide a stronger national defense program.[52]

Since April 1964 a large percentage of NSIA publications have dealt with industrial support for the National Oceanographic Program, a program under which the ships and planes of the US Naval Oceanographic Office have been used for preliminary oil explorations off the shores of Indochina.[53] The same program also supplies a cover for ELINT missions such as *Pueblo*'s.

Nixon's connections with the intelligence and petroleum establishments were more prominent in 1964, when he was one of the earliest and most sustained advocates of "carrying the Vietnam war north." What business interests did Nixon represent during his two visits to the Far East in 1964, one of which lasted twenty-four days? Why was he accompanied by Henry Kearns, a representative of the Japanese Mitsui interests who had contracted in 1963 for a ten-year oil-drilling program in Indonesia?[54] Is it relevant that Nixon's New York law firm represented Mitsui interests in the United States, and that his former law partner Attorney-General John Mitchell was by all accounts the only strong voice inside Nixon's cabinet in support of the 1970 Cambodian invasion?

In raising these questions I do not wish to suggest that Nixon in 1970 was either an omnipotent Machiavellian or a slavish puppet of hidden economic interests. His own inability to envisage the consequences of his escalation, pathetically like that of Johnson in 1964 and 1965, is revealed by his public statement on May 8, 1970: "I would expect that the South Vietnamese would come out approximately at the same time that we do, because when we come out our logistical support and air support will also come out with them."[55] That both of these predictions were soon proved false is no more evidence of outright dishonesty than the Johnson administration's as-

52 Richard D. Terry, *Ocean Engineering* (Washington: National Security Industrial Association, 1966), p. 1.

53 For titles see *National Union Catalogue, Author List, 1963–67*, 39, 50–51.

54 *World Petroleum* (September 1963), p. 66. Henry Kearns served in 1955 on the Hoover Commission Task Force on Intelligence Activities, under General Mark Clark, a sometime business associate of Nixon's who serves on the National Strategy Committee of the ASC.

55 *New York Times*, 9 May 1971, p. 8.

surances in early 1965 that US and Korean forces were being sent to Vietnam for defensive purposes.

But neither should we simply speak, as some have, of the "illusion of presidential command" over recalcitrant generals. In particular Nixon cannot be exempted from responsibility for systematic programs of covert operations against Cambodia, some of which at least emanated from the White House, like the bombings of April–May 1969, and some of which reached their peak under his administration, like the defoliation program of the same two months. Even though one can expect Nixon to be increasingly cool to escalation proposals as the 1972 election approaches,[56] the machinery that will propose (and perhaps engineer) them is machinery strengthened in large part by himself. Next year he will be free to say no, and even to decline renomination, as did Johnson in 1968, even if his decisions cause his party, like Johnson's, to lose most of its vital support from oil and aerospace interests.

The hypothesis, questions, and line of inquiry proposed in these pages are not addressed to the President, a man powerful precisely because of, and within the limits of, his mediocrity. They are addressed to the members of Congress, most of whom unfortunately are also beholden to support from oil and aerospace. Two major Senate committees, stirred to movement by publication of the Pentagon Papers, have finally announced an inquiry into the causes of the Indochina war. The results of that inquiry could indeed help bring the country to grips with its current constitutional crisis. But if that inquiry declines to lift the veil from covert operations and the manipulation of intelligence, if it says nothing about the relevant economic interests which elected many of these same senators, and above all if it turns our attention from the present back to the past, then the cynicism and disaffection of our youth will assuredly be even deeper than before.

---

56 It would appear that Nixon was considerably more restrained in his bombing operations against North Vietnam during the Laos incursion of 1971 than during the Cambodian invasion of 1970. In large part, no doubt, this was due to the blunt warning issued in February 1971 by Peking.

par·a·pol·i·tics (păr′ ə pŏl′ ə tĭks), *n.* **1.** a system or practice of politics in which accountability is consciously diminished. **2.** generally, covert politics, the conduct of public affairs not by rational debate and responsible decision-making but by indirection, collusion, and deceit. Cf. *conspiracy*[1]. **3.** the political exploitation of irresponsible agencies or parastructures, such as intelligence agencies.

Ex. **1.** "The Nixon doctrine, viewed in retrospect, represented the application of parapolitics on a hitherto unprecedented scale." **2.** "Democracy and parapolitics, even in foreign affairs, are ultimately incompatible."

Chapter Seven
Laos: 1971

The last two years of the Indochina war, marked by the Cambodian invasion of May 1970 and the Laos incursion of February 1971, may well appear in retrospect to have been more important for the strategic shifts behind these operations. The US in particular has shifted from short-range to long-range objectives. The US decisions to move the locus of the heavy fighting into the hinterlands of Cambodia and Laos coincided, it is true, with the long-standing recommendations of senior military officers responsible in the past for successful prosecution of the US ground war. However, the manner of their implementation suggests that this overt expansion of the US role into new areas was only the outward manifestation of a new long-range strategy in which the goal of speedy victory has been replaced by the goal of a protracted stand-off or stalemate, defended where necessary by covert operations.

In this new strategy, the US hopes to rely more and more on technology, not as support for decisive infantry operations, but as a substitute for them. Far more than in previous years, the conspicuous military events of 1970–71 only make sense when considered in the light of this transition to a technological strategy. This strategy in turn cannot be fully understood except in the context of emerging US programs for the long-term economic and political "development" or exploitation of all Southeast Asia.

President Nixon hopes to counter the growing anti-war sentiment with repeated statements that he intends "to end this war," and that he is implementing this promise by reductions in US troop levels and casualty figures. But the criterion for the "winding down" of the war is the level not of US casualties but of casualties overall. These remain high, particularly for innocent civilians. The US Senate Sub-committee on Refugees and its staff recently estimated that civilian war deaths in South Vietnam alone were in the order of between 25,000 and 35,000 in 1970, out of some 125–150,000 casualties.[1] This civilian reath rate was perhaps half that of 1969, but only because the US had expanded the center of fighting into Laos and Cambodia. Thus the 1970 figures had also to take into account an estimated 10,000 war dead and 30,000 casualties in Laos, plus uncounted deaths and casualties in Cambodia which might well be even more. As for war dead, a recent White House report by Henry Kissinger justifies the high casualties suffered by the Saigon Army in the Laos incursion by the claim that casualties on the other side were perhaps five times higher.[2]

There are no words that can translate these statistics into their human meaning of agony and destruction. But the figures themselves refute the official US rhetoric that the war is fading away.

That Nixon, despite the rapidly growing disaffection of public opinion in his own country, has as yet no intention of withdrawing from Vietnam has become increasingly apparent in his own more and more candid admissions. While his presidential campaign speeches in 1968 promised a secret plan to end the war by 1972, his remarks of 16 April 1971 to six American journalists specified that US troops will not be totally withdrawn from South Vietnam until it can defend itself. This will not be soon; his earlier speech of 7 April admitted

1 *New York Times,* 15 March 1971, p. 2.
2 *San Francisco Chronicle,* 24 May 1971.

frankly that to end the war precipitately would "give victory to the Communists." One consequence of the expansion of the US war outside South Vietnam has been to render less relevant the significance of US troop withdrawals inside South Vietnam, unless accompanied by concomitant withdrawals from the whole area, and particularly Thailand. It is increasingly the air bases of Thailand and the US aircraft carriers in the South China sea from which the devastating air war is launched against the hinterlands of Cambodia and Laos.

Defense Secretary Laird, who at one time appeared less than enthusiastic about the geographic expansion of America's role in Indochina, has recently given the most explicit indication that US troop withdrawals from South Vietnam do not mean a lessening of the US commitment to remain in Southeast Asia. In his speech of 13 April 1971 Laird made it clear that US ships and planes will remain after the last US soldier has been pulled out of Vietnam, as "part of the realistic deterrent which we shall maintain in Asia." Although he refused to spell out precisely what residual deterrent he envisaged, reporters linked his remarks to the frequent informed reports in Washington that plans for withdrawal from Vietnam would not also cover Thailand and the South China Sea.

On 17 May 1971 it was revealed that while the overall US troop level in South Vietnam had been halved (from 549,500 in April 1969 to 284,000 in May 1971, the level of US combat forces had been reduced 70 percent, to less than 100,000. This fact, while gratifying to the US combat troops affected, is not an indicator that the United States intends to cease fighting in Indochina, or that overall casualty levels will drop at the same dramatic rate as those of US combat troops. On the contrary, the combat troops being withdrawn represent a discarded strategy. Johnson himself never intended that the troop level of 549,500 should be a permanent or stable one. On the contrary, it represented an exaggeratedly high commitment which the US economy could not sustain for more than a short period (witness the US dollar crisis of 1968) in the vain hope that the backbone of Vietnamese resistance could be crushed before the 1968 US election. After the failure of this gamble, it was almost inevitable that US troops would be withdrawn.

Today the statistics of the withdrawal program which best measure US long-range intentions are those which measure US troop support for artillery and air power. The latter in particular seem to be stabilizing. There were 61,000 US Air Force personnel in Vietnam at the 1968 peak, and there were still 44,000 in November 1970; in April 1971 the total number of US troops supporting air activities in South Vietnam was put at 50,000.[3] There were once 800 US planes in Southeast Asia, exclusive of Guam and Okinawa; there are still 500,[4] and those planes which have been withdrawn are often the oldest and most obsolete.

Further reductions in US Air Force levels are explicitly linked to the US goal of doubling the size of the South Vietnamese Air Force, between early 1970 and late 1971, to forty squadrons, or 800 planes.[5] This ambitious program of expanding the South Vietnamese Air Force, to the level utilized by the US at the peak of the greatest air war in history, would if fully implemented give South Vietnam the seventh largest air force in the world today.

At present the South Vietnamese, despite a series of special training programs and close US supervision, are failing to service adequately the more than thirty squadrons already at their disposal. This is only one of several internal factors which may make it impossible to implement the Nixon program for troop withdrawal without weakening America's "realistic deterrent." This major weakness in the technological strategy is balanced by another on the ground: the continuing tendency of Saigon's district chiefs and commanders to reach local understandings or "accommodations," behind the backs of their US "advisers," with their opposite counterparts in the NLF and PRG.

We more clearly understand the Nixon "game plan" for deterrence accompanied by troop withdrawal when we turn from the statistics of withdrawal to those available for measuring the current levels of technological air and artillery support. The tonnages of the US air war in Indochina were reported from Pentagon sources by *Environment* in November 1971 (p. 3):

Munitions Used in Indochina War (in Thousands of Tons)

YEAR	AIR MUNITIONS	SURFACE MUNITIONS	TOTAL
1965	315		315
1966	512	582	1,094
1967	932	1,206	2,139
1968	1,431	1,502	2,933
1969	1,387	1,404	2,791
1970	978	1,194	2,172
Total	5,556	5,888	11,444

3 *Washington Post*, 29 November 1970, A29; *New York Times*, 7 April 1971, p. 14.
4 *San Francisco Examiner*, 25 November 1970.
5 *New York Times*, 29 January 1970, p. 12.

An additional 5,155,700 tons of US ordnance were expended by artillery and troops in the period from 1 January 1968 to 30 May 1970, meaning that in all well over ten million tons of ordnance had been spent in Vietnam. It will be seen that in the Vietnam air war alone the US tonnage dropped has more than doubled that used in World War II (2,119,823 tons), and that the tonnage actually dropped in the first five months of 1970 (594,171 tons) considerably exceeds the punishing total dropped in three years of the Korean war (386,000 tons). One year later, in March 1971, the Pentagon's announced level of tonnage in Indochina showed almost no decline (92,191 tons, or an annual rate of 1,106,000).[6] The average daily tonnage under Nixon is still higher than under Johnson.

Let us for a moment compare these figures to those of the opposition. US sources estimate that the total NLF ordnance expenditures rose from an average of two to three tons a day in calm periods to a peak of twenty-seven tons a day through the Tet offensive of 1968. By April 1969 this level had dropped to an estimated thirteen tons a day. Through the whole of 1969 US ordnance levels averaged 7,551 tons a day.

The latest statistics on the US air war are unfortunately not available to this writer. It is clear, however, that in the 1970–71 period the Nixon administration expanded the range of the air war into Cambodia, the sole part of Indochina hitherto exempted from this rain of destruction. It seems likely that the anomalous "sanctuary" supplied by Cambodia proved quite incompatible with the growing US reliance on air power in place of ground troops, and that this was a prime reason why Cambodia's neutrality and territorial integrity were violated in 1970. Although Nixon first predicted that the US would not supply tactical air support in Cambodia after 30 June 1970, such support, coupled with US helicopter airlifting of South Vietnamese troops, became normal in Cambodia after January 1971, with the first ephemeral clearing of Highway 4 linking Phnom Penh to the ocean port of Kampong Som. In the first twenty days of January US plane and helicopter sorties in Cambodia were put at fifty a day.[7] By April 1971 US air strikes in Cambodia alone were estimated to average 300 a day, or 9,000 a month.[8]

By escalating to this level the air war in Cambodia is now fully integrated into that being fought in Laos and the strategic mountain

6 *New York Review of Books,* 17 June 1971, p. 19.
7 *Wall Street Journal,* 21 January 1971.
8 *New York Times,* 9 April 1971, p. 5.

and jungle areas of South Vietnam. This air war over the hinterland dates back to early 1968, as can be seen by the statistics available for Laos. In early 1968 US air sorties over Laos averaged between 1,000 and 3,500 a month, or between one-ninth and one-third of the current monthly rate in Cambodia. That relatively restricted level of bombing had already destroyed nearly all the Pathet Lao villages in northeastern Laos, and had already generated most of the 750,000 to one million refugees, or some 25 percent of the Laotian population, now estimated by a Senate subcommittee to exist in that country.[9] The *New York Times* estimates that there are five million refugees in South Vietnam, or 30 percent of the population, and one million in Cambodia, or 15 percent. It adds that "the air war . . . is generally accepted as a major cause of the mass displacements."[10]

Despite this success in isolating the Pathet Lao forces from the economic support of the local population, US air strikes against the Laotian mountain areas were sharply augmented both under Johnson in 1968 and again under Nixon in 1969, to levels of some 18,000–27,000 sorties a month. The inspiration for this new air strategy seems to have been the six-week siege of Khe Sanh in early 1968, during which the US Air Force dropped 100,000 tons of bombs in a single area roughly five miles in diameter, converting a jungle into a desert. What really happened at Khe Sanh is unclear (the opposing forces may have withdrawn voluntarily). It is clear that the Pentagon treated the lifting of the siege, in the words of a senior Army general, as "probably the first major ground action won entirely or almost entirely by air power."[11] Since then the US air war has been expanded, in both area and intensity, but also concentrated into a protective and enveloping "umbrella" embracing the spine of the Laotian and Cambodian hinterland and stretching from both sides of the Vietnamese DMZ into areas of northeastern Thailand. The scattered populations of these more sparsely inhabited areas have been largely driven out; where the bombing itself has not achieved this result, the US and local forces, as in the Laotian Plaine des Jarres, northern South Vietnam, and eastern Cambodia, have resorted to forced relocation on a massive scale.

In the resulting free-fire zones the United States has relied heavily

9 *Ibid.*, 15 March 1971, p. 37.

10 *Ibid.*, 21 April 1971, p. 16. The Senate Subcommittee estimated that there had been 1.5 million refugees in Cambodia (25 percent of the total population); cf. also 15 March 1971, p. 37.

11 Townsend Hoopes, *The Limits of Intervention* (McKay), p. 214; quoted with amplification in *New York Review of Books*, 18 June 1970, p. 32.

on B-52s and since early 1971 on huge 7.5-ton bombs, the largest in the US non-nuclear arsenal. Since 1968 there has been an absolute decline in the inventory of planes available (from 800 to 500) and also in the tonnages dropped. But these rates of decline, particularly in tonnages, have lagged considerably behind the rate of "Vietnamization" suggested by the highly publicized statistics for the withdrawal of US troops. The United States is still estimated by many to be dropping over a million tons of bombs a year (in excess of the 1967 level), and the smallest estimate I have seen is 550,000 tons (in excess of the 1966 level). Despite their cost of one million dollars a day, B-52 raids from Thailand have been stabilized since August 1970 at a rate of about 1,000 a month; the B-52s account for a monthly average total of 28,000 tons, or a kiloton equivalent exceeding that of the Hiroshima bomb. This amounts to 336,000 tons a year from B-52s alone, an annual total that comes close to the three-year total of 386,000 tons in the Korean war. Heavy bombs from B-52s have now created over five million bomb craters in the depopulated free-strike zones; this "craterization" of whole areas, which will take years to undo, represents ecological devastation on a scale that renders the old defoliation programs obsolete.

Though the heart of the technological strategy is still clearly the air war, supported to a lesser extent by artillery, it is the intention of the Pentagon to find technological equivalents for infantry as well, through development of the so-called automated or electronic battlefield. The US already uses a variety of acoustic and seismic sensors to pinpoint any target movements along the Ho Chi Minh trail. It has digital computers that can store information even from personnel-detection radars, and is now experimenting with a variety of self-arming and self-detonating anti-personnel weapons. Robots, linked by radio with computers, have reached the stage of mechanical testings. In November 1970 the Senate Armed Services Preparedness Investigating Subcommittee announced that $3.25 billion had already been appropriated for automated battlefield programs, which *Business Week* has estimated will run ultimately to a cost of $20 billion.[12]

Both the Cambodian invasion and the Laotian incursion took the heavy fighting inland, away from South Vietnam's populated areas and into zones of uninhibited air support. Both are thus outward or "high-profile" manifestations of this sustained, larger, but

12 For details, see Paul Dickson and John Rothchild, "Electronic Battlefield: Strangelove's Answer to War Crimes," *Washington Monthly* (May 1971), pp. 6–14; *Electronics,* 26 October 1970.

less newsworthy air strategy. Neither adventure was wholly unprecedented, except in overtness and in scale. Small covert forces of US
and South Vietnamese troops had made sporadic forays and/or
maintained "intelligence" outposts in these supposedly neutral areas
since at least 1964, and Nixon had first ordered bombing strikes
against the Cambodian hinterland in the spring of 1969. What was
new was the flagrant way in which the Americans used South Vietnamese forces to subjugate the ethnically distinct Cambodians and
Laotians; the genocidal repression against civilians, particularly the
ethnic Vietnamese in Cambodia, who had not previously been directly involved; and the scale of the Cambodia and Laos adventures.

Both operations represented temporary tactical re-escalations of
the war to unprecedented levels. Before 1970 the largest ground
operation had been Operation Junction City of February 1967 in
Tayninh province, using 25,000 US and South Vietnamese troops.
The Fishhook phase of the Cambodian invasion alone used the same
number of troops.[13] The February Laotian incursion involved at least
20,000 South Vietnamese and 9,000 US troops, while a simultaneous
coordinated sweep of the Cambodian Fishhook utilized another
10,000 South Vietnamese troops.[14] The totals may have been larger;
it was later revealed that 50,000 South Vietnamese main force units
had been temporarily removed from their role of support for the
pacification program. The Laotian incursion was also marked by an
unprecedented use of helicopters to move and supply troops, and in
this sense can be seen as an experiment in the "Vietnamization" plans
for reducing combat-troop levels by making them more rapidly de-
ployable.

One can assess the many-faceted results of both operations only
by taking into account the emerging US air strategy. In terms of
victory both US initiatives were clearly failures. The Khmer Rouges
are now far stronger, and the Phnom Penh government far weaker,
than ever before. Indeed Phnom Penh is now largely cut off from all
of its territory except that occupied by South Vietnamese invaders.
Rather like the Laotian capital of Luang Prabang to the north, it is
susceptible to being overrun by coalition troops at any time they
might choose. This was illustrated by the ease with which a small
band of Khmer Rouge sappers demolished the Cambodian Air Force
stationed at Phnom Penh's airport.[15]

13 *Wall Street Journal*, 11 May 1970, p. 1.
14 *New York Times*, 4 February 1971, p. 1.
15 *Ibid.*, 22 January 1971, p. 1.

The Laotian incursion, measured by these criteria, was an even more conspicuous failure. Not only were South Vietnam's irreplaceable Ranger battalions decimated, but the rout of these elite forces demonstrated to the world, and more importantly to US politicians and public opinion, that the South Vietnamese army is in no way ready to take over a ground combat role from the Americans. One result, as after the Tet offensive of 1968, has been an accelerated disillusion inside the United States, not only with the war, but also with Nixon's drawn-out procedures for protracting and "Vietnamizing" it. One of the most dramatic features of the Laotian incursion was the inability of the South Vietnamese to support themselves, even with unprecedented helicopter and air support, beyond the twelve-mile range of heavy US artillery. All this has greatly increased political disquiet in the United States about Nixon's program of phased withdrawal without concessions at the conference table. Even US generals, such as General Gavin, are asking whether US air power will be able to protect US troops when they reach the maximum level of 50,000 or so which some White House staff members have projected for late 1972.[16]

In mid-February a US colonel described the Laotian incursion as the biggest battle of the war, one in which the winner would take all.[17] If this were really so, the US and South Vietnamese would now clearly be defeated; yet Nixon's resistance to anti-war sentiment in the United States is now greater and more open than ever. This would suggest that continued instability in the areas of the Cambodian and Laotian campaigns has not dismayed him, since in fact his goal was not swift victory but the continuation of a stand-off. By this criterion the proponents of air war and a technological strategy reached a quite different assessment of both campaigns. Like Henry Kissinger's secret report to the president, they point instead to the large number of casualties inflicted by US air power in fighting where the role of the South Vietnamese forces is reduced to that of "bait" to draw and identify enemy concentrations. They point to the fact that in bringing war closer to the peoples of Cambodia and Laos they have taken the war farther away from the people of South Vietnam, the nation selected by US policy to share with Thailand hegemony over the states of Indochina. This result, they argue, has been accompanied by an end to the acute political instability that paralyzed the Saigon government in 1964.

16 *US News and World Report,* 26 April 1971.
17 *Los Angeles Times,* 16 February 1971, p. 11.

Clearly a major test of this technological strategy will be the success of the so-called pacification program for the elimination of the NLF military and political organization among the Vietnamese people. The PRG in its twelve-point program of action announced on 10 June 1969 indicated that it would continue to put political priorities ("to strengthen the resistance potential of the people in all fields" and "develop the revolutionary power at all levels") ahead of military ones ("to consolidate and widen the liberated zone").[18] That it has continued to make progress in this area is officially denied by Saigon and the US, but conceded by many US officials and observers.

The success of the PRG is reflected in the new billion-dollar pacification program launched by the United States on 1 March 1971, a program marked by dramatic escalation of the violent and repressive phases of past ones, and the virtual absence of any lip-service to the goal of "winning the minds and hearts of the people."[19] In particular the new program calls for an expansion of the controversial Operation Phoenix to provide for the elimination by murder or capture of 14,400 NLF agents in one year. The plan also calls for the expansion of the local "People's Self-Defense Forces" from one-half million to four million, including children over the age of seven, and a stepped-up use of informers.

In announcing this new program, the United States recognized that the NLF apparatus was still what it called a "major problem" in eight out of forty-four provinces. Significantly, however, these eight provinces included four in the delta which allegedly had already been "pacified." This indicates that, as in the past, the United States will give top priority to pacification efforts in selected provinces close to Saigon. This concentrated effort, coupled with the forced relocation of peasants from the northernmost provinces, suggests that by early 1971 the United States had indeed moved to a modified enclave strategy in which the Saigon area would serve, along with Thailand, as a redoubt for the preservation of a superficial US ascendancy in Indochina. One can well ask whether Nixon's determination to hang on in Indochina is related to recent rumors of imminent major offshore oil discoveries in the nearby southern waters of the Mekong delta region.

There are increasing reports of US dissatisfaction with both corruption and false reporting in administering the pacification program

18 *Three Documents of the National Liberation Front* (Introduction by Gabriel Kolko) (Boston: Beacon Press, 1970), p. 35.
19 *New York Times,* 7 April 1971, pp. 1, 15.

by Saigon officials. In most cases, the incredibly high number of hamlets rated as "secure" under the HES (Hamlet Evaluation System) ratings is to be attributed to the lack of candor between local officials and their US advisers, the desire of General Thieu to appear successful as the 1971 Vietnamese election approached and to the increasing number of local "accommodations" between Vietnamese officials on both sides.[20] Many US officials now frankly concede that the NLF and PRG have successfully infiltrated the Saigon government and army itself at the highest levels. To this infiltration is attributed the failure of the United States ever to catch its enemies by surprise, as in the futile prisoner-of-war incursion into North Vietnam. In this context, Nguyen Cao Ky's recent expressions of weariness with the war are reminiscent of apparent "peace feelers" put out by Ngo Dinh Nhu in 1963, and Nguyen Khanh in 1964, in both cases just before they were overthrown in US-encouraged coups. All in all, however, Ky's prediction on 18 April 1971 that it would be fifteen to twenty years before South Vietnam could defend itself[21] seems a realistic appraisal of the present instability of Saigon. As I write (in May 1971), major ground action is reportedly being mounted by NLF forces only twenty-five miles from the garrison city of Saigon itself.

Nixon's game-plan of a technological strategy is threatened by its political bankruptcy on the level of "pacification." It is also inherently unstable on the geopolitical level in that it has threatened to draw Thailand, and possibly other countries, more and more into the war. The concentration of B-52s, electronic data networks, and other costly equipment in Thailand has forced the United States to give exaggerated attention to counterinsurgency efforts there, particularly in endemically dissident areas of ethnic minorities as in northeastern Thailand. Many observers conclude that the repressive bombings, defoliation, and forced relocations of this stepped-up counterinsurgency campaign in Thailand are themselves prime forces in generating a strong regional liberation movement.[22]

Thailand itself is playing a more and more open military role, especially in Laos, where Senator Fulbright has announced that 4,800 Thai troops are engaged in the war.[23] More recently, it has been reported that

20 *Ibid.*, 5 April 1971, p. 8; 21 April 1971, p. 16.

21 *Ibid.*, 19 April 1971, p. 7.

22 Al McCoy, "Subcontracting Counterinsurgency: Academics in Thailand, 1954–1970," *Bulletin of Committee of Concerned Asian Scholars* (February 1971), pp. 56–70.

23 *New York Times,* 22 May 1971, p. 5.

American estimates put the number of Thai troops in Laos at between 5,000 and 6,000 now. The Pathet Lao claim 20,000. Other diplomatic sources estimate 7,000 to 10,000. . . . This means Thai troops will soon approach one-third of the 30,000 American-directed "irregular forces" in Laos.[24]

Thai troops have been reported fighting not only in their losing battle for the Bolovens plateau in the Laotian panhandle,[25] but also at the time of the Laotian incursion close to the borders of North Vietnam in the strategic Plaine des Jarres area. Highway 7, which descends into the Ca valley from the Plaine des Jarres to the North Vietnamese coast near Vinh, is a natural route for the invasion of North Vietnam; and from Saigon at this time there were numerous threats of just such an invasion,[26] while US warships gathered menacingly in the Tonkin Gulf. Whether such an invasion was actually contemplated, or was merely a decoy operation to divert North Vietnamese energies from the relief of Tchepone, Thailand's increasingly provocative threats to liberated Laos, and to North Vietnam itself, are inviting retaliation.

The failure of the Laotian incursion to achieve even its stated objectives suggests that at the outset some greater escalation had originally been contemplated in its support. The *New York Times* wrote at the outset that the incursion "defies all logic," pointing to Pentagon staff reports in the 1960s that a minimum of 75,000 US troops would be required to cut the trail.[27] On 17 February Nixon repeated that apart from the use of tactical nuclear weapons there were no limits on the use of US air power in all Indochina—an obvious threat in the direction of North Vietnam.[28] According to reports from both sides, the bombing of North Vietnam did increase in this period, yet neither as intensively nor as extensively as might have been expected in support of the precarious Laos incursion. The United States appears to have been deterred from more massive air strikes by the unmistakable warnings from Peking in the first two weeks of February, a fact which may have contributed in turn to the "ping-pong" phase of more relaxed US-Chinese relations.

One should not think that with the advent of "ping-pong diplomacy" the threat of great-power confrontation in Indochina has passed. Though there are few outspoken advocates of escalation to-

24 *San Francisco Chronicle,* 7 December 1971, p. 16.

25 *Washington Post,* 21 January 1971, A1.

26 *Christian Science Monitor,* 12 February 1971.

27 *New York Times,* 5 February 1971, p. 30.

28 *Ibid.,* 18 February 1971, p. 1.

day in Saigon, Bangkok, or Washington itself, there are many whose continuance in power depends on at least the achievement of a minimal stand-off through the technological strategy. If, as seems highly possible, that strategy fails to supply a credible degree of protection, there will be those who will seek to induce another US escalation—perhaps through recourse to nuclear weapons, the only significant technological asset as yet untried in the war. To Peking, as to many Americans, an article in the January 1971 issue of *Foreign Affairs* appeared to be a trial balloon "sounding out public opinion" on the use of nuclear weapons in Indochina.[29] As in 1964 and 1968, the bureaucratic pressures to escalate in response to a new "crisis" may well increase, particularly if Nixon makes political concessions in a bid for popularity during the US elections. Thus a covertly induced "crisis" like those involving the *Maddox* and the *Pueblo* seems not impossible. And on 8 May 1970, Nixon warned that if the enemy escalated in the future, "we will move decisively and not step-by-step."

Alternatively, particularly if US public opinion were to prevail, the United States might reverse its policy of two decades in Southeast Asia and accept an unconditional withdrawal of its troops from Indochina. As yet there has been no premonition of such a reversal in the technological strategy as we have described it. On the contrary, US investment in South Vietnam, which Ambassador Bunker recently called an important part of the US "Vietnamization" program,[30] has been stepped up in the wake of the ill-fated Laos incursion. With liberal development subsidies and war-risk insurance supplied by the US government, US companies are clearly being invited to help create the kind of artificially stimulated and superficially prosperous urban economy that one sees today in South Korea. As this investment progresses, the pain and cost of US extrication from Indochina will become greater.

This is especially true of the offshore oil exploration program which is now envisaged for eighteen concessions south of the Mekong delta and westward toward Cambodia. The US Navy has played a key role in the geological and geophysical exploration of this basin of the South China Sea, in various operations dating back to 1957. The interest of major US oil companies in the offshore development of the entire basin has become evident since about 1963. Since about 1968 or 1969 there has been increasing interest in the offshore oil prospects

29 *Peking Review*, 12 February 1971.
30 Department of State, *Bulletin*, 15 February 1971.

of South Vietnam itself, particularly in the waters fronting on Cambodia. Recent US commercial journals have reported speculation that "the ocean floor off South Vietnam . . . may contain the richest petroleum deposits in Southeast Asia" and "that the entire Far East could contain oil deposits rivaling those of the Middle East."[31]

In June 1969, one month after the first public report of South Vietnamese offshore oil possibilities, a bill for petroleum development was introduced in the Saigon parliament, and in December 1970 its promulgation as law opened the way for private US and international bidding on offshore leases. The bill was modeled on a Thailand law drafted by Walter Levy, a New York consultant to major oil companies who during World War II was petroleum chief for the Office of Strategic Services. Ambassador Bunker specifically referred to the opportunities presented by this law in his speech on the importance to "Vietnamization" of "an effective strategy . . . to attract private investment."

It is obvious that major oil discoveries in South Vietnam could help end that country's perennial economic crisis, which remains chronic despite US-supplied and import-support programs on the order of $2 billion a year.[32] The South Vietnamese economy, whose inflation rate is perhaps the worst in the world, was described last fall by a State Department official as "Thieu's Achilles heel."[33] Only such discoveries could rationalize the commitment to Indochina of US resources which in the last seven years has brought simultaneous inflation and recession to the US economy as well. It is thus possible that oil prospects help explain why Nixon, after being elected on a pledge to end the war, has since expanded it to include a permanent South Vietnamese occupation of eastern Cambodia. This invasion, the intensified pacification of the delta provinces, and the transfer of heavy fighting to the hinterlands of Cambodia and Laos, all seem well-suited to favor offshore exploration in the primary area around the island of Poulo Panjang, adjacent to Cambodia and South Vietnam.

I recently spoke to two opposition and supposedly "anti-war" senators from Saigon, who expressed the hope that their civilian slate would win in the fall 1971 elections. They spoke candidly of long-term prospects for the Saigon regime. The NLF, as an "undemocratic force," should not be allowed to participate in the forthcoming

31 *Journal of Commerce,* 1 April 1971; *Forbes,* 15 March 1971.
32 *Christian Science Monitor,* 20 April 1971.
33 *Business Week,* 24 October 1970; *Wall Street Journal,* 24 August 1970, p. 1, 9.

elections, "but maybe in the next ones." The US air war would probably have to continue, "as long as Hanoi receives aid (*sic*) from abroad." Their civilian slate, if elected to power, would solicit US oil investment before a political settlement to the war was reached, "because frankly no Saigon government could afford not to."

In other words, Saigon elections of 1971 offered no challenge to the continuance of US intervention in Southeast Asia, even while Duong van Minh was still a candidate. The future of Thieu seems unalterably vested in the South Vietnamese Army and a sustained war effort; but his replacement by General Duong van Minh and his civilian allies would probably only presage a return to the "low-profile" involvement of the 1950s in which the leading US role would again be given to intelligence and other civilian agencies.

The latter course would ensure the prolongation of the Indochina war and the continued suffering of the peasants, even if a few enclaves around capital cities were outwardly "pacified."

Some 12,000 Nationalist troops fled across the Yunnan border and set up camp in the lush poppy-growing area of northern Burma. Occasionally they conducted hit-and-run raids into Red China, but soon they grew tired of it and decided to settle down and become rich by growing opium. Nevertheless, the CIA saw these troops as a thorn in Mao's side and continued to supply them with arms and money. Many of the supplies were air-dropped by a CIA-backed company called Air America, a firm that still exists today supplementing the US military effort in Vietnam.

George Thayer, *The War Business*

Chapter Eight
Opium, the China Lobby,
and the CIA

Professor Samuel Eliot Morison has written how in 1903 Theodore Roosevelt, "in the face of international law and morality," secretly ordered the US Navy to support the "revolutionary" secession of Panama from Colombia. The secession, which led swiftly to the Canal Zone treaty, is described by him as a plan by "Panama businessmen, agents of the French company [which stood to gain $40 million in compensation under the treaty] and United States army officers."[1] He neglects to add that the "agents" of the French Panama Canal Company were the New York investment bankers J. and W. Seligman and their Washington lobbyist Buneau-Varilla,

1 Samuel Eliot Morison, *The Oxford History of the American People* (New York: Oxford University Press, 1965), pp. 825–26. Pointing to the subsequent impact on all Latin America, Morison concludes that "the United States is paying dear today for Roosevelt's impetuosity in 1903."

who organized and financed the "revolution" out of a suite in the Waldorf-Astoria. The intervention of the US Navy was not Roosevelt's idea but Buneau-Varilla's, who called on the President and spoke to him about "American lives and interests." Even the flag of the new Panamanian Republic, for which later generations of more idealistic nationalists have demonstrated and died, was designed and handstitched by Buneau-Varilla out of Macy's silk, at the summer house of James Seligman in Westchester, New York.[2]

In some ways the Panama exercise in "big stick" partition, with its subsequent thorough but ineffective congressional exposure and its hidden economic interests, including a "French company" financed through Wall Street, is an instructive precedent for the postwar US involvement in Indochina.[3] Legally, however, the picture might appear to be different, for many of Buneau-Varilla's activities in preparing for revolution and war would today be outlawed under section 956–60 of the US Criminal Code. In theory at least, responsibility for this kind of defense of American "interests" is now a monopoly of the CIA, even if the CIA continues to maintain close contact with J. and W. Seligman and similar Wall Street institutions.

These contacts have been powerful, and in 1948 it was pressure from Wall Street that succeeded in pushing the infant CIA into its first covert operations. President Truman has since declared his unhappiness at this deflection of the CIA from its intelligence function: "I never had any thought . . . when I set up the CIA that it would be injected into peacetime cloak-and-dagger operations.[4] His intentions, however, counted for less than those of Allen Dulles, then a New York corporation lawyer and President of the Council on Foreign Relations. The administration became concerned that the Communists might shortly win the Italian elections:

Forrestal felt that secret counteraction was vital, but his initial assessment was that the Italian operation would have to be private.

2 Stephen Birmingham, *"Our Crowd": The Great Jewish Families of New York* (New York: Harper & Row, 1967), pp. 236–38; US Congress Senate Documents, 58th Cong., 2nd Sess., No. 53; House Documents, 58th Cong., 1st Sess., No. 8. The French government was so far from involving itself in this campaign to recuperate the assets of the defunct Paris company that "the French Foreign Minister in Washington wired Buneau-Varilla's brother in Paris, saying that Philippe's [Congressional lobbying] activities were embarrassing to France, and suggesting that Philippe had lost his mind" (Birmingham, p. 237).

3 For example, the "nation-building" activities in Vietnam of the immigrant European liberal Joseph Buttinger can be compared to those of the French Liberal Buneau-Varilla, "who had first caught the attention of the Seligmans through his activities in the Dreyfus case."

4 *Washington Post,* 22 December 1963, A11; quoted in Roger Hilsman, *To Move a Nation* (Garden City, N.Y.: Doubleday, 1967), p. 63.

The wealthy industrialists in Milan were hesitant to provide the money, fearing reprisals if the Communists won, and so the hat was passed at the Brook Club in New York. But Allen Dulles felt the problem could not be handled effectively in private hands. He urged strongly that the government establish a covert organization. Because of the desire to finance the organization with unvouchered funds, the decision was made to create it under the National Security Council.[5]

This fateful essay in nonaccountability is instructive: the Defense Secretary felt the operation should be private, but a private corporation lawyer determined it should be public. By this arrangement, presumably, the men in the Brook Club even got their money back; since then the funds (unvouchered) have been ours.

Truman's lack of sympathy for the way the CIA was being "diverted" into covert operations did not result in any measures to curb control of the CIA by Wall Street Republicans. On the contrary, as the CIA began to burgeon under Bedell Smith, *all seven* persons who are known to have served as deputy directors of the CIA under Smith and Truman came from New York legal and financial circles.[6]

These men used their corporate experience and connections to set up a number of dummy private enterprises, as "proprietaries" or wholly owned fronts for the CIA, particularly for Far Eastern opera-

---

5 David Wise and Thomas B. Ross, *The Espionage Establishment* (New York: Random House, 1967), p. 166.

6 Frank G. Wisner (OSS) came to the government in 1948 from the Wall Street legal firm of Carter, Ledyard and Milburn, which represented various Rockefeller, Whitney, and Standard Oil interests. As director of the "Office of Policy Coordination," which became the CIA's Plans Division on 4 January 1951, Wisner was in charge of the CIA's covert operations.

William Harding Jackson (Republican), Smith's Deputy Director in 1950–51, had been with Carter, Ledyard and Milburn from 1934 to 1947, and was now an investment partner of John Hay Whitney on the board of Bankers Trust.

Allen Welsh Dulles (OSS, Republican), a wartime director of J. Henry Schroder Banking Corporation and longtime partner of Sullivan and Cromwell (linked with various Rockefeller and Schroeder interests), succeeded Jackson as Deputy Director in August 1951.

Murray McConnel, president of the Manufacturers Capital Corporation on Wall Street, was the CIA's Deputy Director for Administration in 1950 and 1951.

Walter Reid Wolf (Republican), a vice-president of the National City Bank of New York and of its investment affiliate City Bank Farmers Trust, was a CIA Deputy Director (presumably McConnel's successor) from 1951 to 1953.

Robert Amory, Jr. (son of a New York manufacturer who was a co-director of at least three Boston firms with directors of United Fruit), came to the CIA as Deputy Director for Intelligence in 1952 (according to *Who's Who*).

Loftus E. Becker, of the Wall Street law firm Cahill, Gordon, Reindel and Ohl (representing the investment firms of Dillon Read and Stone and Webster), went on leave to the CIA in April 1951 and was named Deputy Director "for Intelligence" (according to the Martindale-Hubbard Law Directory, 1965, p. 4707) for a year beginning 21 January 1952.

All of these seven men except Becker were also listed in the select *New York Social Register*, and thus were members not only of New York's financial-legal elite but of its hereditary upper class. The known links between the CIA and Civil Air Transport-Air America date from this period, when New York finance enjoyed a monopoly over the CIA's top civilian appointments.

tions. On the model of William Pawley's CAMCO company which had fronted for General Chennault and the Flying Tigers in 1941, the capital came from government sources, but profits if any are said to have been retained by the proprietary in question.

Thus William Ray Peers, an OSS hand from Burma and China who later was the Army Chief of Staff's Special Assistant for Special Warfare Activities, headed up Western Enterprises, Inc., in Taiwan, a cover for the launching of Kuomintang commando raids from Quemoy and Matsu.[7] Willis Bird (OSS China) headed a Bangkok "trading company" called Sea Supply, Inc., which supplied arms and other supplies to the KMT troops of General Li Mi in Burma,[8] and later trained the Thai border police under Thai Interior Minister Phao Sriyanon.[9]

By far the largest CIA proprietary in Asia was the Delaware corporation CAT Inc., chartered in July 1950 and known since 31 March 1959 as Air America, Inc. General Lansdale's memorandum of July 1961 to Maxwell Taylor on unconventional warfare, published as part of the Pentagon Papers, confirmed this commonly known fact:

> CAT. Civil Air Transport (Chinese Nationalist). CAT is a commercial airline engaged in scheduled and nonscheduled air operations throughout the Far East, with headquarters and large maintenance facilities located in Taiwan. CAT, a CIA proprietary, provides air logistical support under commercial cover to most CIA and other US Government agencies' requirements. . . . During the past ten years, it has had some notable achievements, including support of the Chinese Nationalist withdrawal from the mainland, air drop support to the French at Dien Bien Phu, complete logistical and tactical air support for the [1958] Indonesian operation, air lifts of refugees from North Vietnam, more than 200 overflights of Mainland China and Tibet, and extensive support in Laos during the current [1961] crisis.[10]

General Lansdale erred, however, in failing to distinguish between the Taiwan commercial airline CAT Co., Ltd., alias Civil Air Transport or CATCL, and the American operating firm CAT, Inc., the CIA proprietary which supplied CATCL with pilots and other personnel.

---

7 David Wise and Thomas B. Ross, *The Invisible Government* (New York: Bantam, 1965), pp. 115–16; *New Republic,* 12 April 1969, p. 8.

8 Wise and Ross, *Invisible Government,* p. 140.

9 *New York Times,* 20 September 1957, p. 7.

10 *The Pentagon Papers* (New York: Bantam, 1971), p. 137.

Sixty percent of the capital and control of CATCL was KMT-Chinese Nationalist, represented by officers of the former Kincheng Bank in Shanghai who allegedly fronted for T. V. Soong and/or his sister Madame Chiang Kai-shek.[11]

CATCL had been set up by General Chennault in 1946, after the US State Department cited pressure from T.V. Soong and Madame Chiang as grounds for forcing UNRRA to reverse itself and subsidize the creation of Chennault's airline.[12] Chennault's partner in CAT was Whiting Willauer, a US "economic intelligence" officer who during World War II supplied the Flying Tigers as an officer of China Defense Supplies under T. V. Soong. CAT's treasurer in the 1940s was James J. Brennan, another member of the wartime Chennault-Corcoran-Alsop "Washington squadron," who after the war served as T. V. Soong's personal secretary in China. The lawyer for CAT, as for the Flying Tigers, was Tommy Corcoran, who after the war was rumored to be handling T. V. Soong's multimillion-dollar investments in the United States.[13]

In the late 1940s CAT flew military support missions for the Kuomintang against the Communists, while Chennault lobbied openly from a Washington office against the more cautious China policy of the Truman-Acheson State Department. In November 1949 Chennault, after a similar visit by Chiang, flew to Syngman Rhee in Korea, "to give him a plan for the Korean military air force," even though at this time it was still US official policy to deny Rhee planes, to discourage him from invading North Korea.[14] In December 1949, *Time* later claimed, Dean Acheson told one of its correspondents that "what we must do now is shake loose from the Chinese Nationalists," while in January 1949 George Kennan predicted that "by next year at this time we will have recognized the Chinese Communists."[15] All such thoughts were frustrated by the sudden outbreak of the Korean

11 Arnold Dibble, "The Nine Lives of CAT—II," *Saturday Evening Post,* 18 May 1968, p. 50; *New York Times,* 11 November 1949, p. 14; 5 April 1970, p. 22; *Free China Review,* November 1963, p. 31. In 1949 the Kincheng Bank ostensibly severed its connections with CAT, in the vain hope of continuing to operate on the mainland. But Wang Wen-san, then manager of the Kincheng Bank, is still chairman of CATCL's board, on which the KMT-Chinese Nationalists have three of the five seats. Air America pilots still circulate the rumor that "Madame Chiang owns the planes and we lease them from her" (*San Francisco Chronicle,* 2 April 1970, p. 31).

12 Charles Wertenbaker, "The China Lobby," *Reporter,* 15 April 1952, p. 9.

13 John R. Beal, *Marshall in China* (New York: Doubleday, 1970), p. 85.

14 US Congress, House, Committee on Un-American Activities, *International Communism: Consultation with Major-General Claire Lee Chennault,* 85th Cong., 2nd Sess., 23 April 1958, pp. 9–10; US Department of State, *US Policy in the Korean Crisis* (Washington: GPO, 1950), pp. 21–22.

15 *Time,* 15 October 1951, p. 23.

war on 25 June 1950—an event still imperfectly understood, but which may have been anticipated by certain KMT speculators who because of the war "cleared an estimated profit of about $30,000,-000" in soybeans.[16] President Nixon, as he approaches reelection, would do well to review the history of previous efforts at rapprochement with Peking, which were again frustrated by the Quemoy crises of 1954 and 1958.

Shortly after the outbreak of the Korean war, on 10 July 1950, CAT, Inc. (along with its holding company Airdale Corp.) was chartered in Delaware. The American company CAT, Inc. promptly supplied planes, pilots and US airlift contracts to the Taiwan company CATCL, which in this period was the sole flag air carrier of Chiang's new republic.[17] While Tommy Corcoran continued to represent Soong, Chennault, and CATCL, the aviation law firm of Pogue and Neal handled the incorporation of CAT, Inc., whose later counsel Brackley Shaw was a former Army intelligence officer and general counsel for the Air Force. During this period of formation a vice-president of the National City Bank of New York, Walter Reid Wolf, was recruited briefly as a CIA Deputy Director, from 1951 to 1953; soon afterwards two of Wolf's fellow-directors in the small Empire City Savings Bank (Samuel Sloan Walker and Arthur B. Richardson) were named to the board of CAT, Inc., where they have been sitting ever since.

At the same time, Desmond Fitzgerald entered the CIA from the Citibank-related law firm of Samuel Sloan Duryee, Walker's cousin and a director with Wolf of Citibank's investment subsidiary (City Bank Farmers' Trust). Fitzgerald, a former liaison officer with the Chinese New Sixth Army, spent much of the next decade in Asia, and was in charge of the CIA Laos operatives "in the field" which President Kennedy found so hard to control. But what Hilsman calls the "problem of CIA" arose, not because of the remoteness of Fitzgerald and CAT from the center of power, but because of their proximity to it. For Fitzgerald too was a member of New York's 400-member Brook Club, "perhaps clubdom's richest from the point of

16 *New York Times,* 6 July 1951, p. 9; cf. 9 June 1951, p. 6; I. F. Stone, *The Hidden History of the Korean War* (New York: Monthly Review Press, 1969), p. xi. The *New York Times* wrote that "the soybean is expected to come under any Congressional inquiry of the China Lobby"; but no such inquiry ever took place. It may be relevant that Joe McCarthy himself took part in the profitable soybean speculations, on the advice of a Pepsi-Cola lobbyist.
17 The bulk of US military airlift inside Korea was flown by CATCL, which soon boasted assets of some $5.5 million and income in the order of from $6 to $12 million a year (*Collier's,* 11 August 1951, p. 35).

view of inherited wealth."[18] Other Brook Club members included three directors of CAT, Inc., two directors of Pan Am, and Chiang Kai-shek's promoters Walter S. Robertson, who for six years was Eisenhower's Assistant Secretary of State for Far Eastern Affairs, and Joe Alsop.

In this pyramid the CIA's official control over CATCL was remote and unreliable. Its proprietary Airdale Corp. (in 1957 renamed Pacific Corp.) owned 100 percent of CAT, Inc./Air America, Inc. (which hired pilots), and of CAT Inc.'s subsidiary the Asiatic Aeronautical Company, later Air Asia (which owned both aircraft and "one of the world's largest aircraft maintenance and repair facilities . . . at Tainan in southern Taiwan."[19] But Airdale owned only 40 percent of CATCL, and thus could hardly be called to account when (as frequently occurred) CAT planes flew in support of operations conforming to Taiwan and KMT foreign policy, but at odds with the official foreign policy of the United States.

Even the CIA's control over Airdale/Pacific Corp., which is said to clear profits in the order of $10 million a year, is open to question: it is possible that the proprietary relationship is as useful in supplying an "official" cover for private profit as it is in supplying a "private" cover for the CIA.[20] Air America itself has a private stake in Southeast Asia's burgeoning oil economy, for it "flies prospectors looking for copper and geologists searching for oil in Indonesia, and provides pilots for commercial airlines such as Air Vietnam and Thai Airways and for China Airlines [Taiwan's new Chinese-owned flag airline which since 1968 has taken over CAT's passenger services]."[21] Much larger has been the economic stake of the financial interests represented on the boards of Pacific Corp. and CAT, Inc. over the years (such as Dillon Read, represented by William A. Read, Jr., and the Rockefellers, represented by Laurance Rockefeller's employee Harper Woodward).

Perhaps the most obvious stake has been that of Pan Am (on whose board sit Robert Lehman of Lehman Brothers and James

---

18 Cleveland Amory, *Who Killed Society?* (New York: Pocket Books, 1960), p. 202.

19 Dibble, p. 50.

20 One indication of this mutual advantage between political and economic concerns is the later convergence in the board of one enterprise (Cuno Engineering) of former CIA Director Bedell Smith, of his deputy director Murray McConnel, and of McConnel's successor Walter Reid Wolf, who was involved in setting up CAT, Inc.

21 *New York Times,* 5 April 1970, pp. 1, 22. Air America pilots, like Lockheed's U-2 pilots, are mostly recruited from the USAF, and are said to have the same rights of return into the USAF at the end of their "civilian" tour.

Sterling Rockefeller of the National City Bank). Like the National City Bank itself, and the larger Bank of America which in the early postwar period was still allied with it,[22] so also Pan Am was particularly oriented toward development of a "Pacific rim community," as opposed to an "Atlantic community." It has been shown that Pan Am's staggering profits in the 1960s were built about its early monopoly of commercial air service to Thailand and Indochina. Pan Am's Indochina service was opened with the assistance of the US government "in the national interest" on 22 May 1953, seventeen days after CAT, using planes and pilots "loaned" by the USAF, began its military airlift to Dienbienphu.

The inauguration of CAT's airlift to Laos in September 1959, which has continued with little interruption ever since, was likewise a godsend to Pan Am and the other big US airlines at a time when they were suffering badly. Laos generated a need for additional military airlift which, after considerable lobbying and threats of quitting international service, was awarded by contract to the commercial carriers.[23] Thanks to its Pacific operations, Pan Am saw its charter revenues soar almost 300 percent in four years, and showed a profit in 1961 for the first time since 1956, even though its Atlantic service continued to operate at a loss.[24]

One can note with some cynicism that at the heart of the so-called China Lobby in Congress in the early 1950s (Claire Boothe Luce, Pat McCarran, and Owen Brewster) was to be found the heart of the Pan Am lobby. Senator Pat McCarran of Nevada, who chaired the congressional inquiry into Owen Lattimore and the Institute of Pacific Relations, had first achieved fame as author of the 1938 Civil Aeronautics Act, and later as an oil lobbyist. In his heyday as a China Lobbyist, McCarren was also known as "the gambler's senator" and

22 Transamerica Corp., the Giannini holding corporation, was in the late 1940s the largest stockholder in both banks, owning about 9 percent of Citibank, and 22 percent of the Bank of America.

23 New York Times, 8 April 1960, p. 62; US Congress, House, Committee on Armed Services, Special Subcommittee on National Airlift, Hearings, 86th Cong., 2nd Sess. (Washington: GPO, 1960), pp. 4616–50, 4730–34. The president of Pan Am testified that his company would have to release 300 pilots during the next six months "if traffic—other than normal civil traffic—doesn't become available." It has been noted that the congressional compromise between the Pentagon and the commercial airlines contained "no recommendation about what to do if the combination of more strategic airlift and continuing guarantees to the [airlines] industry produced too much airlift in nonwar situations" (Frederick C. Thayer, Air Transport Policy and National Security, Chapel Hill, N.C., University of North Carolina Press, 1965, p. 225). Thanks to the Laotian airlift and war, that problem was not faced.

24 Angus McDonald and Al McCoy, "Pan Am Makes the Going Great," Scanlon's (April 1970), p. 53. In 1961 Pan Am's Atlantic competitor, TWA, lost $38 million. In 1962 Pan Am's total air cargo load rose 500 percent, thanks in part to the airlift in that year of US troops to Thailand.

is said to have sat in court at the Riverside Hotel in Reno, making deals for syndicate men with criminal records to obtain casino licenses despite the law.[25] Despite such dubious representatives, one cannot call lobbying a conspiracy, any more than one can discern anything illegal in the fact that AirAmerica's top operating personnel were also recruited from Pan Am.[26] When, however, one looks beyond the Washington offices of Air America to the Asian field operations of CAT, with its 60 percent Chinese Nationalist control, the possibility of KMT-criminal connections and activity demands to be explored.

The most questionable of CAT's activities was its sustained supply of arms and other matériel to KMT General Li Mi and his successors in Burma and North Thailand between 1949 and 1961. Li Mi is probably the only major opium-dealer in the world to have been honored with the US Legion of Merit and Medal of Freedom; his 93rd Division began collecting opium from the Meos of northern Laos as early as 1946.[27] Faced with a public scandal after Burma complained about these foreign intruders on its soil, the US hired CAT, Inc. to fly them out in 1954. Nevertheless, the bulk of the troops refused to move and CATCL continued to supply them, possibly using some of the very same planes chartered for the illusory repatriation. According to an informed source, "the CIA saw these troops as a thorn in Mao's side and continued to supply them with arms *and money*," even though they had "decided to settle down and become rich by growing opium."[28]

The decision to finance and supply the remnants of Li Mi's troops had grave consequences for the world opium and heroin traffic, and also for that part of it handled by the so-called National Crime Syn-

25 Ed Reid, *The Grim Reapers* (Chicago: Henry Regnery, 1969), p. 219; Wallace Turner, *Gamblers' Money: The New Force in American Life* (Cambridge, Mass.: Houghton Mifflin, 1965), pp. 10, 274.

26 George A. Doole, Chief Executive Officer of Air America; Amos Hiatt, Treasurer; and Hugh Grundy, President of Air Asia, all were recruited from Pan Am and its foreign subsidiaries, just as William Pawley had worked for Pan Am's China subsidy CNAC before setting up the Flying Tigers in 1941. One also notes that the "American Fliers for Laos" who volunteered in respose to the 1959 Laos "invasion" were recruited by Clifford L. Speer, a "major in the Air Force Reserve and civilian employee at Fort Huachuca, Arizona" (*New York Times,* 27 September 1959, p. 16). Pan Am has a contract at Fort Huachuca to conduct highly secret "electronics weapons" research for the USAF.

27 J. T. McAlister, *Vietnam: The Origins of a Revolution* (New York: Knopf, 1969), p. 228; cited in David Feingold, "Opium and Politics in Laos," in Nina Adams and Al Mc-Coy (eds.), *Laos: War and Revolution* (New York: Harper, 1970), p. 335.

28 George Thayer, *The War Business* (New York: Simon and Schuster, 1969), p. 158, emphasis added. Even the US Government *Area Book for Thailand* (Washington: GPO, 1968) records of the KMT troops that "their principal income allegedly comes from serving as armed escort for the opium caravans moving southward" [to Bangkok] (p. 454).

dicate in the United States. The new right-wing Thai government of Phibun Songgram, having seized power in an 1948 coup (over the issue of controlling the local Chinese),[29] legalized the sale of opium and established an official Thai Government Opium Monopoly on 17 September 1949. This happened just as the Chinese Communists were expelling the last of the KMT-linked warlords who had supplied the Far East and America with opium before World War II. Shortly thereafter, prepared opium in the containers of the Thai Government Opium Monopoly was seized in a raid in Boston, Massachusetts, an event not noted in the US press but duly reported by the US government to the United Nations Commission on Narcotic Drugs.[30] Throughout the 1950s US government representatives continued to notice quietly that Thailand was a source for the opium and heroin imported into the United States, though this relative candor waned in the 1960s with the escalation of the Second Indochina war.[31] They also reported the rapid increase in both opium-trading and opium-growing in northern Thailand, where the KMT troops were established, and noted that most of this opium was exported out of Thailand for illicit traffic abroad.[32]

Up until about 1964, the United States also complained officially and ostentatiously to the UN Narcotics Commission about "Yunnan opium," brand "999" morphine, and heroin from "the Chinese mainland," as part of Peking's "twenty-year plan to finance political activities and spread addiction."[33] In 1958, for example, it reported the smuggling into the United States of 154 pounds of heroin "from mainland China"; and in 1960 that "the principal sources of the diacetylmorphine [heroin] seized in the United States were Hong Kong, Mexico, and communist China."[34] But other delegates and the Commission itself would complete this misleading picture: "Yunnan

29 G. William Skinner, *Chinese Society in Thailand: an Analytical History* (Ithaca, N.Y.: Cornell University Press, 1957), p. 289.

30 UN Document E/CN.7/213 (communicated by the US Representative), 17 November 1950, p. 9.

31 E.g. statement of Harry J. Anslinger, then US Commissioner of Narcotics, before the Senate Committee on the Judiciary, *Illicit Narcotics Traffic, Hearings*, 84th Cong., 2nd Sess. (Washington: GPO, 1955), p. 13; UN Document E/CN.7/394, 29 April 1960, p. 2.

32 US Congress, Senate, Committee on the Judiciary, *Narcotic Control Act of 1956, Hearing*, 84th Cong., 2nd Sess., 4 May 1956, p. 34. Before the Tenth (1955) Session of the UN Narcotics Commission, the US representative noted that from 200 to 400 tons of opium were imported annually south into Thailand across the Burma-Laos border, of which only 100 tons were consumed in Thailand itself (UN Document E/CN.7/303/Rev. 1, p. 34).

33 UN Commission on Narcotic Drugs, *Report of the Ninth Session* (1954), E/CN.7/283, p. 22.

34 UN Commission on Narcotic Drugs, *Report of the Thirteenth Session* (1958), E/CN.-7/354, p. 26, cf. p. 22; *Report of the Fifteenth Session* (1960), E/CN.7/395, p. 19, cf. p. 18.

opium" was opium that came from anywhere in the "fertile triangle" (the Burma-Thai-Laos-Yunnan border area). The Hong Kong authorities "were not aware of a traffic in narcotics from the mainland of China through Hong Kong," but "quantities of narcotics reached Hong Kong via Thailand" (E/CN.7/395, p. 18). The bulk of "Yunnan opium," and the "999" morphine in particular, were in fact trafficked under the protection of the KMT troops in Burma and north Thailand supplied by CAT. In 1960 the UN Commission discreetly noted the presence in the Burmese sector of the "fertile triangle" of "remnants of KMT troops who were maintaining themselves largely on the profits of the opium trade. It was reported that they received their supplies periodically by air" (E/CN.7/395, p. 15).

Why did CAT planes continue until 1961 to support the suppliers of heroin, which was flooding, via Thailand and Hong Kong, into the United States? One reason was indeed military, to use the KMT troops and raids "as a thorn in Mao's side," especially during the CIA/CAT-supported operation in Tibet (adjacent to Yunnan) from 1956–60, for which the CIA agent Tony Poe (later stationed in the Laotian opium center of Ban Houei Sai) trained Tibetan guerrillas in the mountains of Colorado.[35]

But a second reason was political: to maintain contact with the elaborate fabric of Chinese secret societies or "Triads" throughout Southeast Asia. The profits and relationships of the opium trade, in other words, would help to preserve the prewar KMT ascendancy among the Chinese middle class of these countries, and thus challenge their allegiance to the new Chinese People's Republic. This question of Chinese allegiance was particularly acute in the early 1950s in Malaya, where the farming of the opium franchise among Chinese "Triads" had been resorted to by the British authorities since at least the 1870s.[36] The organized opium traffic had become a well-established accommodation and control mechanism, and after World War II the opium was supplied by the "fertile triangle."[37]

Although the British by and large resisted Triad-KMT offers to

---

35 *San Francisco Chronicle*, 4 September 1970, p. 1. *Free China and Asia*, a journal published by the KMT agency responsible for chartering the CAT flights, gave details of Yunnan military operations and wrote of "plans to rise up in coordination with the efforts of the Tibetans against the Communist rule, particularly those in Yunnan and Sikang" (*Free China and Asia*, June 1959, p. 21; cf. January 1959, p. 10).

36 Wilfred Blythe, *Impact of Chinese Secret Societies in Malaya* (London: Oxford University Press, 1969), pp. 190, 250.

37 Cf. (e.g.) UN Commission on Narcotic Drugs, *Report of the Seventeenth Session*, E/CN.7/432, p. 15.

mobilize against the Chinese insurgency in Malaya, they also found it difficult to crack down on the opium and gambling activities of the Wa Kei secret society, "without disrupting the fabric" of the Wa Kei and leaving a vacuum for the Communists to fill.[38] Meanwhile the wealthy Chinese owners of tin mines in the more exposed countryside found it expedient to subsidize a Wa Kei-Triad private army "with strong KMT backing" as a mobile armed force against the Communist guerrillas. This "Kinta Valley Home Guard" is given credit for restoring security to the Malayan tin industry by 1954.[39]

In Thailand, also, the farming of the opium franchise has been used by the government for over a century as a means of controlling the local Chinese population, and the enormous profits from the opium traffic have been a traditional source of corruption inside the Siamese government.[40] In the 1950s the Thai interior minister, General Phao Sriyanon, after an initial phase of anti-Sinitism, "showed every willingness to co-operate with Kuomintang Chinese in the campaign against Communism."[41] At the same time his police, and in particular his border police, collaborated with Li Mi's KMT troops in Burma by officially "confiscating" their contraband opium in return for a reward to KMT "informers." (As early as 1950 a US government representative noted cynical reports that it was profitable for the opium-trader to be seized and to share the reward with police.)[42]

It seems indisputable that some elements in the KMT used opium as a means to organize and finance KMT links with and control over the important Chinese communities of Southeast Asia. This is not surprising: the KMT had relied on the Triads and gangs involved in the opium traffic since as early as 1927, when Chiang Kai-shek, encouraged by foreign bankers, used the Ch'ing Pang "Green Gang" of Tu Yueh-sheng to break the Communist insurrection in Shanghai. (Chiang Kai-shek is said by some authorities to have been a Ch'ing Pang member.)[43]

After the remnants of the Shanghai "Green" and "Red Gangs" had relocated in Hong Kong, one finds increasing references in UN

38 Blythe, pp. 441, 449.
39 *Ibid.*, pp. 441–42.
40 G. William Skinner, *Chinese Society in Thailand*, pp. 120–21.
41 *Ibid.*, p. 337.
42 UN Document E/CN.7/210, 3 November 1950, p. 3.
43 H. R. Isaacs, *The Tragedy of the Chinese Revolution* (Stanford, Cal.: Stanford University Press, 1951), pp. 81, 142–46; Y. C. Wang, *Journal of Asia Studies,* May 1967, p. 437; Blythe, pp. 21, 28–29.

Reports to the narcotics traffic of Triad societies in Hong Kong and throughout the world. In 1963, for example, the US representative to the UN Narcotics Commission "observed that the problem of the Triad organizations (Chinese groups involved in the illicit traffic in the Far East and Europe) appeared to be significant in recent trafficking developments." Other delegates, confirming that "many heroin traffickers . . . had Triad backgrounds," noted the activities of Hong Kong Triad representatives in Germany, Spain, and Switzerland.[44]

This worldwide network of Chinese secret societies in the opium traffic extended both before and after World War II to the Hip Sings, one of the Chinese tongs in the United States, and also to the Bing Kong and other American tongs. In the 1930s the national president of the Hip Sings, Yee On Li, was convicted for a Mafia-linked narcotics operation involving the wife of Lucky Luciano's partner, Thomas Pennachio; Yee was also involved with "Hip Sing dope dealers in Chicago, San Francisco, Pittsburgh, New York, Cleveland, Dallas, and other important cities."[45] In January 1959 a new generation of Hip Sing officials, including San Francisco president George W. Yee, were again indicted for narcotics smuggling. A US government report on the indictments noted that the tong's activities possibly paralleled "the operations of the Triad societies in Hong Kong."[46]

It has been claimed that profits from narcotics smuggling in the United States have been channeled into the China Lobby, thus helping to keep open the opium supply lines through Laos and Thailand. In 1960 Ross Y. Koen, in his book *The China Lobby in American Politics,* wrote that

> There is . . . considerable evidence that a number of [Nationalist] Chinese officials engaged in the illegal smuggling of narcotics into the United States with the full knowledge and connivance of the Nationalist Chinese Government. The evidence indicates that several prominent Americans have participated in and profited from these transactions. It indicates further that the narcotics business has been an important factor in the activities and permutations of the China Lobby.[47]

44 UN Commission on Narcotic Drugs, *Report of the Eighteenth Session,* E/CN.7/455, p. 10.

45 Will Oursler and L. D. Smith, *Narcotics: America's Peril* (Garden City, N.Y.: Doubleday, 1952), p. 87.

46 E/CN.7/394, 29 April 1960, p. 8.

47 Ross Y. Koen, *The China Lobby in American Politics* (New York: Macmillan, 1960), p. ix.

Professor Koen expressed the hope that his charges would lead to a fuller legal investigation; they led, instead, after a denial from Narcotics Commissioner Anslinger, to his book's being recalled by the publisher. But Anslinger's denial, recently published, does not touch upon Mr. Koen's charge about the China Lobby: "I can give you an unqualified statement that this is manufactured out of the whole cloth: that there is no scintilla of evidence that any Chinese officials have engaged in illegal smuggling of narcotics into the United States *with the full knowledge and connivance of the Chinese Nationalist Government.*"[48] And, without the italicized qualification, Mr. Anslinger's refutation is hard to believe. For Chiang's consul general in San Francisco at the time of the Hip Sing arrests in the late 1930s, Huang Chao-chin, himself "narrowly escaped conviction . . . on charges of smuggling narcotics in the US."[49] Since 1952 Huang has been a member of the KMT Central Committee, and today he is chairman of the First Commercial Bank of Taiwan.

The KMT's stake in the CAT airlift to its troops in the "fertile triangle" became obvious in 1961, when Fang Chih, a member of the KMT Central Supervisory Committee and secretary-general of the Free China Relief Agency (FCRA), admitted responsibility for an unlisted CAT plane that had just been shot down over Thailand by the Burmese Air Force.[50] The Asian Peoples' Anti-Communist League (APACL), of which the FCRA at the same address was a member agency, was itself an organization through which the KMT maintained overt contact with right-wing political and financial interests in Europe and America, as well as with overseas Chinese communities.

The chairman of the APACL's secret liaison group in America (in effect the heart of the American China Lobby) was in 1959 Charles Edison, yet another right-wing member of the Brook Club.[51] The APACL also wrote of its collaboration with psychological-warfare experts in the Department of Defense, and with the John Birch Society. The unpublicized visit to Laos of Fang Chih, in the weeks immediately preceding the phony Laos "invasion" of 1959, suggests that the narcotics traffic, as well as Pathet Lao activity, may

48 Joseph Keeley, *The China Lobby Man* (New Rochelle, N.Y.: Arlington House, 1969), p. 148, emphasis added.

49 Michael Straight, "Corruption and Chiang Kai-shek," *New Republic,* 8 October 1951, p. 12.

50 *New York Times,* 16 February 1961, p. 9; *Singapore Straits-Times,* 20 February, 1961, p. 1.

51 *APACL—Its Growth and Outlook* (Taipeh: APACL, 1960).

have been a reason why CAT's planes inaugurated their flights in that year into the opium-growing Meo areas of Sam Neua province. This in turn would explain the extraordinary rumors, reported in the *Christian Science Monitor,* that the Laotian Air Force's "opium runs are made with CIA 'protection.' "[52]

Is it too much to suggest that CAT's entry into Laos in 1959 had less to do with North Vietnam and the nonexistent "invasion" of Laos, reported by Brook Club member Joe Alsop, than with opium? The US government itself, commenting on the nearby rebellion of the same year in the Shan states of Burma, called it "an instance of a rebellion precipitated by the opium traffic."[53] The KMT-sponsored Shan rebellion followed by a crackdown in the summer of 1959 by the Burmese government, after Pai Che-jen and some 2,000 KMT troops had been driven from Sanskyin Mountain in Yunnan into Burma in 1958.[54]

By March 1959, according to Bernard Fall, "some of the Nationalist guerrillas operating in the Shan states of neighboring Burma had crossed into Laotian territory and were being supplied by an airlift of 'unknown planes.' "[55] Their old opium routes were being threatened to the south as well. In July 1959 the Thai government, in response to years of US government pressure, ended its opium monopoly and announced it would clamp down on the narcotics traffic.[56] Shortly after this prohibition heroin, in the place of the bulkier opium, "came to be regarded as the major problem" in Thailand.[57] By September 1959 CAT had commenced charter airlift in Laos at the expense of the American taxpayer.

Meanwhile, in May and June of 1959, Fang Chih of APACL visited KMT camps in Laos, Burma, and Thailand, as he did again in 1960. On 18 August 1959, five days before the arrival of the two

---

52 *Christian Science Monitor,* 16 June 1970, p. 8; cf. 29 May 1970, p. 14: "Clearly the CIA is cognisant of, if not party to, the extensive movement of opium out of Laos. One charter pilot told me that 'friendly' opium shipments get special CIA clearance and monitoring on their flights southward out of the country. The same source alleged two or three flights without this 'protection' crashed under mysterious circumstances."

53 US Note of 29 April 1960 to UN Commission on Narcotic Drugs, E/CN.7/394, p. 2.

54 *Ibid.,* p. 1; *Free China and Asia,* January 1959, p. 10.

55 Bernard Fall, *Anatomy of a Crisis* (Garden City, New York: Doubleday, 1969), p. 99.

56 The Thai police favoritism shown the KMT during 1952–1954 had been disavowed in 1956; and Prime Minister Phibun stated at a public press conference, "The Kuomintang causes too much trouble: they trade in opium and cause Thailand to be blamed in the United Nations" (Skinner, p. 343). The next year Phao was ousted from power by the present military rulers of Thailand, amid reports that Phao, "a sort of local Beria . . . ran the gold exchange and opium trade" (*New York Times,* 6 November 1957, p. 34).

57 UN Commission on Narcotic Drugs: *Report of the Seventeenth Session* (1962), E/CN.-7/432, p. 11.

CAT planes in Vientiane, and twelve days before the alleged "invasion," Ku Cheng-kang, who was president of the FCRA as well as of the Taiwan APACL, received in Taiwan the mysterious but influential Colonel Oudone Sananikone, a member of what was then the ruling Laotian family and nephew of Laotian Premier Phoui Sananikone.[58] On 26 August 1959, in Washington, Oudone's father, Ngon Sananikone, signed the US-Laos emergency aid agreement which would pay to charter the CAT planes, three days after their arrival. This was only a few hours after Eisenhower had left for Europe on the same day, not having had time to study the aid request, for Ngon had only submitted it on 25 August. On 27 August Oudone Sananikone attended the founding in Taiwan of a Sino-Laotian friendship society, whose trustees included Ku Cheng-kang and Fang Chih.[59]

Oudone Sananikone headed a "Laotian" paramilitary airline, Veha Akhat, which in those days serviced the opium-growing areas north of the Plaines des Jarres with Chinese Nationalist planes and personnel (CAT had not yet begun its operations to the Meos in this region, which offered such profitable opportunities for smuggling as a sideline for enterprising pilots).[60] Oudone Sananikone also figured prominently in the secret three-way talks between officers of Laos, South Vietnam, and Taiwan, that preceded the Vientiane coup and resulting crisis of 19 April 1964, the coup that was reported two days in advance by Taiwan Radio.[61]

Another major figure in the 1959 and 1964 Laotian plots was General Ouane Rathikoune, who flew with Joe Alsop to Sam Neua and showed him the staged evidence of the 1959 "invasion." General Ouane is said to have admitted in a recent interview that he was "the real boss" of opium operations in Laos.[62]

What is extraordinary, and quite possibly criminal under US

---

58 APACL, *Free China and Asia,* October 1959, p. 14.

59 *Ibid.,* p. 31.

60 In fact Veha Akhat was little more than a front for the Nationalist Chinese airlines from which it chartered six planes and pilots. On 19 February 1961, four days after the CAT/FCRA plane was shot down by the Burmese, a Veha Akhat C-47 leased from a Taiwan company was shot down over Laos; four of the six personnel aboard were said to be Nationalist Chinese officers (*Bangkok Post,* 22 February 1961, p. 1; *Singapore Straits-Times,* 22 February 1961, p. 3). The same year Taiwan's second airline, Foshing, reported a decrease in its air fleet from three C-47s to two. Foshing Airlines was headed by Moon Chin, a former assistant operating manager of Pan Am's China subsidiary, CNAC, under William Pawley.

61 *Bangkok Post,* 18 April 1964.

62 *San Francisco Chronicle,* 16 August 1971, p. 12.

law, is not the involvement in narcotics of the KMT, nor that of the Taiwan airline CATCL which it controls, but of Americans exercising the authority of the CIA. The CIA as an agency, it is true, cannot be identified with the narcotics trade any more than can the whole of the Kuomintang. In 1955, for example, when the CIA ran airlift to the opium trade in Thailand, General Lansdale in Vietnam used CIA funds to smash the pro-French Binh Xuyen apparatus that controlled the dope and gambling activities of Saigon and its Chinese suburb, much as the Triads operated in Malaya.[63] In 1971 Air America planes are reported to have taken part in the growing US crackdown on the narcotics traffic, while a former-CIA congressman, Robert Steele of Connecticut, has just produced a useful report on "The World Heroin Problem" after a worldwide tour in the company of a former CIA Saigon station chief.[64]

But while General Lansdale was cracking down on narcotics in Vietnam, William H. Bird, the CAT representative in Bangkok, is said to have coordinated CAT airdrops to Li Mi's troops in the "fertile triangle." In 1960, after CAT began flying in Laos through "the great Laos fraud," his private engineering firm Bird and Son began the construction of short airstrips in Meo territory which were soon used for the collection of Laos opium, some of it destined to be manufactured into heroin in Marseilles, and forwarded to the National Crime Syndicate in the United States.[65] Soon Bird and Son had its own airline of fifty planes flying US contract airlift to the opium-growing tribesmen, and rumors soon arose that these planes,

63 It is striking that in 1961, when the CIA inaugurated covert air operations from Saigon against North Vietnam, it spurned the available planes and facilities of CAT at Saigon's Tan Son Nhut Airport and set up a new, unrelated "proprietary," Aviation Investors, Inc., d/b/a Vietnam Air Transport. Vietnam Air Transport is said to have hired Nguyen Cao Ky, then fired him after learning that he used his "Operation Haylift" flights as a cover for opium-smuggling from Laos to Saigon.

64 US Congress, House, Committee on Foreign Affairs, *The World Heroin Problem*, Report of Special Study Mission, House Report No. 92–298, 92nd Cong., 1st Sess. (Washington: GPO, 1971).

65 Stanley Karnow once named a "debonair, pencil-moustached Corsican by the name of Bonaventure Francisci" as one of the top opium runners in Laos ("The Opium Must Go Through," *Life*, 30 August 1963, p. 12). The Francisci family has been linked to the Spirito-Venturi arm of the Corsican Mafia in Marseilles, which in turn reaches to America through Syndicate associate Vincent Cotroni of Montreal (US Congress, Senate, Committee on Government Operations, *Organized Crime and Illicit Traffic in Narcotics, Hearings*, 88th Cong., 2nd Sess. (Washington, GPO, 1964), pp. 956, 961; cited hereafter as *Narcotics Hearings*). This Corsican traffic dates back at least to the 1950s, according to Martin Pera, a senior Narcotics Bureau official: "When French Indochina existed, there were quantities of opium that were shipped to the labs . . . around Marseilles, France, to the Corsican underworld there, and then transshipped to the United States" (US Congress, Senate, Select Committee on Improper Activities in the Labor or Management Field, *Hearings*, 85th Cong., 2nd Sess. (Washington: GPO, 1959), p. 12225 (cited hereafter as *McClellan Hearings*).

like Air America's in the same area, were not infrequently used for smuggling.[66]

William Bird's brother or cousin in Bangkok, China OSS veteran Willis Bird, headed the Bangkok office of a "trading company" called Sea Supply, Inc. As we noted before, Sea Supply first supplied arms to the KMT troops of General Li Mi, and later trained Phao Sriya-non's Thai border police who were also implicated in KMT opium-smuggling activities. Like William, Willis Bird also branched into construction business on his own. In 1959, as vice-president of the "Universal Construction Company," Bird was said by a Congressional committee investigating corruption in Laos to have bribed an ICA aid official in Vientiane.[67] In 1962, when President Kennedy was struggling to bring the CIA hawks in Thailand under control, his brother, the attorney-general, belatedly returned an indictment against Willis Bird, who has never returned to this country to stand trial.[68]

What particularly concerns us is of course not the personal venality of a US construction official or of pilots dabbling in opium on the side, so much as the sustained support by CIA proprietaries of narcotics-smuggling activities which affected the continental United States. It is not at all clear that this policy had official sanction. As I argued in my opening chapter, Eisenhower seems to have been unaware of the airlift operations of Air America and Bird and Son in Laos, which were apparently only authorized by an elaborate conspiracy of deceit. By all accounts the Kennedy administration was exerting pressure to remove the "estimated 4,000 Chinese Nationalists" who "were reportedly operating in western Laos in 1961," having been "flown from Taiwan into bases in northern Thailand."[69]

---

66 In 1965 Bird's air fleet was sold to Continental Air Services, a newly created subsidiary of Continental Air Lines headed by Robert Rousselot, a CAT and Air America veteran. The sale price was said to have been over one million dollars (*Wall Street Journal*, 23 August 1965, p. 20; Continental Airlines, *Annual Report, 1965*, p. 13; *New York Times*, 27 August 1964, p. 6).

67 US Congress, House, Committee on Government Operations, *US Aid Operations in Laos*, House Report No. 546, 86th Cong., 1st Sess. (Washington: GPO, 1959), p. 2; *Hearings*, p. 327; *New York Times*, 24 March 1959, p. 19.

68 *New York Times*, 2 February 1962, p. 8.

69 Stanley Karnow, *Washington Post*, 16 March 1970, A10. Theodore Sorenson records that "Chiang was . . . vexed with Kennedy . . . over our quiet pressure for the removal of his foraging force from Burma" (*Kennedy*. New York: Harper & Row, 1965, p. 661). The KMT lobbied publicly for these troops to be given the job of stopping communism as a "volunteer force" in Laos (*Free China and Asia*, December 1960, pp. 5–6), and were supported in the US by elements in the Pentagon and American Security Council (including Admiral Felix Stump, Air America's board chairman). Western Laos was the area of the celebrated "opium battle" of July 1967, between 800 KMT troops and the forces of the opium-smuggling Laotian general Ouane Rathikoune, who also figures prominently in the Laotian invasion fraud of September 1959; *San Francisco Chronicle*, 16 August 1971, p. 12; Feingold,

Even the Johnson administration announced in February 1964 that it would withdraw Air America (i.e., CATCL) from Laos; this announcement came to naught after the organizer of CAT's American replacement, John Davidson of Seaboard World Services, was "accidentally" killed in a dubious and controversial explosion of a CAT plane.[70]

How could the objectives of a US president be at odds with those of a CIA proprietary? The obvious stake of KMT interests in CATCL is a partial explanation, to which one can perhaps add the stake of private American interests as well. For it is a striking fact that the law firm of Tommy Corcoran, the Washington lawyer for CATCL and T. V. Soong, has had its own links to the interlocking worlds of the China Lobby and of organized crime. His partner W. S. Youngman joined the board of US Life and other domestic insurance companies, controlled by C. V. Starr (OSS China) with the help of Philippine and other Asian capital. Youngman's fellow-directors of Starr's companies have included John S. Woodbridge of Pan Am, Francis F. Randolph of J. and W. Seligman, W. Palmer Dixon of Loeb Rhoades, Charles Edison of the postwar China Lobby, and Alfred B. Jones of the Nationalist Chinese government's registered agency, the Universal Trading Corporation. The McClellan Committee heard that in 1950 US Life (with Edison a director) and a much smaller company (Union Casualty of New York) were allotted a major Teamsters insurance contract, after a lower bid from a larger and safer company had been rejected. Hoffa was accused by a fellow-trustee, testifying under oath before another committee, of intervening on behalf of US Life and Union Casualty, whose agents were Hoffa's close business associates Paul and Allan Dorfman.[71]

The National City Bank itself had once leased its racetrack in Havana (and also, through a subsidiary, the Hotel Nacionale de Cuba's casino) to Meyer Lansky of the organized crime syndicate.[72] In 1950 Citibank's largest shareholder, Transamerica Corporation, was represented, through James F. Cavagnaro, in the shadowy "World Commerce Corporation" organized by several OSS veterans.

---

in Adams and McCoy, *Conflict in Laos,* p. 323; Frank Browning and Banning Garrett, "The New Opium War," *Ramparts,* May 1971, p. 34.

70 *New York Times,* 19 March 1964, p. 4; *Bangkok Post,* 20 March 1964; *New York Times,* 27 August 1964, p. 6; *South China Morning Post,* 22 June 1964, p. 1; *Saturday Review,* 11 May 1968, p. 44.

71 *McClellan Hearings,* pp. 15262–72.

72 Hank Messick, *Lansky* (New York: G. P. Putnam's, 1971), p. 89. In 1968 Citibank refused to produce a $200,000 certificate of deposit which had been subpoenaed in an investigation of stock fraud (*New York Times,* 1 December 1969, p. 42).

In 1950 the World Commerce Corporation was involved in dubious soybean operations[73] while its subsidiary Commerce International (China) sponsored the unauthorized Pawley-Cooke military assistance mission to Taiwan[74] and the illegal smuggling of airplanes from California to the government of Chiang Kai-shek.[75] Satiris "Sonny" Fassoulis, accused of passing bribes as the vice-president of Commerce International, was under indictment ten years later when he surfaced in the syndicate-linked Guterma scandals.[76]

A director of Air America through the years has been Robert Guestier Goelet of the City Investing Co., where his fellow-directors have included Joseph Binns of US Life (Binns was involved in Bahamas and other land speculations with Meyer Lansky's business associate Lou Chesler),[77] and John W. Houser (an intelligence veteran from the Pacific who negotiated the lease of the Havana Hilton hotel casino to Cuban associates of the syndicate).[78]

We find the same network linking CIA proprietaries, war lobbies, and organized crime, when we turn our attention from CAT to the other identified supporter of opium activities, Sea Supply, Inc. Sea Supply, Inc. was organized in Miami, Florida, where its counsel, Paul L. E. Helliwell, doubled after 1951 as the counsel for C. V. Starr insurance interests, and also as Thai consul in Miami. It would be hard to say whether Helliwell (the former OSS Chief of Special Intelligence in China) was more active in representing US or Thai government interests; in 1955 and 1956, for example, the Thai consulate in Miami (operating out of Helliwell's office as secretary for the American Bankers' Insurance Company of Florida) passed over

73 *New York Times,* 23 May 1950, p. 34.

74 Pawley, on the advice of President Roosevelt and Tommy Corcoran, set up the Flying Tigers under a secret presidential executive order, exempting him from the neutrality provisions of the US code (Anna Chan Chennault, *Chennault and the Flying Tigers.* New York: P. S. Eriksson, 1963, pp. 76–83). In 1949 Pawley petitioned the State Department to secure similar authorization for the Commerce International (China) mission, but was turned down (US Congress, Senate, Committee on Judiciary, *Communist Threat to the United States through the Caribbean, Hearings,* 86th Cong., 2nd Sess., testimony of William D. Pawley, 2 September 1960, p. 729). Admiral Charles Cooke, later a member of the American Security Council, proceeded anyway.

75 *Washington Post,* 9 September 1951, A1, A8; reprinted in Congressional Record, Senate, 10 September 1951, p. 11066–67; *Reporter,* 29 April 1952, pp. 10–11; Koen, p. 50.

76 T. A. Wise, "The World of Alexander Guterma," *Fortune,* December 1959, p. 160. Also figuring in the Guterma scandals were Matthew Fox, a former registered lobbyist for Indonesia with possible CIA connections (Chester Cooper, *The Lost Crusade.* New York: Dodd Mead, 1970, p. 52), and Herman Brann, a US intelligence agent in World War II. Guterma himself came from Shanghai and the Philippines, and used Philippine capital to launch himself into Florida land development.

77 Through Chesler's Seven Arts Productions, Ltd.; cf. Messick, *Lansky,* p. 228; Ed Reid, *The Grim Reapers,* p. 107.

78 Messick, *Lansky,* p. 211.

thirty thousand dollars to its registered foreign lobbyist in Washington, Tommy Corcoran's law partner James Rowe. Inasmuch as Corcoran and Rowe were two of the closest personal advisers to Lyndon Baines Johnson, then the rapidly rising Senate majority leader, Helliwell's lobbying activities for the opium-dealing government of Phibun and Phao Sriyanon may well have had a more powerful impact on US policy than his legal activities for the CIA.

Miami of course has been frequently identified as "a point where many of the more important United States and Canadian and even the French [narcotics] traffickers congregate."[79] American Bankers' Insurance, the company from whose office Helliwell doubled as Thai Consul General and counsel for Sea Supply, Inc., appears to have maintained its own marginal links with the institutions servicing the world of organized crime and narcotics.[80] The most striking interlock is that of its director Jack L. King, who in 1964 was also a director of the Miami National Bank. The Miami National Bank was identified in 1969 as having served between 1963 and 1967 as a conduit through which "hot" syndicate money was exported by Meyer Lansky's couriers, and "laundered" through the interlocking Exchange and Investment Bank in Geneva.[81] (Lou Poller, King's fellow-director of the Miami National Bank and a director also of the Swiss Exchange and Investment Bank, was investigated by the McClellan committee about his use of Teamster capital to acquire the Miami National Bank, and subsequently indicted for perjury.)[82]

It is said that rich Thai and other Asian capitalists, like wealthy syndicate gangsters such as "Trigger Mike" Coppola, have invested heavily in Florida's postwar land boom, through companies such as the General Development Corporation of Meyer Lansky's business associate Lou Chesler.[83] Such business associations might help ex-

---

79 *McClellan Hearings*, p. 12246.

80 The company's president was an officer for the realty investment interests of Lindsey Hopkins, Jr., himself an officer of CIA proprietaries in Miami (e.g., Zenith Enterprises and Melmar, Inc. in the 1960s). As a director of Sperry Corp. and its subsidiaries, Hopkins had been linked to William Pawley's establishment of the Flying Tigers in 1941 (through a Sperry subsidiary, Intercontinent Corp., of which Pawley was president). Through the Carl G. Fisher Corporation, Hopkins inherited a fortune in Miami Beach hotels, and took part in the postwar land boom in the Bahamas.

81 *New York Times*, 1 December 1969, p. 42.

82 *Ibid.*, 14 August 1959, p. 9; Messick, *Lansky*, p. 269. Allan Dorfman, whose friendship with Hoffa helped win the Teamsters' insurance contract for US Life in 1950, has recently been indicted for accepting kickbacks on a Teamster loan to the Neisco Corp. (*San Francisco Chronicle*, 15 July 1971, p. 5). Neisco's chairman, G. A. Horvath, was board chairman and principal owner of the Miami National Bank in 1964.

83 The Thai king's general counsel in New York from 1945 to 1950, Carl O. Hoffmann of OSS, is today board chairman of the First Florida Resource Corp.

plain why, for example, Prince Puchartra of Thailand became the only royal representative at the 1966 opening of Caesar's Palace in Las Vegas, a hotel-casino said to be controlled by Jimmy Hoffa.[84] The same associations, if they were exposed, might cast light on the unexplained 1968 business trip to Hong Kong and Southeast Asia of Santo Trafficante, an old Lansky associate named in narcotics investigations.[85] Trafficante had been preceded in 1965 by John Pullman, Meyer Lansky's courier to the Miami National Bank. In April 1965 Pullman visited "the Peninsular Hotel in Hong Kong, where the syndicate had casinos and obtained much of its narcotics."[86]

The apparent involvement of CIA proprietaries with foreign narcotics operations is paralleled by their apparent interlock with the domestic institutions serving organized crime. The need to understand such involvements more fully may well become more urgent in the future, as the Indochina war is "Vietnamized" and handed over increasingly to CIA proprietaries such as Air America. For the thrust of this admittedly sketchy inquiry has been to suggest that, with the maturation of both capitalism and third-world nationalism, and with the outlawing of private war operations like those financed by the Seligmans in 1903, wealthy US interests (using the secret authorities delegated to the CIA) have resorted systematically to organized outlaws to pursue their operations.

It is true that the embarrassing links between Air America and CATCL have diminished in the last five years. But the opium-based economy of Laos is still being protected by a coalition of opium-growing CIA mercenaries, Air America planes, and Thai troops.[87] The recent crackdown on Turkish opium production handled by Corsicans in France can of course only increase the importance of heroin deriving from (and refined in) the "fertile triangle," which is already estimated to supply possibly 25 percent of American heroin consumption.[88]

Official US doubletalk about the domestic heroin problem and the reluctance since about 1963 to recognize the "fertile triangle" as a source for it, is only one further symptom that the public sanctions of

---

84 Reid, *Grim Reapers*, pp. 225–26.

85 *Ibid.*, p. 296.

86 Messick, *Lansky*, p. 241.

87 In March 1970, for example, Air America flew in several hundred Thai troops to defend the CIA's Meo outpost at Long Cheng (*New York Times*, 5 April 1970, p. 22; *Flight International*, 16 July 1970).

88 Eliot Marshall, "Heroin: The Source of Supply," *New Republic*, 24 and 31 July 1971, p. 24: "Shutting down the Turkish opium route . . . is likely to do no more than drive the industry further east."

law and the constitution have yielded ground to private interests and the secret sanctions provided through the CIA. More specifically, the use of illegal narcotics networks to fight communism, resorted to by capitalists in Shanghai in 1927 and in Southeast Asia in the 1950s, seems without our knowledge to have been sanctioned inside the United States.

EPILOGUE:
The Pentagon Papers as Drama

This book attacks a subject of enduring obscurity. Its conclusion must suggest, not so much what is the case, as what is to be done. The conspiratorial escalations of the US war in Indochina will not be properly understood and brought under control until the role of our intelligence agencies and their secret allies has been properly understood and brought under control. This will not be an easy task: it is a challenge to the system governing the relations between the United States and the rest of the world. I see, however, no alternative if either America or Asia is truly to experience peace.

One conclusion of fact can be stated categorically. It is that the truth about the US involvement in Southeast Asia has been system-

215

atically distorted for more than two decades, while certain ugly but central features (such as CIA logistic support of the KMT drug traffic) have been systematically suppressed. "Responsible" newspapers like the *New York Times,* area specialists in the universities, foundations, and congressional committees have all contributed to this systematic disinformation. No matter how deeply one may believe in the American people, one can hardly expect these media of information to lead a crusade for the exposure of their own disservice. One will have to look elsewhere, above all to the new generation of concerned and radical scholars who have already shown that they value truth above bureaucratic advancement.

Their task will not be easy, for their opponents are formidable. Time after time, the ultimate source of our disinformation about Southeast Asia has proved to be US intelligence agencies, without whose helpful assistance many journalists and scholars might cease to be noted authorities. And intelligence agencies and personnel, above all those charged with covert operations from ELINT missions to clandestine warfare, carry perhaps the greatest burden of responsibility and guilt for the second Indochina war.

It may be, as has been argued, that the covert operations of the intelligence agencies were a less lethal option than the massive retaliation policies dear to some of the Joint Chiefs of Staff. The fact remains that the secret practices of the intelligence community have institutionalized and made permanently viable the flagrant discrepancy between American democratic ideals and American imperialist practice. In crisis after crisis, the Indochina war has illustrated the dictum that in the control of intelligence lies the control of policy (which is not to suggest that any single group has ever monopolized the control of intelligence). This control has been rendered far greater by the same agencies' control over covert operations, which could provoke (as in the first Tonkin incident) or perhaps even simulate (as in the second) whatever critical intelligence was desired. This overconcentration of power would be dangerous and undemocratic in any context. It has been particularly dangerous in Southeast Asia, where it has become aligned with a reactionary status quo characterized by narcotics traffic, secret societies, and internationally organized crime.

To free ourselves from this legacy we must understand it. And to understand it means to expose, not only the sycophancy of certain journalists and professors and congressmen, but also the conspiratorial manipulation of truth and events by intelligence personnel and their allies. This conspiratorial manipulation, I have suggested, was on occasion not only unauthorized but quite possibly illegal under domestic US law. The spoor of conspiracy can be traced back to the first commitment of US (plus KMT) planes and pilots to the second Indochina war, in "the great Laos fraud" of September 1959. When the Fulbright committee investigated Laos a decade later, I both wrote and telephoned to urge that this incident be reopened. My letters went unanswered, my phone calls unreturned. This is not surprising, when one considers that the fateful emergency authorization of 4 September 1959 (when by "coincidence" President Eisenhower was isolated in Scotland) was almost certainly approved by Richard Nixon, now himself President of the United States.

Among many Americans Mr. Nixon's "Vietnamization" policy has fostered the hope that the Indochina war is ending. They apparently believe that our monstrous bombing of Laos and Cambodia is about to cease, despite Secretary Laird's solemn assurances that "Vietnamization" means nothing of the sort. Or they cling to the hope that Mr. Nixon's impending visit to Peking will by itself mean an end to the revolutionary conflict in Indochina—as if Mr. Khrushchev's visit to America had not been followed promptly by the U-2 incident of 1960, the Berlin crisis of 1961, and the Cuban missiles emergency of 1962.

I do not wish to belittle the importance of Mr. Nixon's visit to Peking. A visit by Nixon, the American leader with the longest and closest record of collaboration with the KMT, APACL, China Lobby, and Vietnam Lobby, will be more meaningful than a comparable journey by any Democrat. If his trip leads to constructive official relations with the world's most populous nation, then the influence of KMT irredentism, with its fantasy of "rolling back" communism in Asia, may be defunct in this country for all time. Thus one hopes that there will be no new election-year crisis, in Korea or South Asia or elsewhere, arising like the U-2 incident to frustrate this progressive policy.

But the Nixon strategy which underlies both Vietnamization and the Peking visit envisages a return from overt to covert operations in Southeast Asia. The US Army is being withdrawn from Vietnam to the accompaniment of congressional exposures of Mafia influence behind the corruption there of its senior personnel.[1] But the Army's

1 US Congress, Senate, Committee on Government Operations, *Fraud and Corruption in Management of Military Club Systems, Hearings*, 92nd Cong., 1st Sess. (8 October 1969) pp. 275–79. Capital for the supply and kickback operations of Sgt. William Higdon and Sgt. Major William Wooldridge, the Army's senior noncommissioned officer, came "from Deak

place is being filled by a billion-dollar "pacification" program, including an expansion of the CIA's controversial assassination project, Operation Phoenix.[2] Generally speaking, the responsibility for Indochina is being taken from the regular military and given back to the various US intelligence agencies, particularly the CIA. The political success of the anti-war movement at this point is thus being harnessed to a further strengthening of the agency which, perhaps more than any other, helped bring about the war in the first place.

This amazing capacity of the intelligence apparatus to gather strength from its defeats was illustrated earlier after the Bay of Pigs fiasco. Then as now the response of the government to the fiasco (an inter-agency fiasco, involving not only CIA but also Air America, Air Force, and Special Forces personnel) was to strengthen, consolidate, and rationalize the "Special Group" or "303 Committee" apparatus which had produced it.[3] In 1971 there are similar signs that the Vietnam fiasco is being used to strengthen the case for relying on the "expertise" of the intelligence professionals.

The elaborate drama of the Pentagon Papers must be assessed in the light of this bureaucratic retrenchment and consolidation. One feels about their publication as one does about Mr. Nixon's Peking visit (which was announced just fifteen days after the courtroom drama of the Pentagon Papers had brought public support for the Vietnam military adventure to an all-time low). It is possible to approve of both events, while fearing that they will help to perpetuate the imperialist intervention which superficially they appear to challenge. Daniel Ellsberg is undoubtedly a powerful and moving critic of conventional warfare in Vietnam, and one does not wish to sound ungrateful for his courageous revelations. When, however, he tells the American nation on television that "for the first time we are hearing the truth" about the war, he is proclaiming a false millennium.

& Co. . . . in Hong Kong . . . through an individual name[d] Frank Furci." Frank's father, Dominic Furci, was a lieutenant in the Florida Mafia family of Santos Trafficante, allegedly a major narcotics trafficker. Trafficante and Dominic Furci visited Frank Furci in Hong Kong in 1968 (p. 279; cf. US, Congress, Senate, Committee on Government Operations, *Organized Crime and Illicit Traffic in Narcotics, Hearings,* 88th Cong. 1st Session, Washington: GPO, 1964, pp. 522–23, 928).

2 *New York Times,* 7 April 1971, pp. 1, 15; *supra,* p. 182.

3 Ralph Stavins, "Kennedy's Private War," *New York Review of Books,* 22 July 1971, p. 26. While Mr. Stavins' account is useful, he is wrong in asserting that the "303 Committee . . . came into being as a direct consequence of the egregious blundering at the Bay of Pigs." In fact this committee of deputy secretaries, known earlier as the "54–12 Committee" had been established in December 1954; Kennedy's innovation was to bureaucratize and expand its activities, particularly by establishing a Special Group (Counter-Insurgency) to insure the development of programs for it (NSAM 124, 18 January 1962). Cf. Harry Howe Ransom, *The Intelligence Establishment* (Cambridge, Mass.: 1970), p. 89.

The Pentagon Papers are of value, but more for what they reveal inadvertently than for what they reveal by design. It would be foolish to expect candor from any government documents, whether written for internal or external consumption: at least one disaffected veteran from the White House staff has commmented that he would have had a less biased picture of the war if he had confined his reading to the newspapers. As an example of outright dishonesty among the published Pentagon documents, we have already noted General Lansdale's memorandum of 1961 on "Unconventional Warfare," whose information "was compiled within Defense and CIA" for the use of General Maxwell Taylor. That memorandum describes CAT as "a CIA proprietary," suppressing the important fact of its being 60 percent owned and controlled by Chinese Nationalist capital (to say nothing of its long involvement with the KMT narcotics traffickers in opposition to public US policy).[4]

More serious than such particular instances of self-serving disinformation is the overall inherent bias in a record of Defense Department papers. Though the true history of our escalating involvement in Indochina is a history of covert and intelligence operations, most of the recent ones are barely recorded (two striking exceptions, the anti-Diem coup of 1963 and the 34-A Operations Plan of 1964, had already been amply publicized). Needless to say, there is even less documentation of those key escalation decisions (such as Johnson's decision of 12 November 1966 to bomb Hanoi, *supra*, p. 106), which the President arrived at privately—either alone, or after consulting with his political intimates, such as Ed Weisl, Tommy Corcoran, and James Rowe, who represented the highest financial interests in the nation.

The inherent bias in the documents themselves, furthermore, is surpassed by that of the Pentagon study which carefully edits and selects them. The dubious and possibly conspiratorial escalations of September 1959 and December 1960 are passed over in total silence, the chronicle being resumed with the officially authorized escalations of early 1961. Two separate volumes of the original Pentagon study, in chronicling the escalations of 1964, skip from 25 July 1964 to the Tonkin Gulf reprisals of 5 August, thus minimizing discussion of the Tonkin Gulf incidents themselves. (The discussion was so inadequate that the *New York Times,* in its summary of the Pentagon study made up the deficiency from another source.)

Having recently examined some of the original Xerox volumes, I

---

4 *The Pentagon Papers* (New York: Bantam, 1971), pp. 131, 137; *supra,* pp. 194–97.

must report that the Pentagon study's discriminatory bias is occasionally reinforced by outright falsehoods. Two separate portions of the original Pentagon study (I, "US Programs in South Vietnam, November 1963–April 1965," and VII, "The Advisory Build-up") are carefully edited so as to create a false illusion of continuity between the last days of President Kennedy's presidency and the first days of President Johnson's:

> . . . National Security Action Memorandum 273, approved 26 November 1963. The immediate cause for NSAM 273 was the assassination of President Kennedy four days earlier; newly-installed President Johnson needed to reaffirm or modify the policy lines pursued by his predecessor. President Johnson quickly chose to reaffirm the Kennedy policies. . . . Military operations should be initiated, under close political control, up to within fifty kilometers inside of Laos. *U.S. assistance programs should be maintained at levels at least equal to those under the Diem government so that the new GVN would not be tempted to regard the U.S. as seeking to disengage.*
>
> The same document also revalidated the planned phased withdrawal of U.S. forces announced publicly in broad terms by President Kennedy shortly before his death: "The *objective* of the United States with respect to the withdrawal of U.S. military personnel remains as stated in the White House statement of October 2, 1963." No new programs were proposed or endorsed, no increases in the level or nature of U.S. assistance suggested or foreseen.[5]

The Pentagon study thus implies that Kennedy's implementation of a 1,000-man withdrawal from Vietnam had not proceeded beyond the *objective* (of withdrawing 1,000 US advisers by the end of 1963 and the bulk of them by 1965) announced from the White House on 2 October. But this carefully laid impression is false, as is the claim that NSAM 273 reaffirmed Kennedy's policies. A specific *plan* for withdrawing 1,000 men had been authorized by Kennedy's NSAM 263 of 11 October 1963, and then worked out and announced by a high-level Honolulu conference on 20 November 1963, two days before the President's assassination.[6]

5 Pentagon ms., "The Advisory Build-up, 1961–1967," p. 70, emphasis added; cf. "US Programs in South Vietnam, November 1963-April 1965," Summary, p. 2: "President Johnson's first policy announcement on the Vietnamese war, contained in NSAM 273 (26 November 1963), . . . was intended primarily to endorse the policies pursued by President Kennedy and to ratify provisional decisions reached in Honolulu just before the assassination."

6 Richard P. Stebbins, *The United States in World Affairs, 1963* (New York: Harper & Row, for the Council on Foreign Relations, 1964), p. 193: "In a meeting at Honolulu on November 20, the principal US authorities concerned with the war could still detect enough evidence of improvement to justify the repatriation of a certain number of specialized troops."

This symbolic reduction of US support had more political than military importance; it might indeed have encouraged the Saigon junta to explore General de Gaulle's disengagement and neutralization proposals. Kennedy's authorized plan was quietly annulled by the deliberately misleading language of NSAM 273, which "emphasized that the level of effort, economic and military, would be maintained at least as high as to Diem."[7] This tacit reversal of the 20 November decisions was approved only four days later, on Sunday, 24 November, by an informal meeting of many of the same personnel.[8] But three new officials were present, including Lyndon Johnson, holding his first business meeting with his advisers as President.[9]

The full text of NSAM 273 of 26 November 1963 remains unknown. In both the Bantam and the Beacon editions of the Pentagon Papers there are no complete documents between the five cables of 30 October 1963 and McNamara's memorandum of 21 December. This in itself is a striking lacuna. We know, however, that it was "in keeping with the guidance in NSAM 273" that the Joint Chiefs of Staff, on 22 January 1964, proposed an escalation of intelligence operations, an abandonment of "self-imposed restrictions," and preparations "for whatever level of activity may be required."[10] This corroborates Tom Wicker's judgment that the subsequent expansion of the Vietnam war "had been determined in that hour of political decision" on 24 November 1963.[11]

NSAM 273 appears to be an important document in the history of the 1964 escalations, as well as in the reversal of President Kennedy's late and ill-fated program of "Vietnamization" by 1965. The systematic censorship and distortion of NSAM 273, first by the Pen-

Jim Bishop (*The Day Kennedy Was Shot.* New York: Funk and Wagnalls, 1968, p. 107) goes further: "They may also have discussed how best to extricate the US from Saigon; in fact it was a probable topic and the President may have asked the military for a timetable of withdrawal."

7 Pentagon ms., "US Programs in South Vietnam, November 1963–April 1965," Chronology, p. 1. There is no trace of this language in the Bantam (*New York Times*) edition of *The Pentagon Papers*, which reprints only the misleading reiteration of "the objectives of the United States with respect to the withdrawal . . . of October 2, 1963 . . ." (p. 233). Such censorship, which must be deliberate, creates an impression the opposite of the truth.

8 *New York Times*, 25 November 1963, p. 1. Chester Cooper reports that President Johnson did not hold an official meeting of the National Security Council before 5 December 1963 (*The Lost Crusade*, p. 222; cf. p. 216). Taking part in both the 20 and 24 November meetings were Rusk, McNamara, Lodge, and McGeorge Bundy.

9 Alfred Steinberg, *Sam Johnson's Boy* (New York: Macmillan, 1968), p. 761. The other new faces were Averell Harriman, whose deputy represented State in the "303 Committee," and George Ball.

10 *Pentagon Papers*, pp. 274–77.

11 Tom Wicker, *JFK and LBJ: The Influence of Personality Upon Politics* (New York: William Morrow, 1968), p. 206; cf. I. F. Stone, *New York Review of Books*, 28 March 1968, p. 11.

tagon study and later by the *New York Times,* suggests that the Kennedy assassination was itself an important, perhaps a crucial, event in the history of the Indochina war conspiracy.[12]

Assuredly there is much truth in the Pentagon Papers. Nevertheless, their editing, if not the drama of their release, represents one more manipulation of "intelligence" in order to influence public policy. Someone is being carefully protected by the censorship of NSAM 273, and by the concealment of the way in which the assassination of President Kennedy affected the escalation of the Indochina war. It is almost certain that McCone, the leading hawk in the Kennedy entourage, played a role in this secret policy reversal.[13]

Elsewhere in the *New York Times* version of the Pentagon Papers one finds the intelligence community, and the CIA in particular, depicted as a group of lonely men who challenged the bureaucratic beliefs of their time, but whose percipient warnings were not listened to. In June 1964, we are told, the CIA "challenged the domino theory, widely *believed* in one form or another within the Administration," but the President unfortunately was "not inclined to adjust policy along the lines of this *analysis* challenging the domino theory."[14] In late 1964 the "intelligence community," with George Ball and almost no one else, " 'tended toward a pessimistic view' of the effect of bombing on the Hanoi leaders. . . . As in the case of earlier intelligence findings that contradicted policy intentions, the study

---

12 Another such event may have been the court drama preceding the release of the Pentagon Papers, which has been compared to the drama of William Manchester's trivial book, *The Death of a President.* Three of the principals in the *New York Times* trial had clear connections with the CIA/intelligence community. Daniel Ellsberg, the sometime fugitive who for six weeks advised Henry Kissinger in the Nixon White House, was also a former member of General Lansdale's "pacification" staff in Vietnam. Whitney North Seymour, the prosecutor for the US government, a long-time member of Ed Weisl's law firm, Simpson, Thacher and Bartlett, was also a one-time vice-president of the CIA's Fund for Free Jurists. And Judge Murray Gurfein, hearing his first case during his first week on the bench as a Nixon-appointed judge, was a wartime member of OSS; in 1942 he helped negotiate with Meyer Lansky the "Operation Underworld" which led to the postwar release of Lucky Luciano. (US, Congress, Senate, Special Committee to Investigate Organized Crime in Interstate Commerce, *Hearings,* 81st Cong., 2nd Sess. [Washington: GPO, 1950–51], Part 7, pp. 607–08, 1188–91.) After the war, as Lucky Luciano went on to become the acknowledged overlord of the international narcotics traffic, so Murray Gurfein became associated in business ventures with directors of the Bank of America (perhaps the leading institutional backer of the China Lobby) and with Seymour Weiss, recently named as one of the two men (the other being Carlos Marcello) left by Meyer Lansky "to run New Orleans" (Hank Messick, *Lansky,* 1971, p. 87; Dun and Bradstreet, *Million Dollar Directory,* 1964, s.vv. "Goldring, Inc.," p. 504; "Seymour Weiss," p. 5024).

13 One of the unanswered questions about the 24 November meeting, by most accounts an important if not a crucial one, is why it was called so quickly. If Kennedy had lived, he would have had lunch that Sunday alone with Lodge at his Virginia country estate (Tom Wicker, *JFK and LBJ,* p. 183). Dean Rusk, another important participant, would have been in Japan.

14 *Pentagon Papers,* p. 254 (Summary by Neil Sheehan), emphasis added.

indicates no effort on the part of the President or his most trusted advisers to reshape their policy along the lines of this analysis."[15]

In part, no doubt, this is true. The intelligence community did include within it some of the administration's more informed and objective advisers. But once again the impression created by such partial truth is wholly misleading, for throughout this period McCone used his authority as CIA director to recommend a sharp escalation of the war. In March 1964 he recommended "that North Vietnam be bombed immediately and that the Nationalist Chinese Army be invited to enter the war."[16] A year later he criticized McNamara's draft guidelines for the war by saying we must hit North Vietnam "harder, more frequently, and inflict greater damage."[17] Meanwhile, at the very time that some CIA intelligence personnel discreetly revived the possibility of a Vietnam disengagement, other CIA operations personnel proceeded with the planning which led to the Tonkin Gulf incidents.

As presented by the *New York Times,* the Pentagon Papers suggest the model that we rejected at the beginning of this book— that the Indochina war was the result of a series of mistakes. According to this model, the war is to be analyzed as a sequence of official decisions reached by public officials through constitutional procedures, and these officials (now almost all departed from office) erred in their determination of the national interest. The Pentagon Papers suggest further that good intelligence was in fact available at the time, but was unfortunately ignored in a sequence of bad decisions. One is invited to conclude that the intelligence community should have greater influence in the future.

In this book I have reached almost precisely the opposite conclusion. The public apparatus of government with respect to Indochina has been manipulated for the furtherance of private advantage, whether bureaucratic or financial, or both simultaneously. The policies that led to escalation after escalation, though disastrous when evaluated publicly, served the private purposes of the individuals who consciously pursued them. And the collective influence of the so-called intelligence community (no community, in fact, but a cockpit of competing and overlapping cabals) has been, not to oppose these disasters, but to make them possible.

---

15 *Pentagon Papers,* pp. 331–32. A similar story of good intelligence neglected is told by General Lansdale's friend and admirer, Robert Shaplen, in *The Lost Revolution* (New York: Harper, 1966, e.g. pp. 393–94), a work frequently cited by the Pentagon study.

16 Edward Weintal and Charles Bartlett, *Facing the Brink: An Intimate Study of Crisis Diplomacy* (New York: Scribner's, 1967), p. 72.

17 *Pentagon Papers,* p. 441.

This is not a blanket accusation against all intelligence personnel, least of all against the relatively enlightened professionals of the CIA. It is a blanket challenge to the system of secret powers which permits the manipulation of intelligence and the staging of so-called political scenarios in other nations with impunity and without public control. This country's Constitution will be still further weakened if, as after the Bay of Pigs, the exposure of an intelligence "fiasco" becomes the prelude for a further rationalization and reinforcement of the intelligence apparatus.

In the evolution of the Indochina war, the impact of the intelligence community has not been represented by the neglected memoranda of cautious and scholarly analysts. The power and influence of these agencies has lain in the convergence of intelligence and covert operations, and even more in the proximities of the agencies and their "proprietaries" (like Air America) to ultimate centers of private power such as the firms of Wall Street and the fortunes of the Brook Club. If the American public is to gain control of its own government, then it must expose, and hopefully repeal, those secret sanctions by which ostensibly public agencies can engage us in private wars.

After the Bay of Pigs, Congress allowed the executive to clean its own house. This time it must struggle to recover its lost control of the power to make war. It is obvious that at present the majority of congressmen are not so inclined. There may, however, be some who will exercise their investigatory powers to pursue, expose, and ultimately end, the full story of the war conspiracy.

And if not, then, in the name of peace, others must do it for them.

INDEX